KU-798-396

COMING HOME

One man's return to the Irish language

Michael McCaughan

Gill Books

Gill Books
Hume Avenue
Park West
Dublin 12
www.gillbooks.ie

Gill Books is an imprint of M.H. Gill & Co.

© Michael McCaughan 2017

978 07171 7159 0

Print origination by O'K Graphic Design, Dublin
Printed by CPI Group (UK) Ltd, Croydon, CRO 4YY

This book is typeset in 11/15 pt Minion with titles in Champion HTF

The paper used in this book comes from the wood pulp of managed forests.
For every tree felled, at least one tree is planted, thereby renewing natural
resources.

All rights reserved.
No part of this publication may be copied, reproduced or transmitted in any
form or by any means, without written permission of the publishers.

A CIP catalogue record for this book is available from the British Library.

5 4 3 2 1

Michael McCaughan is an Irish author and journalist best known for his work in Latin America. He has written extensively for *The Irish Times, The Guardian, Hot Press* and *Village Magazine.* He is the author of *True Crimes* (2002), *The Battle of Venezuela* (2005), *The Price of Our Souls* (2008) and *Rodolfo Walsh, Periodista, escritor y revolucionario, 1927–1977* (2016). He lives in Móinín na gCloigeann, Co. Clare.

Acknowledgements

This book owes its existence to the 46 people who agreed to sit down and be interviewed for it along with dozens more who shared their wisdom during informal conversations around the country. I am also grateful for the many out-of-print books and documents that arrived in the post or were pressed into my hands by trusting strangers keen to assist my research.

There are too many individuals involved in this effort to possibly thank by name but they know who they are.

My family has been a rock of support and good cheer throughout this process.

Thanks also to Conor Nagle and Catherine Gough at Gill, for all their advice and support.

Go raibh míle maith agaibh.

'There is scarcely a single word in the Irish (barring, possibly, *Sasanach*) that is simple and explicit. Apart from words with endless shades of cognate meaning, there are many with so complete a spectrum of graduated ambiguity that each of them can be made to express two directly contrary meanings, as well as a plethora of intermediate concepts that have no bearing on either ... Superimpose on all that the miasma of ironic usage, poetic licence, oxymoron, *plámás*, Celtic evasion, Irish bullery and Paddy Whackery, and it's a safe bet you will find yourself very far from home.'

Flann O'Brien

'Irish is a language of enormous elasticity and emotional sensitivity; of quick and hilarious banter and full of a welter of references both historical and mythological; it is an instrument of great imaginative depth and scope, which has been tempered by the community for generations until it can pick up and sing out every hint of a tint of emotional modulation that can occur between people.'

Nuala Ní Dhomhnaill

'[A] modest proposal. I – and there are hundreds of thousands of Irishmen who feel on this subject as I do – have always liked my Celtic countrymen and disliked the English nation; it is a national trait of character and I cannot well help it ... Englishmen have very noble and excellent qualities which I should like to see imitated here, but I should not like to imitate them in everything ... I like our own turn of thought ... if by ceasing to speak Irish our peasantry could learn to appreciate Shakespeare and Milton, to study Wordsworth or Tennyson, then I would certainly say adieu to it. But this is not the case ... they replace it by another which they learn badly and speak with an atrocious accent, interlarding it with barbarisms and vulgarity ... I say to you and

I repeat it, that there is no other way to keep the language alive than by speaking it among yourselves … around the blazing bog fire of a winter's night Dermot O'Duibhne of the love spot, Finn with his coat of hairy skin, Conán the Thersites of the Fenians, the old blinded giant Esheen (Ossian), the speckled bull with the moveable horn, the enchanted cat of Rathcroghan, and all the other wild and poetic offspring of the Bardic imagination pass in review before us.'

Douglas Hyde

Contents

CHAPTER 1

From Yearning to Learning, Mo Scéal Féin

On a damp Burren afternoon a little over three years ago I switched on Raidió na Gaeltachta (RnaG), the Irish language radio station. The idea had been simmering for years, a vague curiosity finally reaching some sort of turning point. As a journalist based in Latin America I would return home each summer and hear friends speaking Irish to each other and to their children. The language came alive in these casual, everyday interactions, and I always recognised words, even phrases from my school days, but my brain seemed incapable of stitching any of these together for myself. There was no progress from visit to visit, nothing seemed to stick, just the same old notion that it would be nice to speak Irish if only it could be achieved without any effort.

I was about to turn 50 years of age – a threshold. I held a party in a field to celebrate. The last time I had invited friends to share a birthday was when I turned 21. The future had arrived. My idea of personal ambition had shifted in those years and at times the mere act of getting out of bed each morning seemed a worthy enough achievement. Until it didn't. The Irish language, normally meandering harmlessly around the edges of my consciousness, suddenly demanded my full attention. Some part of me believed I would become a more complete person if I spoke Irish, more in tune with my roots, my identity, my very being. I had an utterly romantic attachment to the language. I would hear someone speak Irish and imagine myself joining in at full pelt. It felt wonderful.

My first forays into Irish language radio were wildlife safaris in which I drove into the jungle in an armoured vehicle, rolled down the windows and listened from a safe distance, absorbing the exotic sounds. I was drawn to the long, guttural *ch* sound, a sort of *hhckkkhhhhhh*, as if clearing your throat to spit, '*chhhhhuaigh mé*', '*chhhhhonaic mé*', '*chhhhhuala mé*'. Then I heard the incomprehensible singsong Donegal lilt, with its *seachtain* 'swee hart' and mysterious *fadoodas* and that oh so natural use of English words grafted onto Connemara Irish: '*mo bhicycle*' and '*tá mé all right*'.

I wondered would I ever be able to speak with such natural ease. I was also hearing that the language of Peig Sayers had become a little bit hip and sexy. Call it the TG4 factor, after the Irish language TV station. The country discovered, through *Ros na Rún* and other contemporary dramas, that Irish speakers led ordinary lives, had sex and used the Internet. Parents who don't speak Irish and may have hated it at school are elbowing each other out of the way to enrol their children in one of the growing number of gaelscoileanna, the rapidly expanding network of Irish language primary schools. Thousands of teenagers visit the Gaeltacht each summer, crying inconsolably when their parents come to pick them up after three weeks. Every town and city has a *ciorcal comhrá*, an informal Irish language meet-up, frequently held in a café or pub, where all comers and all levels of competence are welcome.

I was one of the 1.8 million people who claimed to speak Irish in the 2011 census – 41 per cent of the population – but like most of that cohort I was faking it. We all like the idea of having the language but cannot bear the idea of actually taking the time and effort to learn it. There had been many failed attempts on my part. I signed up for a season of night classes at Áras na nGael in Galway City about 10 years ago. I paid for the 10-week course but attended just two classes. It was a grim ritual, listening to a bad-quality tape recording while the teacher helped trainee teachers learn what they needed to pass some state exam. There was no *spraoi* (fun) in the classroom and far too little conversation. Before that I tried another method, asking friends to recommend a good book. I bought a small Irish–English dictionary and a novel, *An Dochtúir Áthais*, by Liam Mac Cóil, about a psychotherapist in Connemara. I couldn't get any flow to my reading as I was busy looking up every second word. It was a tiresome process and after a few pages that method was abandoned.

Unlike TG4, RnaG broadcasts without subtitles. This is the deep end. I heard a few familiar words and sounds but failed to catch the gist of conversations. After less than 10 minutes I returned to the safety of Sean O'Rourke and Pat Kenny and Matt Cooper. I have no television but love the radio; there is comfort in the familiar voices, even if the ads and the pundits drive me insane. There was no comfort in RnaG. I wasn't familiar with the presenters, had no idea what the schedule was, and the Irish was simply overwhelming. There were no concessions to the learner, just a tidal wave of sounds glued tightly together, forming one endless, incomprehensible utterance.

As a born Taurean with an extra streak of stubbornness I kept listening to RnaG, just a few minutes at a time, dictionary in hand, chasing down words even as the conversation sped ahead of me. After a few weeks of this I returned to my work in Colombia and found RnaG was still accessible with an Internet connection. I discovered one feature that cropped up repeatedly: the death notices. The vocabulary was more or less identical each day, the only change being the names of the deceased. Every morning I would take my laptop to a park in Cartagena, buy a *tinto* from the nearest coffee seller and find a bench, following the funeral arrangements in small towns around the Gaeltacht: Leitir Mealláin, Baile an Fheirtéaraigh, Na Cealla Beaga, all the while soaking up the Caribbean sun. The surreal nature of the exercise kept me at it. Paddy Joe Fat, died in London, body coming home *Dé Luain*, wake on Friday, Socree na Tory, funeral on Sunday, son of Mike Joe Fat and Maire Wore Johnny of Rosmuck, *far shingle* or *ban hingle* aged *ceithre* score or more, survived by two daughters and a son. Immediately after the deaths came this sentence – 'Nee bhooey ayn dinnah an puta R.'

I soon understood the basic vocabulary of death in the Gaeltacht.

I found a few broadcasters with less rapid Irish who interviewed hesitant learners as well as native speakers. I found myself listening in a more assured, relaxed way. The more I understood, the more I was inclined to tune in. When I praised these helpful programmes one Irish-speaking friend informed me that the presenter in question had 'awful' Irish and really shouldn't be allowed to pollute the airwaves. There is a big difference between speaking Irish, it seems, and total *líofacht*, or fluency. Irish speakers keep a close eye on their ambassadors of the airwaves, monitoring grammar and accent in some unwritten yet rigorous register of judgement. When I finally learned enough Irish to follow these debates, which occupy a remarkable amount of time among Irish speakers, I came to realise it formed part of a broader discussion on the survival of the language itself. It spoke of the struggle to maintain the richness of a minority language beside a giant, English, the language of almost everything.

I had always made it my business to talk up the language while living abroad, where no one could challenge my limited knowledge of the issue. Latin Americans have more or less the same level of insight into our country as we have into theirs. In the 1990s Irish people associated Colombia with cocaine, Pablo Escobar and that goalkeeper shot dead after the World Cup. Likewise, in Colombia, Ireland meant the IRA, U2 and leprechauns. 'What language do you speak over there?' asked new acquaintances. 'English,' I'd say, before explaining that we also had our native Irish, an ancient tongue tattooed onto goat hides 10,000 years ago until trampled underfoot by the Saxon invader. I may have laid it on a bit thick. The Irish language was beaten out of the natives under pain of execution, I said, as the wonder grew.

'Say something in Irish'.

'*Sé do bheatha a Mhuire*,' dramatic pause, '*atá lán de ghrásta*', turning the Hail Mary into a conversation piece. If the audience didn't tire I turned to the Our Father for succour. My rote Irish may have sown some doubts among the listeners, who then asked me to say something specific, like 'Any chance of a ride?' Ah, easy, '*An bhfuil cead agam dul amach go dtí an leithreas.*' My efforts were greeted with collective awe but I simply felt awful. Once more I would swear by all things holy that as soon as I got back to Ireland, *le cúnamh Dé*, I would enrol in some course and start a real conversation. There was always one over-interested straggler who would ask the final question in the inevitable chain: 'Does everyone speak Irish?' It's complicated, I would say, everyone learns it but no one speaks it. This sounded reasonable to the Colombians. They all learned English at school but could barely say hello to each other in it.

I should admit at this point that I had unfinished business with the Irish language. I liked it at school, had good teachers, worked hard and achieved high marks. Father Sammy Soffe had a terrifying reputation. He would fling heavy wooden blackboard dusters at distracted students and physically threw anyone guilty of 'cheek' out of the class. Occasionally even he was left at a loss for words. He once asked a pupil where the sun went at night. 'Behind the clouds, sir,' a response deemed too risible to merit punishment. However the forbidding Father Soffe turned into a teddy bear when it came to students who showed even a passing interest in the Irish language. Once in a while I would drop into him during the summer holidays, knocking on the door of the imposing red brick residential quarters, which were strictly out of bounds during term time. Years later I even arranged to meet him in Dún Laoghaire for a cup of tea and introduced him to my girlfriend. By then, however, French and Spanish had taken over my life, and with them the prospect of global adventures. Irish fell by the wayside.

I spurned several more great opportunities to learn Irish outside the classroom. My childhood years were spent in the company of brothers Seán and Breandán Delap, natives of Gweedore, County Donegal, who spoke Irish at home, just a short walk from my own. Both of them have spent their working life using the language, Breandán at TG4 and Seán now deputy principal of Coláiste Íosagáin, a well-known *gaelcholáiste*. I can't recall ever hearing them speak Irish, however, until I called them up recently, seeking advice on writing this book.

It gets worse.

While still a teenager I fell in love with a girl who spoke Irish. I really should have been getting the hint by now. This was the golden opportunity. I would have done anything for her at the time, and I undertook some dubious quests on her behalf. But I never did cross that border into her world of Irish. As the epic Meatloaf song says, 'I would do anything for love, but I won't do that.' As I grappled with *an Ghaeilge* once more I made a rough and forlorn calculation of the hours spent learning Irish at school. It came to about 2,000, but if you add in the hours spent with Breandán and Seán, let's say another 2,000 at least (we shared soccer, punk and other obsessions over a 10-year period) plus the five-year relationship with Mairéad, I was well over the estimated 10,000 hours required for learning any skill to perfection. If I had spent that time with the fiddle I could be Martin Hayes; if I'd spent it on the soccer field you could call me Messi. As a budding writer, I could have been the next Máirtín Ó Cadhain. If only I'd been paying attention.

And then there was Irish college one summer, or maybe two summers, at Baile Bhuirne in West Cork. Oddly, I can't remember ever speaking Irish there. Since then I have lived most of my life in Latin America, speaking Spanish. Irish haunted me. On my annual trip home I would stay with my close friends Éamonn and Deirdre, enjoying a break from the pressures of reporting from Mexico, Colombia and elsewhere. Éamonn, from Belfast, spoke Irish, while Deirdre, his partner, did not. When their first child Aoife was on the way, in 1994, they decided to shift the family language to Irish, a major, life-changing decision. Deirdre worked on the language, picking it up rapidly, boosted by visits to the Donegal Gaeltacht. I continued to visit each summer but made no effort to learn or speak Irish. As I reflect back on that era, I realise that not only did I fail to contribute to the Irish-speaking household, but I forced English on everyone else. Then I recalled the frequent dinners at Mairéad's house, years earlier, the nine members of her family sitting down together, plus me, Mister *Béarla*. The language of the family shifted to English. Irish almost always cedes to English in company.

My inability to conduct a basic conversation in Irish could almost be seen as an achievement in the face of so much potential help in the opposite direction. I could have learned basic household expressions, the limited, repetitive language of mealtimes and bedtimes and morning times, that would have been child's play, literally. I didn't bother because I didn't need to. English was always at hand. Now imagine for a second my one-man wrecking ball on a far bigger scale inside the Gaeltacht, where English insinuates itself into the heartlands, a comfortable commute from Galway City. The newbies send their kids to local schools and before long English has seized control of the schoolyard like Japanese knotweed devouring the surrounding countryside.

If the universe has a special place reserved for language killers my rap sheet will be extensive, my sentence painful. I could perhaps find myself reincarnated as Hector Ó hEochagáin. That fear undoubtedly helped set in motion my return to the language. As I listened to the death notices and little more, I realised that I had started at the end. The initial work had to be done, the slow accumulation of vocabulary, the tuning in to the language, patiently listening and repeating. Among the random conversations heard on RnaG, the voice of Alex Hijmans stood out. He spoke clearly but sounded like he was imitating an old man from Connemara, and although I thought he was mocking it I soon realised he had simply mastered that area's speech. I found Hijmans' short story collection, *Gonta*, a dozen tales from the shantytowns and beaches of Brazil, perfect fare for the likes of me. Hijmans, it transpired, is a Dutch national who came to Ireland, learned Irish and opened an Irish language café, Banana Phoblacht in Galway City. He has since moved to Brazil, adding another language to his growing collection. He still works as a journalist with Irish language media. I was impressed to discover that Hijmans' fiction featured on the Leaving Cert Irish paper in 2012.

I had gained a foothold but feared that might be the end of the journey. It was time for further exploration. I looked for shortcuts, finding a website that listed the most frequently used words in Irish. How many words do you need to understand a language anyway? Peig Sayers apparently had 30,000 words at her disposal, but I wasn't planning to write my life story in Irish. I would be satisfied with the ability to enjoy a relaxed conversation. According to wordsmith and satirist Flann O'Brien, a grasp of English required just 400 words, as it functioned mainly as a language for sorting out daily necessities. In Irish the word *agus* (and) is the fourth most common word in the language, but that didn't mean I understood 25 per cent of each conversation. I checked out the top 100 words in Irish and discovered that even that modest number allows simple conversations using atrocious grammar. A knowledge of the top 300 words helps erode the giant granite block of incomprehension.

Soon after these modest beginnings I tried out my freshened-up Irish on an old friend and fluent speaker. I didn't get far. Once more the whole damn thing looked like a foolish chore, tackling an Everest of a language with no pressing reason to undertake the challenge. Maybe it was true what people said, that it simply *was* a difficult language. But even as I talked myself in and out of it a part of me knew deep down that the journey had begun. There was no turning back. Each new word was quietly added to the growing store, or *stór focal* (vocabulary). I soon realised that what went in did not necessarily come out, at least not for a long time, and that patience and perseverance were better medicine than frustration and fluster.

Then my older brother got in on the act. Gerry, a mathematician, is cut from a different cloth to my own. He is methodical and persistent, and when he takes on something new, he sees it through. He is also eight years older than me, and I have always struggled to be better than him at something. The teachers at school would sometimes call me by his name and, when corrected, remind me of the medals he had won in the classroom and on the rugby pitch. A competitive edge danced around our close friendship. Gerry became interested in Irish around the same time as me, listening to RnaG with a consistency that irritated me. He didn't understand any more Irish than I did, but he kept listening anyway. I wasn't about to let him get the better of me.

The radio went back on.

As time passed I began listening to programmes on a regular basis, establishing a daily practice. The balance began to shift a small bit in my favour. I live alone in the Burren, County Clare, surrounded by large rocks, a Dutch vegetable grower and a Spanish Flamenco dancer. I could have worked on my Dutch or Spanish any day of the week, but there was no Irish within walking distance, unless you count the signs for the nearby national park. I weighed up my options. Soon afterwards I spotted a letter in *The Irish Times*, written by Liam de Paor in County Mayo. 'For years I had convinced myself that I was unable to understand Irish,' he wrote. 'Then I discovered Raidió Na Gaeltachta, or rather I heard Áine Hensey presenting a late night radio programme called *An Ghealach Ghorm* and my ears were opened.' My own ears were wide open now. 'I do not know why this is so, but Ms Hensey's Irish and enunciation are so exquisite as to make understanding almost unnecessary.' I liked the idea of a voice so rich it rendered understanding unnecessary. I tuned in to *An Ghealach Ghorm* the following week, and Hensey was as good as the word of de Paor, speaking slowly and clearly between tracks, a little background here and there, but no machine gun bursts of enemy fire. I could follow a lot of what she said. A couple of years later I came across Hensey again on RnaG as she was doing the commentary for the Ireland–Sweden soccer match at the Euro 2016 tournament. I watched the match but listened to the radio, picking up new vocabulary – *taobhlíne* (touchline), *cárta buí* (yellow card), *Na Sualannaigh* (the Swedes) – as Hensey maintained her impeccable

Irish enunciation despite the pressures of a fast-moving match.

In the meantime I checked the schedule and found *Cruinneog*, meaning 'globe', a programme aimed at the diaspora, on Saturday mornings. Presenter Cearbhall Ó Síocháin helmed a relaxed programme that travelled round the world, from Paris to Beijing, digging up learners and native speakers alike. Through these voices *an Ghaeilge* became a more friendly language, a warm, welcoming place with more familiar voices.

The slow but steady language shift had begun, my faltering efforts greeted with unwavering encouragement. Those native speakers with fearsome reputations, the brutal taskmasters roused to immediate anger over a missing *séimhiú* or an overlooked *urú* existed solely in my own head. And the *séimhiú* (aspiration), as in *an fHuinneog*, and *urú* (eclipse), as in *i nGaillimh*, aren't as difficult as I had imagined. The sounds are simple when you break them down. *An fhuinneog*, with its added 'h', becomes 'i', like 'in', while *i nGaillimh* takes the 'ng' we use in 'song' and 'wrong', and places it at the start of the word. Try it now.

While the world seemed satisfied with my progress I could only hear flat Irish riddled with *botún*. The Irish language, when properly spoken, has a lilting rhythm, a curl of the tongue around shifting vowels cohabiting with harsher throat sounds that summon vague notions of Arabic. Comedian Des Bishop joked that when he wanted to work on his Irish pronunciation, he turned to Al Jazeera for tips. The language has a word for this shifting rhythm, '*an blas*' – the flavour, taste or relish. I have the opposite, the flat, tasteless tones of the 'wet sandwich', as in 'taw gayhlge agum'. My Irish was becoming reasonably effective but it wasn't *filíocht* (poetry).

In 2015 I found that *an Ghaeilge* had come over me like a fever. People asked why – why Irish and why now? The answer kept changing along with my feelings for the language. Friends suspected some variation of the mid-life crisis, while Irish-speaking friends viewed my return to the language with a degree of pride, evidence perhaps that all was not lost, even if the language is dying in its Gaeltacht home. Now I fear that I am going to wake up in the morning and find myself tired of the language, done with it, disappointing my new allies. In Irish begins responsibilities. I tried out more (very) brief chats with Irish-speaking friends but they quickly tired of the baby talk. The return to the language had not brought me as far as I thought. I was not merely relearning the language, as I first imagined, but tackling it virtually from scratch. I had climbed this hill once before and I knew the terrain. I had managed to develop my beginner Spanish and take it all the way to fluency. *An féidir liom?* Could it be done again?

CHAPTER 2

Buried Alive

Ask any Irish adult '*An bhfuil cead agam?*' and they will probably finish the thought with '*dul amach go dtí an leithreas*'. Irish children spend 14 years learning the language at school at a rate of about 45 minutes per day for about 180 days each year. The final tally is more than 2,000 hours, but the sum total of our comprehension involves little more than asking permission to go to the toilet. Probe a little further and you may be rewarded with the beginning of a prayer, '*Sé do bheatha a Mhuire*', and as a last resort, '*tiocfaidh ár lá*'. After almost a century of compulsory Irish we have acquired a prayer, permission to go to the bathroom and an empty slogan.

Many pupils remember more about the marks left on their bodies than the ones they got in their final exams. 'I didn't spend a single day at school without being walloped, slapped, thumped and picked up by the ears,' Eugene Hayes, 59, told me. Hayes, an accountant, maintained the books for a small company I used to have. We never met in person, but when he heard about my interest in Irish he was keen to recount his own experience. 'We did every subject through Irish and I may as well not have been there.' Hayes struggled and the priests responded, but not with understanding. Six months before he was due to sit his Intermediate Certificate exam, the principal interrupted class to announce the names of six boys who would not be eligible to continue due to their lack of ability in Irish. Hayes was among them. If they had sat the exams in the school, the principal feared they would bring down the all-important average mark. Irish classes around the country were subject to periodic inspections, and teachers could lose salary increments if the required level wasn't achieved. If Hayes failed his Irish exam he failed the entire Inter Cert, dashing any prospect of entry to university. He was forced to leave school and family and attend boarding school far from home, in Castlebar, County Mayo. In a further attempt to awaken the sleeping Gael, he was dispatched to the Irish college one summer. 'We were stacked like shelves in a supermarket,' he recalled, referring to the traditional pile-em-high, rake-it-in policy of host families, squeezing extra state payments per student housed. After a week Hayes ran away and hitched home.

As the conversation came to a close Hayes informed me that his paternal grandmother was a first cousin of independence hero Michael Collins, and some other relative was a bigwig in the Department of Foreign Affairs. I sensed an urgency behind this information, his family's revolutionary bona fides mitigating his failure to learn Irish. Unsurprisingly, his *focal scoir*, or parting word, was about the compulsory nature of Irish at schools. 'I hate the compulsion of anything,' he said.

Of course Eugene Hayes was raised in prehistoric, priest-ridden 1960s Ireland. We live in another country now, in which kinder, gentler teachers kindle a loving awareness of *an teanga náisiúnta* (the national language). Or so we like to believe. I wandered into a shop in Limerick where a boy, maybe 10 years old, sat with a soccer ball, his mother working behind the counter. '*Cad is ainm duit?*' I said, asking him his name in Irish. He didn't respond until his mother repeated the question. He looked uncomfortable and I regretted my curiosity. Then he told me that Irish hadn't gone well for him at school. His father had helped him with homework one night, teaching him the word '*gluaisteán*' for 'car'. In school the following day, the child was upbraided and told the proper word for car was '*carr*'.

Sometimes it feels like the language is *faoi gheasa*, under a spell, serving 300 years in the wilderness like the children of Lir, jinxed by a jealous stepmother. It's a dismal fate for a language that has given us the lyrical beauty of 'Caoineadh Airt Uí Laoghaire' and 'Cúirt an Mheánoíche'.

Yet despite the beatings, the irrelevant syllabus and general turnoff, Irish people like the idea of having a language of their own. I have always ticked the box on the census form out of sympathy for the language, even when I didn't speak it. The 2011 census form was blunt: Do you speak Irish, yes or no? The only follow-up question was about frequency of use – daily (inside or outside the education system), weekly, less often or never. But there is a world of difference between a *cúpla focal* and a competent speaker. In my own experience, the competent speaker is a rare thing, and yet census figures suggest that between 2002 and 2011, 200,000 new speakers joined the ranks. With the exception of Des Bishop, I wonder where they came from and how frequently they are speaking Irish. It is one thing to tick the box but quite another to sign up for a *dianchúrsa* (intensive course) at an adult learning centre.

People often experience their first hint of pride in the language and shame at their own ignorance of it when they meet someone in New York or Adelaide who says, 'Say something in Irish.' The excitement of others prompts a rethink, along with the discovery that the language actually does have a practical use: it allows you to talk about strangers in their company. When it comes to languages other than Irish and English, the census asks residents of the Republic of Ireland whether they can speak such languages 'very well, well, not well, not at all'. Even that level of detail would be helpful in gaining a more accurate map of Irish language use. In Northern Ireland, 185,000 people claimed some knowledge of the language in the 2011 census – nearly 11 per cent of the population. More than half that number said they could speak the language to some degree, with 4,130 using Irish as their main home language. The figures in Northern Ireland are probably more reliable, as the census question is more specific, asking whether the person can read, write and speak the language.

While even the most fanatical enthusiast will acknowledge that there are nowhere near 1.8 million Irish speakers, the figures hint at a greater respect for and identification with the language than might be assumed from media discussion on the topic. That attention tends to focus on the cost of maintaining the language and the occasional public scandals arising in its wake. The popular assumption surrounding *an Ghaeilge* is that truckloads of money have been tossed in its general direction since the foundation of the state, to no avail, and that as soon as the cash plug is pulled, the language will expire.

Douglas Hyde, language enthusiast, Gaelic League founder and Ireland's first president, was universally regarded as a moderate. He rejected violence and took no part in the Easter Rising in 1916. When it came to the defence of the Irish language, however, the tranquil Hyde was easily moved to rage. A diligent collector of stories and words, he travelled the country and once met a young man who, when asked if he spoke Irish, responded thus: 'Neither my father nor my mother has one word of English and still I can't spake and I won't spake Irish.' Hyde lost his temper and hit the youth 'one good kick' which went unanswered, prompting Hyde to conclude that such a passive attitude 'shows you what the loss of your native language does to you'.

When I came back to Irish in recent years, I was often asked how and when the language ceased to be spoken by the Irish people. I didn't know. Despite all those years of Irish language instruction at school I never learned anything about the history of the language itself. I was surprised to discover that Irish, this

Celtic tongue blown across Europe by a people on the move, was once spoken by all the inhabitants of Ireland, that it was the oldest language in Western Europe and served as the language of everyday life on this island for more than a thousand years. It is also the oldest *written* language in Western Europe, starting in the 5th century and flourishing with a manuscript tradition throughout the Middle Ages.

The decline began with the Norman invasion of Ireland in the 12th century, but the initial shift was not from Irish to English but the other way round, as Anglo-Norman settlers learned Irish and married into the community. The Statutes of Kilkenny (1366) were aimed at these new settlers: 'If any English or Irish living among the English use the Irish language amongst themselves, contrary to this ordinance, and thereof be attainted, his lands and tenements, if he have any, shall be seized into the hands of his immediate Lord.' As threatening as this sounds, the actual purpose of these early statutes was not to dissuade the Irish from speaking their language but to arrest the process whereby descendants of the Anglo-Norman occupiers had rapidly assimilated into the Gaelic-speaking majority, becoming 'more Irish than the Irish themselves'.

Once the dissident Irish speaker had his lands and tenements seized by the nearest lord, things would stay that way 'until he come to one of the places of our lord the king and find sufficient surety to adopt and use the English language and then that he have restitution of his said lands by writ to issue out of the same place'. If the person in question had no lands to be seized, 'then his body shall be taken by some of the Officers of our lord the king and committed to the next gaol, there to remain until he or another in his name find sufficient surety in the manner aforesaid'. When you strip away the quaint English, the 'aforesaids' and 'thereof be attaints', this piece of legislation is simply a death threat. The tone bears a striking similarity to that of the Spanish invaders landing in the Americas in the 15th century: *la biblia o la espada,* the bible or the sword – submit or face the consequences. The Irish resisted, however, and by 1536 Henry Vlll was moved to send a missive to the colonial rulers of Galway City, ordering not just settlers but 'every inhabitant within said town ... to speak English' and teach it to their children, and warned to 'fail not to fulfil this, our commandment, as you tender our favour and would avoid our indignation and high displeasure'. This was a period in history in which high displeasure easily translated into headless corpses. The occupying forces accompanied this fatwa with a campaign of psychological warfare, blaming the Irish people's attachment to Gaelic as the chief cause of a 'certain savage and wild kind and manner of living'. The task of destroying the language would begin with 'babes from their cradles' instructed 'with a pure English tongue, habit, fashion, discipline', so that in time they would 'utterly forget the affinity' to their traditions and lose the ability 'to infect others'. Jonathan Swift, the great Irish writer, added his voice to the chorus: 'I am deceived if any thing hath more contributed to prevent the Irish from being tamed, than this encouragement of their language, which might easily be abolished, and become a dead one in half an age, with little expence, and less trouble.'

If there is anything surprising about the evolution of the Irish language, it lies not in its decline but in the fact that it survived at all. The laws against the language, combined with confiscation, plantation, transportation, religious persecution, devastation and military intimidation, reduced the native population to serfdom. The language of infection and illness would evolve into the *Punch* magazine cartoons of the 19th century depicting the Irish as lazy savages with simian features.

The language went into decline during the 16th and 17th centuries as the British replaced a native aristocracy with its own administration, yet an estimated 80 per cent of the people still spoke Irish as late as 1801. The English-speaking elite spread out around the country, through the courts, police and landlords, while all legal contracts were drawn up in English. Between 1820 and 1840, a very short period, the occupying power set up a nationwide police force (1822), the Board of Works, circuit courts and local district courts (1826) and schools (1831). Suddenly the state was everywhere, and knowledge of English was beneficial to get an education and useful to access the court system if necessary. 'In any kind of legal affair,' wrote Peadar Ó Laoire, born into this era, 'the man with English was able to turn black into white on them and they had no means of defending themselves. If they gave their own account in Gaelic, none would understand them – except perhaps the man who was planning to do them an injustice.' If the Irish speaker found an interpreter, they also stood a chance of being tricked should the interpreter have taken a bribe. In brief, 'the man without English was in disastrous straits'.

This power imbalance was painfully clear in 1882 when an innocent man was hanged and four others imprisoned after being wrongfully convicted of the Mám Trasna murders, a brutal crime in which five members of the Seoighe family were murdered in their home in a remote Connemara village, shocking the nation. In the ensuing trial, the judge, jury and lawyers on both sides spoke only English while defendant Maolra Sheáin Seoighe, subsequently hanged, spoke only Irish. All evidence and testimony in Irish fell on deaf ears. Four fellow defendants spent twenty years in prison, one of them dying behind bars.

I was surprised to learn that Daniel O'Connell, the liberator, instigator of the 'monster meetings' around Ireland and perhaps the most popular politician of the 19th century, always spoke in English, a language just one fifth of his crowd understood.

O'Connell's legendary speeches and public meetings addressed not so much the local peasantry, intimately acquainted with the nature of British repression, but rather the visiting British journalists. 'Although the Irish language is connected with many recollections that twine around the hearts of Irishmen,' said O'Connell, the 'superior utility' of the English tongue was so great 'that I can witness without a sigh the gradual disuse of the Irish'. It would be hard to find a more pithy description of the fate of Irish today.

Thomas Davis, a founding member of the Young Ireland movement, was a leader of the 1848 rebellion. A keen advocate for the language, he stated that 'a people without a language of its own is only half a nation'. Davis himself didn't speak the language, and made no attempt to learn it. When he set up a paper, *The Nation*, it became a huge success, being read aloud in villages all over the country – in English, of course. The Irish language declined but the population grew, and with it the number of speakers. There were upwards of 4 million Irish speakers in 1845, more than at any other time in history, almost half the population. However, these figures don't tell the full story, as the English speakers controlled the country while the Irish speakers remained a peasant underclass. Irish was the language of daily life, of the fair and the market, of the field and of Sunday mass. But increasingly, as the association with shame and poverty deepened, parents opted not to pass the language on to their children.

Once the Great Hunger struck in 1845 the Great Silence quickly followed. The language shift occurred at a dizzying pace. The slow erosion and decline became a traumatic overnight upheaval. The vast majority of famine victims, perhaps as many as 90 per cent, were Irish speakers living in the west of the country. In addition, more than 2 million people emigrated in the years that followed, most of them poor and disproportionately Irish speakers. As Hyde travelled the country in 1890 he observed with sadness that 'in most circles in Ireland it is a disgrace to be known to talk Irish; and in the capital, if one makes use of an Irish word to express one's meaning, as one sometimes does of a French or German word, one would be looked upon as positively outside the pale of decency'.

This was the era in which children wore a *bata scóir*, or tally stick, tied around their necks with a piece of string, like a goat with a bell attached. Each time the child spoke Irish, a notch was carved into the stick. Children spied on each other like East Germans in the time of the Stasi, only this programme was enthusiastically enforced by parents who spoke only Irish. Children admitted to speaking Irish, as a sin, in the confessional, valuable Irish manuscripts were thrown out as rubbish, used to wrap groceries, cut up for tailors' patterns and scrapbooks for kids.

The occasional testimony of a sympathetic observer revealed the scale of the pain inflicted during the language shift. Oscar Wilde's father, William Wilde, travelled around the Irish countryside in the early 19th century and observed the *bata scóir* in action:

> The children gathered round to have a look at the stranger, and one of them, a little boy about eight years of age, addressed a short sentence in Irish to his sister, but meeting the father's eye, he immediately cowered back, having to all appearance committed some heinous fault. The man called the child to him, said nothing, but drawing forth from its dress a little stick ... which was suspended by a string around the neck, put an additional notch in it with his penknife. [We] were told that it was done to prevent the child speaking Irish, for every time he attempted to do so a new nick was put on his tally, and when these amounted to a certain

number, summary punishment was inflicted upon him by
the schoolmaster ... when questioned, the father, who spoke
little English, enthusiastically expressed his affection for
the Irish language but explained that the children needed
education and, since no Irish was taught in the schools,
they had to be encouraged to speak English. The school was
more than three miles distant, across river fords and over
mountain passes, and an adult escorted the children there
and back each day, occasionally carrying the weak.

The National School system introduced compulsory English
into the classroom in the 1830s. When it comes to discussing
the Irish language the issue of 'compulsory' learning is never far
behind, but never in the context of English forcibly replacing
Irish. The language shift speeded up as English became firmly
established as the language of power and prosperity, jobs and
commerce, emigration and getting ahead. English was the
language of the oppressor but from the famine era onwards it
was, at least in places such as the US and Canada, the language
of freedom and opportunity. The census of 1851 indicated a
widespread under-reporting or denial of Irish, a sign of the
times, just as recent census data in Ireland suggests a massive
over-reporting of Irish language proficiency, a sign of very
different times.

In the 19th century grown-ups made a sane, rational choice
around the language for themselves and their kids, based on
a calculation of odds and possibilities. The children, however,
had the language beaten out of them, literally, with a stick, and
the trauma beaten into them. The marks on the body may have
healed over time, but not necessarily the deeper ones within.

In his novel *Caisleáin Óir*, Donegal writer Séamus Ó
Grianna described the confusion arising when children turned
up for school and were punished when they failed to respond

to the roll call, their names utterly unrecognisable to them. 'Didn't I always believe that my name was Séimí Phádraig Duibh, isn't that the name I was always called?' the young child asks his mother. This is your new name in English, she said, adding 'would you leave yourself unable to communicate and to read and write your own letters when you move out among strangers?'

These children were our great-great-grandparents, less than a blink of an eye in genetic terms. No one knows for sure just what impact that trauma might transmit to current generations, but it can hardly have disappeared without trace. I sense a connection of some sort in the black-and-white attitudes expressed on the subject, that fierce, aggressive attachment to the language, and an equally fierce and aggressive rejection by others. It seems we are almost unaware of this process even as we act it out. In the context of this sudden shift it is hardly surprising that a small group of determined dreamers emerged within a generation, the poets, teachers and creatives who made 1916 happen, painfully aware of what was lost.

When the Gaelic League was founded in 1893, even the most passionate enthusiasts believed that restoration of the Irish language was a lost cause. There was broad support for the revival movement but learning Irish was regarded as a pastime, part of the wider aspiration towards independence from England. The existence of a separate language was critical to the concept of a separate nation and with it, the right to independence. There were, however, a significant number of activists who learned Irish to a high standard, and who consciously set about giving it a fresh prominence in public life. Father Eugene O'Growney's *Simple Lessons in Irish*, the first grammar book to enjoy national distribution, sold more than 300,000 copies in a decade. James Joyce and Jim Larkin attended lessons, while even W.B. Yeats made a half-hearted attempt to get to grips with *an Ghaeilge*.

This was the generation that turned out for the Easter Rising, discovering the literature, music, drama, art and sport of an ancient nation, alongside its language. Of the 16 men executed in the wake of Easter 1916, 12 spoke Irish, while six of the seven signatories to the proclamation spoke or taught Irish. The first volunteer to die in battle, Sean Connolly, was an Irish speaker and frequent visitor to the Gaeltacht.

St Enda's School, the brainchild of Pádraig Pearse, served as a kind of laboratory for a future, idealised Gaelic society. Interestingly, it was highly successful as a school but permanently bankrupt as an economic enterprise. Four of the signatories to the proclamation had taught at the school while more than 30 former pupils turned up for battle at the GPO.

Why did Irish speakers disproportionately turn out for the Rising and risk all on a doomed military adventure? The answer may lie in Hyde's reference to the youth he kicked: a hunger for the language frequently inspired a hunger for independence, generating a spirit of rebellion. Language shapes our reality, and just as the shift to English brought with it a changed mindset in Ireland in the 19th century, the Gaelic revival prompted a rethink. The rebel mind had been progressively de-anglicised in the run-up to the Rising, not by refusing to speak English or rejecting the rich literary tradition in that language, but by discovering pride in Irish music, word and song, a connection to a native root. The British occupiers understood this process in the preceding centuries, aggressively de-Gaelicising Ireland, an essential part of the colonisation process.

Douglas Hyde's best-known speech, 'The Necessity for De-Anglicising Ireland', marked the launch of the Gaelic League. That speech, delivered to a small and sceptical audience in 1892, was a call to resist creeping British influence and encourage the use of the Irish language. It would eventually come to define the era. Hyde had nothing against the British, but he lamented the surrender of a classically learned Gaelic people to a slavish imitation of the English. Hyde said he would gladly swap the Irish language for English it if meant embracing the wordplay of Shakespeare, but he disliked and rejected the popular English culture, which added no richness to the language. Hyde also made reference to that particular Irish habit, when it comes to our powerful neighbour, 'to grieve when she prospers, and joy when she is hurt'.

Every Irish person recognises this particular quirk of the Irish character. I celebrate when the English soccer team is beaten in international games even as I celebrate the victories of another English team, Liverpool, in the British Premier League, week in and week out. I wince when an English accent comes on the radio to speak of an Irish matter, even if it is something as trivial as selling car insurance. I feel this as an inexplicable, instinctive, ancestral rejection, which, regardless of changed historic times, cannot be uprooted or removed. I can only explain it as some permanent vestige of conquest, a genetic defiance, a necessary distrust against the risk of further injury and a mark of respect to the memory of those who came before and suffered.

And all this in the context of not knowing for sure if my predecessors, the McCaughans of County Antrim, were part of Gaelic society or Scottish settlers arriving from Britain. The origins of the McCabes, my maternal connection, lie further south in Ireland. My resentment of England's overarching influence over Irish society is completely dissociated from the quality of my close friendships or casual interactions with English people wherever I meet them, once they are not wearing an army uniform. I am not alone in feeling this learned antipathy, but like so many issues surrounding the past, there is an expectation that we should guard silence lest we offend. I have witnessed on several occasions the reaction of an audience to John Spillane, singer-songwriter, when he shifts tack during a gig, moving from English to Irish: 'That's enough songs in the language of the oppressor,' he'll say, straight-faced, without further comment. There is a titter of laughter in the audience and a sense of unease as we reflect on a throwaway line hinting at a deeper truth. The Irish language reflects a fundamental expression of a native culture; however irrelevant it seems today, it still forms a core element of our being. Something valuable has been lost. When the Free State was established in 1922, the new government set about restoring the Irish language, granting it official status alongside English. After centuries of prohibition and violence, Irish was now hailed as the highest expression of a risen people. The language became compulsory, not just at school but for entry to the national university, the civil service, the teaching profession and a range of other careers, as famine became feast. And in a final twist worthy of Orwell's *Animal Farm*, the new language bosses held on to the *bata scóir*, emulating the old bosses, beating the language into less-than-enthusiastic scholars.

The new leaders of the country believed that coercion had robbed the country of its language so surely if you coerced the other way round, the outcome would be an Irish-speaking nation. The entire responsibility for the revival was offloaded onto the schools. This policy proved disastrous, as almost every Irish person of a certain age can attest. Children are required by law to study the language all the way to their final school exams. This measure has failed miserably in its goal of producing Irish speakers. Indeed it has produced the opposite effect at school: a widespread resentment of the language.

Éamon de Valera, independence hero, prime minister, president and language enthusiast, was a major figure across 20th-century Ireland. If there was ever an influential individual who might have helped to revitalise the language, it was him. 'All that we require is a suitable scheme,' said de Valera, before adding his own awkward conclusion, 'no such scheme has come to my notice.' The fate of the language was also tied to economic circumstance, and the lack of any scheme to improve the lives of Gaeltacht residents meant the logic of emigration held fast.

De Valera might have shown leadership from the top, inviting cabinet colleagues to conduct sessions through Irish. The first session of the Irish parliament, sitting in rebellion in 1918, was conducted entirely in Irish. There was, perhaps, an opportunity for consensus and a major switch, not overnight but within a generation. This shift would have required leadership in Dáil Éireann alongside a major effort in the schools. The Israeli example is often upheld, with its switch to Hebrew. More recently, Rwanda replaced one official language, French, with another, English, in a phased but dramatic changeover. 'The challenge was not to compel all children to speak Irish but for they [the politicians] themselves to speak it, read it and write it,' observed historian J.J. Lee. Instead de Valera washed his hands of the language, lamented the lack of a 'magic wand' that might replace more prosaic tasks like coming up with creative ideas and applying them with rigour. The education system struggled with its responsibility. 'You might as well be putting wooden legs on hens as trying to restore Irish through the school system,' commented Eoin MacNeill, Minister for Education and, yes, co-founder of the Gaelic League.

The system struggled valiantly on. By 1939, competence had officially improved and the Cosgrave government launched a plan whereby the first two years of primary school would be in Irish, for all children aged five to seven years. Prior to that, in 1934 Minister for Education Thomas Derrig decreed more time for Irish and less for other subjects. The Irish National Teachers Organisation concluded, by 1941, that all-Irish education resulted in 'the relative retardation of the child', while numbers of speakers in the Gaeltacht dwindled rapidly, from

200,000 (1922) to 100,000 (1939) and half that number again in 1964. A recent report, written by Conchúr Ó Giollagáin and Brian Ó Curnáin (2015) suggests that within 10 years Irish will no longer be the language of daily life in the Gaeltacht.

Commissions were commissioned over the years and reports delivered, but any serious proposals involving financial commitment were sabotaged and strangled at birth. Irish was fine as a distant aspiration and an occasional performance piece but there was no appetite for the type of collective action that might help it prosper. It was taught as a dead language, a flowery, literary relic with no bearing on everyday life. There was of course the ritual charade of civil service tests, but the aspiring bureaucrat cramming for a brief, perfunctory exam knew as well as the examiner sitting opposite that once through this formal hurdle they would likely never be called upon to use the language again.

For the brave souls who through family ties or school or individual enthusiasm managed to master the language, there was no social life outside the Gaeltacht, a situation that still holds true today. Dublin city has a leprechaun museum, dozens of McDonald's 'restaurants', the Guinness factory and several hundred cafés, but no dedicated network of social spaces for the Irish speaker to sit down and enjoy a coffee or a chat with something to read at hand and an Irish language radio station or music playing in the background. These days the Irish language is safely imprisoned within the confines of *Seachtain na Gaeilge*, an annual series of public events *as Gaeilge* that take place nationwide over the course of a fortnight. This token official gesture allows the language to be safely forgotten for the remaining 50 weeks of the year. During the course of *Seachtain na Gaeilge*, the state charade is briefly amplified, and for one day the order of business in Dáil Éireann is conducted in Irish, along with opposition leaders' questions to the Taoiseach.

Even this symbolic act of linguistic theatre has been hijacked for political ends. In 2015 Taoiseach Enda Kenny faced a question from opposition TD Mick Wallace as to whether the prime minister would raise questions regarding human rights abuses when he met President Obama on St Patrick's Day. Kenny answered in Irish, at which Wallace apologised for his inability to speak the language. Kenny ordered him to put on his headphones and access the simultaneous translation service. Wallace couldn't find the headphones, offering Kenny further opportunity to humiliate his opponent. The purpose of Seachtain na Gaeilge, to motivate and encourage the use of the Irish language in a welcoming atmosphere, was set aside in favour of a cheap political kick in the shins.

The Irish language was born of an oral tradition, a language passed down through song and story, dressed up in exuberant, lyrical finery. Up until the famine era in the 1840s, Irish was the language of everyday life, of lovemaking, of putting your kids to bed, telling them stories, the language of grief and sorrow, the language of farming and fighting and joking and so much more. A Hawaiian woman, whose people share the experience of a language lost, was visiting Ireland when she met an Irish speaker and nearly passed out with excitement, describing the gift as 'the unbroken connection to our ancestors'. That connection was broken but is being remade, one word at a time, by a network of learners and speakers around Ireland and further afield.

CHAPTER 3

Anyone Can Learn Irish

can't build a bookshelf or change a plug. I can drive a car but have no idea what lies under the bonnet. I use the shower but as soon as it stops working I call a plumber. The mysterious DIY universe lies way beyond my reach. My friends berate me every now and again, not for my lack of practical skills but for the laziness they see behind it. A man of my intelligence (*plámás*, meaning flattery or soft talk, is one Irish word they won't need explained to them) must surely be capable of fixing things, if only I were patient enough. And they are probably right. This flattering approach has produced occasional results. I successfully hammered a small spice rack to the wall in my kitchen. It is still there, if slightly uneven. I derived a huge sense of achievement from completing this small task. I subsequently tried to erect a fence post to secure a gate. Somehow the hammer struck my index finger and I ended up in the Accident and Emergency department in my local hospital. My friends insist that my negative attitude produced the negative outcome. I'm never going to win that argument. The point is I simply don't want to learn that stuff. I will pay someone to do things I cannot or will not do myself.

'*An bhfuil cead agam … ?*' has an instant effect and usually triggers the second half of a familiar phrase, '*dul amach go dtí an leithreas*'. The word '*cead*', meaning permission, holds a deeper significance due to the complex relationship between the Irish and their language. Who gives permission to speak? The notion of permission cropped up repeatedly in my conversations about Irish, as learners and speakers alike doubted themselves and their abilities before others. The title of this chapter, 'anyone can learn Irish', was self-explanatory.

Or so I thought.

When my DIY-friendly friends hear me speak Spanish or pick up a book I have written they declare those talents a mystical gift, a magic wand waved in my general direction. Yet I work like a *madra* at these so-called gifts. And when people marvel at my Spanish I accept the compliment and remind them how long I've been learning – 40 years and counting, hardly an overnight success. We can do things we think we cannot. Each day my gaze falls upon the spice rack and it gives me a sense of satisfaction that still surprises me. I could do more DIY if I worked at it. I would need help and guidance and I would never build a home extension on my own. That doesn't matter. In my own writing I don't compare myself to Borges or Joyce; in learning an instrument you don't have to become a Keith Jarrett and in speaking a language you don't have to attain native speaker status. The sights shouldn't be set too high. Each of us can cross a threshold and develop skills at something we firmly believed we could not master and enjoy it at the same time.

Nothing can convince Irish people that learning the Irish language fits into this pattern. Many people have a desire to speak Irish just as people want shelving or spice racks. There is, however, a psychological barrier to be crossed before tackling Irish *arís*. We have been there before. Most of us failed miserably in the attempt. Why would I expect a different result now? After all those hours in the classroom, after visiting the Gaeltacht and trying again as an adult, surely there comes a time to leave well enough alone? This nagging self-doubt produces the sensation, even the certainty, that Irish is 'too difficult', that as a language it belongs in a unique category of its own, with impenetrable codes rather than a limited number of sounds.

I used to believe that language begets language. The pattern seemed unmistakeable: Úna was raised through Irish and also speaks Italian, German and Spanish. Éamonn learned Irish and subsequently picked up good Spanish despite making only fleeting visits to Spain. Paul has no Irish and has spent extensive periods in Mexico and Italy, failing to pick up Spanish or Italian, despite considerable effort. Sarah gave up on Irish at an early age and has made little headway in learning French, despite spending a year in France. A friend phoned as I was writing these lines, speaking from her office. She mentioned that there were two native Irish speakers working alongside her. 'Do they speak any other languages?' I asked. She consulted them. One of them speaks Spanish, along with Irish and English, the other speaks French, Ulster Scots and Scots Gaelic. This random sample has no scientific significance whatsoever, yet it seems obvious that language competence feeds on language practice and that taking up a second or third language improves overall capacity.

Éamonn Ó Dónaill, director of Gaelchultúr, an Irish language learning centre, is uniquely placed to answer the question, but there is no definitive answer. 'It depends entirely on the individual,' he says. 'Some people learn very quickly and some absolutely brilliant people I know have never managed to grasp the language at all.' Ó Dónaill contrasts the frustration of a friend who earned a doctorate in linguistics but failed to make any progress in Irish with José, a visitor from Madrid who could converse, 'not fluently, but able to engage in conversations' after just six weeks of immersion in the Gaeltacht. If you are already bilingual, observed Ó Dónaill, you pick up new languages quicker, as you already have prior learning strategies built into your brain.

This could be cold comfort if, like most learners, you speak only English. You need to develop a system, some combination of practice, repetition and immersion. I began to learn Spanish at school at the age of 12. When the teacher arrived into class we opened our books. The first page showed a couple visiting a bar, ordering drinks from a waiter. There was one problem. The script on the page was entirely in Spanish. How were we supposed to learn? 'Miss! Miss! Miss!' we shouted, skipping ahead through the book. There must be some mistake, we thought, amazed at the absence of English assistance. Bernie Cosgrove, our new teacher, an attractive, cheerful young woman (yes, it helped, in a roomful of adolescent boys – let's face it, my science teacher was an unpleasant grump and I learned nothing from him), put us to work learning how to ask questions and order food. It was immediate and effective. In contrast, my Irish classes were conducted almost entirely through English and the teacher, even the good one, did almost all the talking. The Spanish system worked for me. Mrs Cosgrove was an inspiring teacher but that didn't mean the whole class embraced the subject. Most of my classmates stumbled along, learning just enough to get by.

It is often said that languages can only be acquired by putting them to use, a tough call in 1970s Ireland. The Spanish Embassy was located directly across the road from my school and occasionally a group of us would stroll through the gate and quietly make our way to the entrance. We eased the heavy door open and, holding our breath, tiptoed up to the unattended reception desk, pocketing bundles of leaflets displayed on the counter. This small act of senseless larceny cheered us up immensely after a day at school, and even though the leaflets invariably ended up in a bin, I would first have a read, working out the advice to tourists contained within.

I soon got myself a red-and-black foolscap notebook and

began writing every new Spanish word in it. The following summer, now a teenager, I began going to a local disco, 7.30pm to 10.30pm, three times a week, strutting my stuff to 'Staying Alive' while waiting for The Clash and The Adverts to put in an appearance. This was the summer of Thin Lizzy's 'Dancing in the Moonlight'; I was finding my feet and not just on the dance floor. The south side of Dublin was invaded each summer by gangs of Spanish kids, their parents keen to have them learn English in a proper Catholic environment. These arrivals were the subject of great fascination for me and my friends, these exotic, olive-skinned creatures, and now, *Gracias a Dios* (aka Mrs Cosgrove) and my new secret weapon, the red-and-black book, I could talk to them. Not much, of course, but enough to break the ice.

A year later I took off to Kerry with a couple of friends for a week of youth hostelling. We spent the first night in Killarney, where I met a young woman from Bilbao in the Basque country who was travelling around with a couple of Irish friends. Both of us had recently turned 13. That evening we began chatting, mixing Spanish and English. Several hours and many cups of tea later (it's true, mother, no alcohol was involved) we noticed that everyone had gone to bed apart from a group of bikers at a nearby table. The chat spread out, and by the time I went to bed the sun was coming up and I had a new, special friend, Tixiar Gallastegui. I also had a copy of *Zen and the Art of Motorcycle Maintenance*, which one of the bikers had given me. It still ranks as one of the most memorable nights of my life. Tixiar convinced her friends to change their schedule and we met again at the next hostel. It felt like something from a fairy tale, unexpected, innocent and unforgettable. I had just read Hemingway's *For Whom the Bell Tolls*, and this was my Pilar. I could almost hear the machine gun fire echo in the Spanish hills on a night full of rain. Tixiar and I exchanged letters for a while before settling back into our own lives. That brief moment of *draíocht* was enough.

Right from the beginning Spanish was connected with the unexpected, with real life encounters stimulating me to learn more. This was my reward and motivation. I edged forward into the language, verb by verb, noun by noun, but the spoken word still lagged well behind. I left school and continued with Spanish at college, where I had the unexpected pleasure of encountering Bernie Cosgrove's husband, Dr Ciaran Cosgrove, another inspirational figure. The opportunity arose to visit Nicaragua in 1985, the time of the Sandinista revolution. This was to be my first visit to a Spanish-speaking country, and I was ready. Only I wasn't. The buzz of Spanish conversation flew around me when I landed in Managua, the overheard snatches that fill public spaces in big cities. Someone directed a comment towards me but I failed to grasp it. A day later, out on the street trying to engage with locals, it hit me with a bang. I had been learning Spanish for nine years, at school and at college, but casual conversations among native speakers were beyond me.

I found work as a volunteer with a group of Guatemalan exiles and after a few weeks I could unglue most of the sounds whizzing around me. I returned to Ireland and finished my degree before beginning life as a journalist in Latin America, relishing the experience of wrapping my tongue around the exotic sounds of Colombian, Cuban and Argentinian Spanish, one phrase at a time, as proficiency edged towards fluency. As I look back at that linguistic journey I am aware of the distinct stages: frustration, giving up, coming back, language grazing, breaking through the pain barrier and then suddenly, as if overnight and when least expected, fluency.

Older and wiser, my approach to learning Irish became systematic, a rigorous daily practice: some radio, a little reading and music in Irish. I listened in to the news in English first, familiarising myself with the day's topics, and after that I was able to decipher the bones of a story on RnaG. I also attended events conducted in Irish and launched myself into brief chats with other speakers. The reading seemed particularly important. When you read Séamus Ó Grianna, Tomás Ó Criomhthain and Pádraig Ó Conaire, you are not just picking up language but discovering how life was lived in Ireland over the past 100 years or more.

As time passed I felt I was discovering a part of myself that had been hidden away, unlocking some doorway into an unexplored part of my psyche. When I read over that sentence it sounds utterly vague and ethereal, but something was stirring in me. The journey became more than just an exercise in language. When I took up Spanish, I had discovered a wider world beyond Ireland, but with Irish it felt like I was drilling down into the depths of something close at hand. There was a connection growing to a parallel world, planet Gaelach, which exists, almost imperceptibly, underneath the surface of English-speaking Ireland. There are glimpses of this world on RnaG each day, some echo of another way of being that has disappeared through the decades. I can't put my finger on it yet, and I may never figure it out, but the curiosity is growing. For now, the small steps, the growing confidence and the immense pleasure are more than enough. I don't want this to stop. I need more Irish.

A few years ago, after the death of my father, I sifted through papers and books left behind in the family home. I came across that familiar, large, hardback notepad from my school days: the red-and-black book. I was immediately transported back to another time when I sat on the same bed in the same room, as a teenager, staring out at the flashing red dot in the distance, a place across Dublin Bay known as Pigeon House B. I had my growing collection of records and books and the pirate radio stations I listened to under the bed covers. I also had this ledger where I wrote down new Spanish words as I learned them, reciting them to myself. *El Sistema.* No one obliged me to do it and I can find no explanation for it. Perhaps the immediate rewards of adventure and intrigue, already gifted to me, motivated me to go back to the books and learn the grammar. My Irish is developing along the same lines, new friendships growing along with my *stór focal* as notebooks fill up and hesitant conversations breathe life into the written and spoken word. I am convinced that a personal interest is more important than innate talent when it comes to learning a language. That interest requires a system adapted to your lifestyle and temperament if it is to work. It takes time to find it but once you have it, in whatever form, you have started the journey. If this is true then anyone can learn Irish.

I wasn't sure if I could rely on my own instincts so I consulted others. I asked them all the same question: What would you say to someone who came to you and said, How can I learn Irish?

In West Cork, composer, visionary and philosopher Peadar Ó Riada fixed me his scary look and knitted his brows.

'How can I learn Irish?'

He repeated the question with a tone that implied it was probably the stupidest question he had ever heard.

'How do you give up cigarettes?'

'You stop smoking them.'

'How do you learn Irish? You start speaking it. That's the answer to that.'

'What if you live in the middle of nowhere?' I continued, feeling short-changed, seeking something more concrete.

'Don't bullshit me,' he said. 'There are plenty of ways and means of doing it, even if you are on the moon you can get on the Internet and Skype people who will teach you the Irish language in any dialect you like.' Peadar recommended reading in the language 'not in a modern book but in the older books, because the modern books are actually English through Irish'.

I moved on to Manchán Magan, broadcaster and activist, someone who has dedicated time and energy to figuring out ways and means of learning the language. 'Des Bishop is the answer to your question,' he said, mentioning the Irish-American comedian who spent a year in the Gaeltacht and learned enough of the language to perform his stand-up *as Gaeilge*. 'He showed the world, yeah, I can learn it, that's the answer to the title of your book, of course you can learn it, just fucking learn it.'

Right so – go to the moon, read old books and just fucking learn it.

I didn't think that would stand up in a book costing 15 euro.

There had to be more to it. I soon discovered that when it came to the language, bribery seems to have played a role. 'My father said I'll give you a tenner if you read *An tOileánach*,' recalled poet Nuala Ní Dhomhnaill, who was 15 years of age at the time. 'I read it and he gave me the tenner and I bought a Beatles record.' Manchán remembered that his grandmother paid cash for every *seanfhocal* he learned. Ailbhe Ní Ghearbhuigh, a lecturer in Galway University, recalled that 'if you wanted 50p to go to the shop you did better if you asked in Irish'.

As adult learners, however, we probably need different ways to immerse ourselves. Diarmuid Johnson, linguist, musician and teacher, was succinct. 'It's simple,' he says, 'you have to stop speaking English.' I don't think he meant forever, just long enough to breathe another language into your life. Johnson compared the process to preparing for a marathon. 'You'd better start training, that means you're going to sweat and break your heart, and in a year's time you're going to run the marathon like thousands of people do.' The first step is establishing priorities, creating time every day. 'It's a sacrifice, because the hour you do Irish is the hour when you don't do something else,' he says. 'Then you become part of the circle of people, a community; Irish speakers are a global community.'

This way Irish becomes a shared, social opportunity. 'You find people, you find a class, a teacher, books, RnaG, you find everything.' This process will take three years, according to Johnson, and anyone can do it, 'but the difference between anyone can do it and it's easy to do it – those two things are not the same'. The state can invest all the money in the world, he says, but money is not the answer. 'You have to want it badly enough,' he adds, like winning the All-Ireland: 'whoever wants it most is going to win'. If you start learning Irish for other reasons, some abstract ideal or historic principle, it's not going to work. 'That is going to impede you, in fact,' he concludes. 'You want to learn the language just because you *want* to speak it, not because you should.'

Johnson mentioned the *ulpan*, an Israeli language-immersion method, which helped achieve a speedy language shift after the Israeli state was declared in 1948. 'I know almost nobody who knows how best to teach Irish; it's a mystery,' added Johnson. He argues that the time available for Irish is insufficient at school, and the methodology inadequate. Johnson calculated a total of 800 hours to learn Irish, but the system wouldn't work in a classroom with large numbers and mixed abilities. The 800-hour system would only work if each hour had a structure and each lesson a clear goal, with each session building on the previous one.

Diarmuid Lyng, a Wexford hurler who learned the language inside and outside the classroom, contrasted learning by technology (lessons and apps) with the direct experience of going to the Gaeltacht: 'The technology route is like going into the mechanics, where the learning of the language becomes the focus', whereas a visit to the Gaeltacht allows the language to happen. 'It opens up a layer beneath that learning. It opens up a love for it, an experience that is deeper in you, the connection to yourself, to your soul, to your Irishness, whatever that is.'

If you are still reading you are probably ready to get started.

CHAPTER 4

Essentials for the Language Cupboard

When you take up a new hobby, from kayaking to cooking, you need the essential kit to get going. Your kitchen needs sharp knives and a cutting board, oil and spices, peeler and grater. If it is music you crave, an instrument is costly – a fiddle or concertina will set you back anything from 300 to 3,000 euro, not to mention the lessons that are also required. However, learning the Irish language is not a costly undertaking, requiring, *i dtús báire*, just a hint of resolve and a personal practice of some sort. It all begins with a dictionary.

Dictionary

A learner without a *foclóir* (dictionary, pronounced 'fucklore') is like a kayaker without a paddle – you simply can't survive. The *foclóir* is your best friend, and as anyone knows who has lost a best friend to a job in Australia or a sudden row, it's best to have more than one on the go. The great-granddaddy of all dictionaries is the classic *Foclóir Gaeilge agus Béarla*, Dinneen's finest, first published in 1904. Some people remember where they were when J.F.K. died; others recall the killing of John Lennon or even the week when Queen's

'Bohemian Rhapsody' reached number one in the charts, but I remember that Saturday afternoon, on 25 June 2016, when I purchased Dinneen in Dublin. I held it close, resisting with difficulty the temptation to open it up and roar out some of the more colourful words.

Patrick S. Dinneen (1860–1934) was an eccentric and conservative priest whose classic book *The Queen of the Hearth* served as a *buntéacs* or key inspiration for the articles relating to home life in Éamon de Valera's 1937 Constitution. Dinneen, born on Christmas Day, joined the Jesuits but abandoned the ranks 'without canonical stain' in 1900. He wrote plays, essays, school texts and a novel, and claimed that he was the only person in Ireland making his living entirely from writing in Irish, a remarkable feat at the time. Dinneen worried about all aspects of womanhood in the wake of the First World War, fearing it would be difficult to get *na mná* back into the kitchen after their spell in the workforce. The Suffragettes were one of his favourite targets, and he insisted that 'a large proportion of adult women are not anxious to become parliamentary voters', and that when it came to domestic drudgery, 'such a life of self-sacrifice, is a natural, if heroic outcome of the training of a good mother'. My mother, who forgave everyone their sins, would have called him 'a man of his times'. He stared out at me from the dictionary, arms folded, steely gaze, wide, thin lips clamped firmly shut. A friend of mine spotted the image of Dinneen and said it reminded him of the Mona Lisa.

Dinneen can't have been all bad, surely? I sought a second opinion: 'Dinneen was as amicable a man as you could meet,' wrote one contemporary, sounding a more hopeful note, 'so long as he got his own way'. A bit like Stalin, I suppose. Dinneen had several brushes with Pádraig Pearse, unsuccessfully attempting to prevent him securing the post of editor of *An Claidheamh Soluis*, the newspaper of the Gaelic League. On another occasion Pearse published a short story, 'Poll an Phíobaire', under a pseudonym, an adventure story about two boys exploring a cave. It was well received, ending up on the school curriculum. However, Dinneen took exception to this 'storyette with a nauseous name' ('Poll an Phíobaire' could also mean 'the Piper's Hole'). Dinneen dismissed the story as *béarlachas*, too reliant on English language structures, but ended with a pun that challenges his reputation as a humourless crank: 'it is to be hoped that the Píobaire will continue to draw from the stores of his capacious and well-filled arsenal'.

Irish speakers, like English and German speakers, don't agree on much, but it is widely acknowledged that Dinneen's dedication to collecting Irish words and phrases, notably from the spoken language, produced a rich archive, a critical *stór focal* for anyone going deeper into the language. All the plates and printing were destroyed by fire during the 1916 Rising but Dinneen, undeterred, rose again, writing a bigger, expanded version that was published in 1927 and is still available today. Dinneen includes such vital terms as *geataire*, whose many meanings include 'a long rush, a splinter of bogdeal for lighting, a man of slight build, a small cake, a small missile'. Or try *fo-Dhord*, a murmuring of bees, back-biting, a conspiracy.

These days Dinneen is enjoying a retro-chic revival, like old LP records. Poet Biddy Jenkinson cast Dinneen as a detective in her short story collection, *An tAthair Pádraig Ó Duinnín Bleachtaire*. The wily priest solves a range of puzzling crimes but falls a little short of the moral high ground expected from his profession. In one tale, 'Duinnín agus Professor Moriarty', legendary sleuth Searbhlach de Hoilm, better known by his English moniker Sherlock Holmes, tracks down Dinneen, *sagart na bhfocal*, in the National Library to work out clues to an apparent plot to kidnap the Queen, clues written in Irish on a scrap of paper. Dinneen, unfazed by the famous de Hoilm, works it all out with casual aplomb, and teaches the young pup a lesson along the way.

Dinneen's ghost also rides again on Twitter. Each day, a new word is released into the virtual wild. Better still, Dinneen's playful linguistic spirit has flourished among a fresh generation of language lovers, his archive interactive and open to suggestion. On 9 May 2016 John O'Donovan added his Dinneen for the day, *mo bhia-grá* ('muh vee-ah grah') – my lovefood? – that would be Viagra. And before you screen addicts even ask, yes, it is available online. Peadar Ó Riada suggested that all children, on leaving senior infants, be issued with a copy of Dinneen's dictionary. The idea seemed preposterous. The book itself weighs in at two kilos, a fifth of your Ryanair luggage allowance. However, Dinneen is fun, and the old font, with its curling letters and dots (the G looks like a soccer player in mid-bicycle kick) imposes the intended pace and rhythm of the language. In addition, the dictionary includes terms from specific Gaeltacht areas, allowing kids in those areas to seek out words attached to their locality and even their family. The book begins with a pronunciation guide, and it doesn't take long to get used to the old Gaelic script. Start with familiar words – *fuinneog, doras, cailín* – to get used to it.

All the major Irish language dictionaries are available for free on the Internet. But the feel and smell of the books cannot be obtained online. For a handy but substantial working dictionary, most speakers and learners choose Niall Ó Dónaill's *Foclóir Gaeilge–Béarla*, more words than you can learn in a lifetime for a mere 30 euros.

Post-its

In Gabriel García Márquez's novel *One Hundred Years of Solitude*, the people of Macondo are afflicted by amnesia and forced to label everyday objects or forget them forever. The Irish language has suffered a similar fate, a language once spoken by everyone, its *saibhreas*, or wealth of expression, rapidly declining as words disappear from use, dying along with older speakers. Apply the Macondo remedy to everyday objects in the home and you'll find that it's by far the quickest and most painless way to learn, as the sheets, pillows, toilet paper, wardrobe, table, carrots, lentils and rooms all acquire a new identity.

If you have children, get them involved. The greatest predictor of a bad attitude to Irish among kids is the bad attitude of their parents. Children soak up the prejudices and preferences of their parents; the younger they are, the more powerful the effect. If you actively demonstrate that the language means something to you, you are doing your kids a great favour. They may end up disliking Irish for their own reasons, but at least they will have reached that viewpoint without your active assistance. Researchers who studied attitudes towards Irish among more than 2,000 pupils confirmed that active participation by parents, 'in the form of encouragement, praise or help with homework', led to more positive attitudes among pupils and a higher achievement in Irish. This approach also spares you the whining that all too often accompanies a subject that for now at least remains compulsory to the bitter end of school days. Yes, parents, this is part of your job description.

You don't need to be an expert in Irish to encourage your offspring. Get a large slab of post-its and get to work. If you require a pronunciation guide, go to www.abair.ie, where you can feed any word into a search engine and a synthesiser will speak it back to you. It's not the same as gazing into someone else's eyes, *cois tine*, but it's a start. Each time I tried and failed to learn Irish, it came down to both sloth and lack of opportunity. This is an immediate and effective step towards making Irish visible – by surrounding yourself with it.

Do not fear copulation

Like all languages Irish has its own structures, stitching words
and verbs together into its own unique tapestry of sound. We
are so dependent on English language structures that it takes a
conscious effort to undo those habits and begin a new linguistic
adventure. *An chopail* (no, it's not a horse, that's a *capall*), or
copula, is a connector, particularly with the verb 'to be'. The Latin
root means 'fastening together'. Irish, like Spanish, has two ways
to be, one permanent, one temporary. *Táim sa chistin anois*, I am
in the kitchen right now, but *Is rapcheoltóir mé*, I am a rapper.
This is a critical feature of the Irish language, and when used,
however hesitantly, it signals an intention to go beyond the basics
with the language. The English speaker says 'I'm a tennis player',
'I'm here', 'I'm happy', etc., whereas Irish demands a different
construction, giving a different balance to a sentence.

Is iriseoir mé, it's a journalist me, or even *is iriseoir atá
ionam*, there is a journalist inside me. *Is as Baile Atha Cliath
mé*, it is out of Dublin I am. There is very little to it, *is* in the
present, *ba* in the past, *nach*, as in *nach deas é sin?*, meaning 'isn't
that lovely'? Then comes the *orm*, *ort* and the like, emotions
that come upon me and you, as in *tá áthas orm*, happiness is
upon me. Getting into the habit of using these forms starts the
process of de-anglicising your tongue and your brain, just as
Spanish and French require their own adaptation out of English
linguistic habits. If you remain wedded to English language
structures, you miss out, not only on the entertaining ways in
which Irish is expressed but on the different *meon*, or mindset,
that comes with understanding another language. *An múinteoir
tú? Ní múinteoir mé.* Teacher you? No teacher me. It sounds
like Tarzan and Jane, which may explain why one of the Tarzan
programmes featured a jungle tribe speaking Connemara
Irish. I kid you not. Sean McClory, a former stage actor born
in Galway, played the role of Red McGeehan in 'The Golden

Runaway' (1966), and persuaded director Lawrence Dobkin to use *an Ghaeilge* as the language of the pygmies.

Challenge: Using *an chopail*, build a brief, personal profile: an introduction to yourself, where you live and what you do.

RnaG

The Irish language radio station was conceded after many decades of struggle, and began with just three hours of programming per day. Yet the first language ever heard on Irish radio was *an Ghaeilge*, when President Douglas Hyde formally launched Radio Éireann on 1 January 1926, with a speech emphasising the importance of Irish. In the first decade of broadcasting, there was a grand average of one hour and 45 minutes of Irish language programming per week. The main debate over programming pitted those who viewed Irish programmes as a source of news and entertainment against those who saw Irish as an educational tool for the majority who spoke little or none.

The hours dedicated to Irish rose in the 1950s, to 10 per cent of total airtime, or about 11 hours per week. When television arrived in 1962, the time devoted to the Irish language was minimal, an hour or two per week, out of a total of 42 hours each week. The Irish language programmes on television achieved remarkable ratings, notably *Féach*, a current affairs programme with an audience of 650,000, and *Amuigh Faoin Spéir*, a nature programme that commanded an audience of 780,000. Admittedly the viewing options were a little narrower back then and the 'opposition' to *Amuigh Faoin Spéir* might well have been *Wanderly Wagon*, for all I know.

The *Gluaiseacht Chearta Sibhialta na Gaeltachta*, a civil rights organisation based in the Gaeltacht, played a key role in lobbying for an Irish language radio station, launching their own pirate station in Connemara while politicians dithered and delayed. The growing militant mood of the Gaeltacht, a key Fianna Fáil heartland, helped push the issue ahead, and Raidió na Gaeltachta began broadcasting in 1972.

I knew nothing about RnaG before switching it on, having assumed it was a narrow, parochial and conservative station. It has since become the *bunchloch* (foundation) of my own practice, three hours or more of RnaG *gach lá*, apart from weekends, when the endless sport becomes unbearable. For the price of a radio or any device with Internet attached you can have a living, talking Gaeltacht in your kitchen, in your bedroom, all day, every day. In my own case, this has been the single most important instrument in advancing my knowledge of Irish. It began as a penance but has since become a pleasure, marking the pace and rhythm of the day. You take your own time, listen when it suits, switching on and off as you please. In the beginning, you will understand almost nothing. It doesn't matter. No one talks back to you and no one gives out to you and you can pick and choose your programmes and listen back on the RTÉ player if you need a second turn at a particular item. Over time, like a runner preparing for a marathon, you build up stamina.

Another great advantage: there are no ads. I mentioned this to a friend and she responded, 'God help them they must be in dire straits.' Actually they're in a privileged place that is all too rare these days, a commercial-free zone where no loud, insistent voices are selling you useless stuff and more useless stuff – endless useless stuff, in cheery, loud, insistent voices, every 15 minutes.

When the day arrives that you can understand most of what's going on, *comhghairdeachas leat*, you have arrived, at least in terms of comprehension. If you are overseas and far from other Irish speakers, it is incredibly helpful. I probably understood no more than 5 per cent of the language spoken at the outset, but that figure has crept steadily upwards, providing one of the most satisfactory, tangible achievements in this process. Language does not grow in a straight line, it curves and loops and twists and turns. There are days when Irish comes easy and days when it seems to run backwards. There are programmes I now understand 100 per cent, but there are others that still leave me guessing. Switch it on and let it soak in, absorbing it as you go about your daily life.

Everyday phrases, breakfast, dinner and night-time

The Irish language disappeared out of the lives of our families one word at a time. This erosion can be reversed, one common phrase at a time. The smallest phrase thrown into everyday conversation is like adding a fresh ingredient to a salad, a hint of mint, a murmur of marigold. Watch out for the response: *Fáilte*, you're welcome, *go raibh maith agat*, thank you, *dia duit*, how are you, *dia is muire duit*, just fine, *codladh sámh*, sleep tight. After a week spent in Buenos Aires, my Argentinian friends can pronounce those phrases to perfection. Every morning I got up and greeted them in Irish, thanked them when appropriate and said 'sleep tight' at night. Despite my offers, Amanda, a teenager, resolutely refuses to speak any English to me, a subject she learns at school. But she gets into the spirit of the Irish phrases. You don't have to wait for a grant from the Irish government to begin the reverse language shift.

Irish dwells here

Find out your address in Irish and use it. I live in Boston, Tubber, County Clare. What does that mean? Somehow Móinin na gCloigeann, the original name, became Boston, a meaningless nothing of a name. *Móinín*, a meadow, *cloigeann*, head, something like 'the top of the meadow', summoning an entire landscape into existence as you approach this tiny village. Tubber sounds like a tyre factory, whereas *tobar*, the Irish word for a well, conjures images of holy wells and ancient rituals. It is a small but significant pleasure to receive post addressed to me in Irish. Begin the shift with anyone who sends you post, especially bills.

But be warned – you will meet a range of responses, from blank incomprehension to outright hostility. I phoned up my insurance company to renew my car insurance in July 2016, advising them of a change of address. I spelt it out carefully. The woman on the other end of the phone hesitated. 'I can't find it,' she said. 'It's the same place, just the Irish version,' I assured her. She told me it wasn't coming up on her GPS instrument, that it wasn't a recognised address. I assured her that all my official post arrived to this address in Irish but she remained unconvinced. 'I can't do it,' she said. 'Fine,' I replied, before I had a chance to think, 'then I can't renew the policy.'

As soon as I hung up the phone I began to doubt my impulsive action. All the other insurers probably worked off the same GPS identification system. I prepared myself for a meek return to my original insurer and with it, grey, miserable Boston, Tubber, while possibly disguising my voice on the phone. First, however, I called up another broker, who gave me a quote. I spelt out the address. 'That's fine,' she said, and the policy arrived a couple of days later to Móinín na gCloigeann. The quote was also 10 euro cheaper than that offered by the company I had been insured with.

Begin emails with a greeting in Irish and close them with a Gaelic farewell. Ronan, *a chara*, that's it, for masculine or feminine, *a chara*, Hi there. For the signing off, try *sonas ort, slán is beannacht, is mise le meas, le gach dea-ghuí*. There are risks attached to this approach. A friend in California responded to my greetings with entire Google-translated 'Gaelic' emails, which threatened my sanity for weeks on end. I also transferred my computer commands in Firefox to Irish, a task that takes less than five minutes. I am so familiar with the drop-down menu, the edit, print, save and so on that I soon switch them in my head to their Irish equivalents.

Tune in to Fuaimeanna na Gaeilge, the sounds of Irish

If RnaG is simply too much to handle for starters, and it may well be, start out with a CD or two of Irish language sounds. My own particular favourite is *Gugalaí Gug*, a collection of songs and rhymes produced by Futa Fata publishers in An Spidéal, Connemara. There are 29 tracks, most of them no longer than a couple of minutes, spoken and sung by children and adults. The language is beautiful, the range of ages and styles is broad, the music top class, and it comes with a booklet should you want to decipher the words and rhymes. Put it on in the background, in the car, at night, especially if you have children. The tracks focus on *fuaimeanna na Gaeilge*, the all-important phonetic sounds of Irish. If you prefer Munster Irish opt for *Rabhlaí Rabhlaí*, and if Ulster Irish is your thing *Ící Pící* will do the job. No home should be without them all.

Once you master the sounds you can pronounce anything. It becomes a question of 'ungluing' the words into smaller units of speech and practising them. The Irish language, when properly spoken, murmurs and wraps itself round the listener. Songs and rhymes have an irresistible contagion effect. In Shaw's Road, west Belfast, where a handful of families came together to form a Gaeltacht, they found that friends' kids, playing in the street, learned the Gaelic rhymes used by their own Irish-speaking kids. There was no conscious effort involved, just the joy of play and the impact of repetition.

The lyrics of Kila's albums are another vital tool in cracking the sounds of Irish. Find a copy of their 1997 *Tóg É Go Bog É* and listen to tracks 9 and 10, 'Bí ann' and 'Leanfaidh Mé'. All their albums are worth a close listen, and the solo records made by singer Rónán Ó Snodaigh are also a great way of warming up and tuning into the language in a creative setting. Kila also manage another remarkable feat – their instruments sound like they are speaking in Irish. If in doubt, listen to 'Crann na bPinginí', track 11 on the same album as above. It's a slow air, an instrumental lament that hurls mournful Irish at the listener.

John Spillane is another great source of light around the Irish language, an easy-going bard with a wicked sense of humour. While his original albums are, without exception, and to borrow a word of his own, *brilliant* (start with 'My Dark Rosaleen'), he has also recorded two albums of songs we learned at school, in Irish. If, like me, you went to a west British school in south Dublin, you probably didn't learn any of them, making this an even tastier discovery. The experience is particularly enjoyable because Spillane found school kids to sing along, adding a welcome burst of child energy to the mix.

Beware the FGWA: Fíor Ghaeilgeoirs With Attitude

Our old friend Dinneen, of the dictionary, defined an Irish speaker as 'an unsophisticated, generous, easy-going, simple' type of person. We wish. He got it wrong on that one, but then again the concept of a Gaeilgeoir was unheard of until after his death, so he can hardly be blamed for the oversight. In Dinneen's day there were no Gaeilgeoirs, just Gaedhealaighe (Gaels). While Irish speakers are simply that – speakers of Irish – there is a small subset of Irish speakers whose main motive in speaking the language seems to be lobbying on its behalf. These Gaeilgeoirs are monothematic and tireless, and no issue is too trivial for it to be adopted as a badge of struggle.

The Ó Dónaill *foclóir*, successor to Dinneen's classic, defined the Gaeilgeoir as 'an Irish speaker' and 'an Irish learner', anticipating perhaps the emergence of the Gael-bore, whose motivation and talent for the language seems to extend only as far as talking about the injustices visited upon it. Before I bothered to check it out, I had assumed that a Gaeilgeoir was anyone who spoke Irish, including native speakers. This was a terrible mistake on my part and takes me to what is probably the most significant book written in the Irish language (not to be confused with the giants of the literary canon, where Máirtín Ó Cadhain and others rule the roost), required reading for anyone needing a detox from the misery memoirs of their school days.

An Béal Bocht

Nothing about the Irish language can ever be the same once you've read this book, *An Béal Bocht*, the poor mouth, written in 1941 by satirist Myles na gCopaleen, aka Flann O'Brien, aka Brian O'Nolan. *An Béal Bocht* is the Irish language literary equivalent of *Father Ted*, a savvy satire on the misery memoir exemplified by Peig Sayers and Muiris Ó Súilleabháin, penned by a person with enormous respect and admiration for the original texts in a homage that strikes every possible sore point, in absurd, exaggerated fashion.

It is the perfect antidote to the toxic legacy of Peig Sayers, which unjustly forms the basis of an entire generation's distaste for the language. The book brings the three main Gaeltachtaí into one grim Irish-speaking landmass – Corca Dhorca, its inhabitants at the mercy of grinding poverty, endless rain and occasional visits from Gaeilgeoirí, those fervent revivalists from Dublin who revel in the authentic Gaelic poverty of the authentic Gaelic-speaking natives in their authentic Gaelic hovels. Bonaparte O'Coonnassa takes us on a breathless ride through the diverse aspects of authentic Gaelic life, its traditions, its annual carnival, in which eight people die of exhaustion provoked by authentic loyalty to Irish dancing, as they literally dance until they drop. A local chieftain is named Gael of the Year and makes a long acceptance speech, taking a day or two to say his piece. I have left the word *fíor*, meaning true or truly, but pronounced like the English word 'fear', because it engages so cleverly with the spirit of the text:

> Gaels! It delights my Gaelic heart to be here today speaking Gaelic with you at this Gaelic feis in the centre of the Gaeltacht. May I state that I am a Gael. I'm Gaelic from the crown of my head to the soles of my feet … If we're fíor Gaelic, we must constantly discuss the question of the Gaelic revival and the question of Gaelicism. There is no use in having Gaelic, if we converse in it on non-Gaelic topics. He who speaks Gaelic but fails to discuss the language question is not fíor Gaelic in his heart; such conduct is of no benefit to Gaelicism because he only jeers at Gaelic and reviles the Gaels. There is nothing in this life so nice and so Gaelic as fíor fíor Gaelic Gaels who speak in fíor Gaelic Gaelic about the fíor Gaelic language.

An Béal Bocht builds a bonfire of Irish language enthusiasms and happily puts a torch to it. I tried reading it in English, seeking a juicy quote or two, but the English version lacks the richness of the original. It is a relatively easy read, and with Gael and fíor-Ghael appearing in every other phrase, you will quickly get the hang of it. Some fíor-Ghaeilgeoirí view *An Béal Bocht* as a hostile text serving to undermine the language, but in the context of a troubled past it seems a joyful text, a labour of love and a necessary antidote to the Gaelbores of yore. If there was such a thing as restorative linguistic justice then this should be on the Leaving Cert syllabus.

Challenge: Get the book, read the book.

Dialect: a public warning

The next person who comes up to me and tells me a) they can't learn Irish because they don't have a dialect or b) Donegal Irish is impossible for reasons so obvious they require no articulation, is going to get a copy of the Dinneen dictionary over the head. It will hurt and you have been warned. Imagine being told you probably shouldn't go to Mexico or Cuba or Argentina to learn Spanish because it's too difficult and too different from Madrid Spanish. Spanish in Latin America does indeed sound different, just as English spoken in Glasgow, Cork or Belize City takes some getting used to. It's all English though, and we adapt to it.

Irish has three major dialects, and if Connacht or Munster Irish are perceived as easier than Donegal it is only because people have more exposure to them, especially at school. Irish people have many pieces of language baggage, and dialect is in everyone's carry-on luggage. Irish has a written standard but no spoken standard, so the spoken language is always up for grabs, and the Donegal people take full advantage. Beware the *bolsairí*, or whingers. Tune in and enjoy whatever Irish comes your way. When I visit Mexico I quickly recover my Mexican accent and local store of words, aligning myself with the local speech. In my own daily practice, I listen to *Iris Aniar* (Mon–Fri, 9.15–10.15am), based on Connemara Irish, *Rónán Beo* (Tues–Fri 3–4pm) from Gaoth Dobhair in Donegal and *Cormac ag a Cúig* (Mon–Fri 5–6pm), from Dublin. I occasionally drop in to *An Saol Ó Dheas*, broadcast from the Kerry Gaeltacht and *Barrscéalta*, a Donegal production.

If you don't have any Irish they are all as bloody difficult as each other, but with Irish and a patient ear, they all come to life and make sound sense over time. Spare me the *seafóid* about dialect. The issue only becomes relevant if you move into a particular Gaeltacht, and if you have taken that great leap forward then dialect is coming your way of its own accord in the language of everyday life around you.

CHAPTER 5

Fever

Outbreaks of Irish language fever occur when least expected: My niece Caroline attended an Irish-medium school and in early 2016 she watched the first episode of *Rebellion*, a dramatic re-enactment of the events surrounding the Easter Rising of 1916, made for television. Soon after this she told me she was changing her surname, Skelly, to the Irish version, Ní Scealaí. Right after St Patrick's Day 2016, a friend informed me that fiddle player Martin Hayes had changed his Facebook identity to Máirtín Ó hAodha. The closer I get to the language the more excited I get about these small victories, confirming some vague notion of a rising Gaelic tide. David McWilliams, prominent economist and author, fresh from a visit to the Irish-speaking island of Inis Oírr, caught a touch of this fever, tweeting a request for advice on how best to learn the language. Then it was broadcaster Vincent Browne's turn, as he signed up for a *dianchúrsa* in Corca Dhuibhne. Friends who attended the course recalled the pleasure they had in harassing Browne during class; '*Freagair an cheist*', they would insist when he had difficulty answering the teacher, 'Just *freagair an cheist*'. Not to be outdone, broadcaster Miriam O'Callaghan announced in August 2016 that she was keen on Irish and would be interested in presenting a show *as Gaeilge* once she improved her skills in the language. Comedian Tommy Tiernan then announced a stand-up show in Irish at a comedy festival in Galway. Any day now Blind Boy Boatclub will announce a date for the

Rubberbandits *dianchúrsa* at their own Coláiste Samhraidh in Limerick in 2017.

Beidh mé ann.

My return to Irish ripened and blossomed in 2016, coinciding with the centenary of the Rising, and with it an avalanche of radio and TV programmes, books, public events and exhibitions. Ireland is examining itself in the light of the promises made at the birth of the state, the sacrifices of that generation and notions of identity and aspiration that accompanied the struggle for independence. There is some debate on the role of *an Ghaeilge* in the movement for freedom. The 1916 rebel proclamation contained just one phrase in Irish, *Poblacht na hÉireann,* the Republic of Ireland, minus the required *fada,* or accent. This brief document, written in haste, has the shape and style of a press release rather than a blueprint for a new society. It was understood that the Irish language would be a key pillar of the emerging nation, 'not free merely, but Gaelic as well, not Gaelic merely but free as well', as Pearse insisted.

Unfortunately Pearse left no instructions behind.

According to the 1891 census, just 3.1 per cent of children under the age of 10 spoke Irish, marking the end of intergenerational transmission, the key marker measuring language handed on from mothers to their newborn infants, suckled at birth alongside the milk that nourishes them.

This was, literally, the end of the line.

The language revival was a critical foundation stone in the emergence of a collective national consciousness. 'If the Irish language is allowed to perish the life of the Irish Nation as a separate nation ceases,' wrote Micheál Ó hAnnracháin, one of the executed men. On the eve of another execution, Seán Mac Diarmada wrote a letter to his brothers and sisters, urging them to pass on the following message to his children: 'counsel them to always practise truth, honesty and straightforwardness in all things, and sobriety, if they do this and remember their country they will be all right. Insist on their learning the language and history.'

The language revival took hold of the popular imagination in the years before the Rising, and in 1902, when the Gaelic League held its annual 'language procession' march in Dublin city centre, 100,000 people attended. This was a language on the move, a key part of a broad social movement that recognised the central role it might play in forging national identity. If ever there was a moment in which *an Ghaeilge* might have been restored, 1916 and its aftermath was it. Survivors of the independence war set about building the Free State, but the immediate outbreak of civil war (1922–3) and the failure to negotiate a better deal for the Nationalist population in Northern Ireland left a bitter, divisive legacy, shattering any hope of a shared national moment. The chronic economic crisis and lack of creative spirit saw the Irish language relegated to a ceremonial role, an adornment to be displayed on special occasions.

In other countries, the birth of a new state or the overthrow of a dictator have historically been times of positive, collective energy, in which great undertakings might be attempted. In Nicaragua, 1980, one half of the country, largely urban, taught the other half, largely rural, how to read and write. The Sandinista government, fresh from toppling dictator Anastasio Somoza in 1979, rallied the nation to a literacy campaign, supported by UNESCO. Some 90,000 people, most of them under 18 years of age and several thousand as young as 12, volunteered to teach adults how to read and write. The country's schools and universities closed down and parents were given leave from work to help coordinate the effort. A two-week training course was followed by a five-month literacy programme, for which volunteers stayed with host families and worked alongside them in their small plots of subsistence agriculture. The campaign was successful in that illiteracy was reduced from 50 per cent to about 12 per cent of the population, but it also created a shared sense of citizenship and a meeting of two Nicaraguas whose paths rarely crossed.

I wonder what might have happened if the Irish state had coordinated a nationwide language programme soon after independence, inviting native Irish speakers to spend time in the homes of willing learners around the country or inviting learners to stay for an extended period in Gaeltacht homes. A major effort was made to teach school subjects through Irish in the 1950s and 1960s, but the initiative occurred in a vacuum, as Irish had little or no presence outside the school system. In Israel, fresh from the declaration of the new state, the government implemented a Hebrew language programme in 1949, achieving a language shift within a generation. The *ulpan*, a Hebrew word for studio, is a rapid language acquisition system combining individual sessions with a personal coach, group interaction and self-study sessions. The system produced rapid results.

It makes you think.

What if the Irish state had determined that Irish would be the language of the people alongside English within 10 years? The cabinet could have led by example, the civil service upskilled to accommodate Irish, the Gaeltachtaí granted special status in facilitating the transition. It would have been challenging but possible, the pain long forgotten by now. In Ireland, however, as Éamon de Valera observed, the state waited for a big idea that never came along. There were no revolutionary changes in post-independence Ireland, just a handover of power from one conservative elite to another. The same social structures remained in place while the Catholic Church deepened its control over cultural and state affairs, dampening creativity.

The Irish language remained on the sidelines but had a habit of showing up without invitation, a ghostly presence, a spectre haunting school children by day, engaging poets by night: 'If we regard self-understanding, mutual understanding, imaginative enhancement, cultural diversity and a tolerant political atmosphere as desirable attainments, we should remember that a knowledge of the Irish language is an essential element in their realisation.' There is nothing like a quote from Seamus Heaney to put manners on an argument. Is the Irish language important to us as a people? Heaney says it is essential to our being. *Ab shin an méid? Sin an méid.* Is that it? Yes, it is. When people ask me what Irish means to me, words, normally my most reliable companions, suddenly dry up. I end up talking in vague terms about the beauty of the language, the breadth of expression in place names, the longing and belonging expressed through a native tongue that holds the life experience of the generations before us.

In Ireland there is a distinction to be made between native and mother tongue. English was my mother's tongue, the language that raised me, but Irish is an expression of an older tongue inhabiting an older body and a deeper identity. The exact nature of this connection is difficult to pin down. In Colombia I first came to understand this attachment to place and language in dramatic fashion. The Colombian U'wa, an indigenous people living close to the border with Venezuela, treat the land around them with extreme care. When it comes to planting their own crops, they work the land so carefully that their crops cannot be detected from the air. Another way they protect the diversity around them is by prohibiting all human access, including their own, to large tracts of forest inside their recognised territory. This area is a reserve protecting jaguars, bears and toucans. The U'wa have no written language, their experience passed on through story and song.

I visited the U'wa in 1999, meeting Roberto Cobaria, a tribal elder, who explained how his people maintain harmony with nature by 'singing the world into existence'. At the time of my visit the U'wa were in a state of emergency, as they resisted an attempt by US oil company Occidental to drill for oil and gas on their land. Members of the U'wa threatened to commit collective suicide rather than allow the drilling to go ahead. There was a historic precedent; when the Europeans arrived in the 16th century some members of the community opted to throw themselves off a cliff rather than submit to the Spanish invaders. On the threshold of the 21st century the U'wa told me the oil exploration process would irretrievably alter not just the landscape but the imprint of the U'wa across time. If that was to happen, they would no longer recognise themselves as a people, and their stories and lives would have no meaning. I spent several days in this beautiful, remote place, staying in a hut on a mountainside above the low-hanging clouds. I came under the spell of a warm people living in close proximity to nature. On an intellectual level, I understood their campaign to preserve their way of life, but it was light years removed from my own experience as a middle-class product of south Dublin.

In similar fashion, my return to the Irish language was an intellectual exercise at first, my attention focused on finding an efficient and speedy method to learn it. As the months passed, however, I sensed a shift within me as the language became more heartfelt, increasingly connected to nature and the landscape around me. The U'wa visit came back to me as I grappled with the language and its significance. As yet, I had no words for this shift.

I met Manchán Magan, travel writer and native Irish speaker. He was raised in Dublin but spent holidays in the Corca Dhuibhne Gaeltacht in west Kerry, enjoying childhood trips to the Blasket Islands, where the local women sang to him and told him stories, enchanted by the visiting fair-haired child dressed in elegant French clothes. Manchán's grandmother, Sheila Humphreys (1899–1994), was a prominent, lifelong Republican and a key figure during his childhood years, nurturing a love for the Irish language. Humphreys was a member of Cumann na mBan who spent three years in prison, including 31 days on one of several hunger strikes, 'for nationalism and the language'. At the age of 11 or 12, Manchán was tasked with writing 'comms' on Rizla papers – tiny messages meant for Republican prisoners, smuggled into the H-Blocks in Belfast. 'Every word you spoke was a bullet aimed at England,' he recalled. 'We were living every day for what Bobby Sands was doing then.' Manchán rebelled against his family's Republican orthodoxy and drifted away from the language. Once he left school he travelled to Africa and Latin America, learning other languages. When he visited India he took up residence in a cowshed to devote himself to meditation. 'I wanted a cave,' he said, 'but they wouldn't give me a cave.' His brother, a Hollywood film producer, interrupted his reveries with a commission from the new Irish language TV station, Teilifís na Gaeilge (renamed TG4 in 1999) to make a series of travel programmes. Manchán would be the presenter. One of the programmes took them to an island off Taiwan where they met a Yami man, one of the Polynesian sea people living in underground caves. As they prepared to film, the cave dweller approached Manchán, brandishing a ceremonial sword. He grew frightened. The man noticed and began to sing in his native language before saying 'Don't be scared, these are our birth songs, our songs of creation from the sea, you have your songs of creation too, you can understand me even if you don't understand the words.' Manchán was instantly transported back to the Blasket Islands, where the local women sang him songs that carried the memory of a people, back through the ages. 'I suddenly got it, this direct link to another native culture.'

I was becoming involved with a community of Irish speakers, despite my lack of fluency. The sudden awareness of the interconnectedness of language, place and people felt like an anchor grounding my return to the language in something lasting and firm.

When pressed about my feelings for the language I stumble over terms like 'connection', 'link' and 'ancestors' before reaching for slippery concepts of 'identity', 'healing' and 'wisdom'. I realise I am trotting out motives and explanations that have been over-rehearsed or borrowed, ringing hollow after so much use. I turn to more seasoned thinkers: Heaney wrote that 'not to learn Irish is to miss the opportunity of understanding what life in this country has meant and could mean in a better future', an unequivocal call to language as a source of self-knowledge and collective inspiration. Not learning Irish, concluded the poet, would 'cut oneself off from ways of being at home'.

Peadar Ó Riada acknowledges the usefulness of English as a language of communication, but regards it as secondary to the Irish language, an 'ill-fitting coat' that he believes cannot express our complete selves. One of the characters in Brian Friel's play *Translations* describes the feeling of arriving in to an Irish-speaking village as one of 'a sense of recognition, of confirmation of something I half-knew instinctively'. The Irish language, its hidden depths, its secret constructions, are half-known to me, and in that recognition, I feel more at home with myself. Former President Mary McAleese said that learning Irish was like transitioning from black-and-white television to colour: 'Irish life came into view in technicolour.' I caught the tail end of the era of black-and-white television and how normal it seemed until the colours arrived. After that, there was no going back.

The poets seem particularly adept at putting their finger on it. Paul Durcan spoke of his relationship with *an Ghaeilge*: 'Irish, which once I could read, and even speak a little, is buried ten fathoms of bones inside me.' This is *an fhadbh*, the crux of the matter. It doesn't feel like an alien language, it feels like a secret living inside me, waiting to be revealed. I don't know whether this feeling has taken root because of the time spent learning the language as a schoolchild or if it comes down to reasons of mystic trace or mythic forebear. If the Irish language is a revelation it is a rather slow-moving one, all hard work and no flashes of lightning, word for word combat rather than burning bushes. McAleese said that Irish played an important part in her identity even before she could speak it. I grew up with Catholicism, which covered me like a second skin, something powerful and ever-present but surprisingly superficial and easily cast off once adulthood arrived. The language, however, adheres to the bones, the very marrow.

The Oxford English Dictionary informs me that a fever is 'an abnormally high body temperature, usually accompanied by shivering, headache, and in severe instances, delirium'. My current infatuation with the language feels like this, more a delirium than a desire to master the mechanics of the language itself. I savour obscure words in the dictionary and feel a strange delight on dipping into the *Duanaire*, a collection of poems of the dispossessed Gaelic scholars dating from 1600 to 1900. I have discovered a doorway into another world, but then what? Where does the language go? Where do I go? Who has walked this path before me?

A farewell to English

Over the past 50 years a number of people have responded to the challenge of a return to Irish, symbolic gestures aimed at self-knowledge and perhaps inspiring others into making similar gestures. Michael Hartnett (1941–1999), a distinguished Irish poet, fell in love with the Irish language, which he first heard from his grandmother, 'a woman who embodied a thousand years of Gaelic history'. His relationship with the language deepened as a teenager, after a visit to Cúil Aodha: 'I began to think in Gaelic, to dream in it, and even, as I was told, to speak it in my sleep.' As an adult he reached the following conclusion: 'revival of the Irish language [is] too important to be left to any government'.

Hartnett spoke of the language as a 'spectre haunting the twilight of the imagination', and declared his grand gesture in 'A Farewell to English', a bilingual poem that marked the end of his writing in English. Hartnett's gesture was on a par with folk singer Bob Dylan going electric, only it was the intrusion of the ancient rather than the shock of the new with which he struck a chord. Unlike Dylan, however, Hartnett had a small following within a notoriously small clique of marginalised writers and their readers. The announcement was made on the stage of the Peacock Theatre in June 1974, and he moved to Templeglantine, County Limerick, to be closer to the land and the language:

I have made my choice and leave with little weeping:
I have come with meagre voice
to court the language of my people.

Hartnett was a lone rebel taking to the hillsides to pursue his dream of a bilingual state in which English would be the language of trade and commerce ('a great language to sell pigs in,' he wrote), while Irish would preside over matters of philosophy, love and poetry. He phased out his English poetry readings, first with bilingual performances and finally *an Ghaeilge* alone. However, his life carried on in English at home and in everyday life and in retrospect his gesture seemed more like a missing chapter from the pages of *An Béal Bocht* than any serious attempt to revitalise the declining *teanga*. One could easily imagine Hartnett's solemn announcement, the End of English, at the annual Oireachtas language festival, the fíor Ghaels cheering his decision to cut all ties with the enemy Saxon tongue. Later that evening the 're-racinated' hero would return home to his English-speaking family and friends.

In later years Hartnett's wife Rosemary strengthened that notion of a Quixotic, deluded battle when she spoke of her feelings of exclusion from the new life of her husband, who entertained a circle of Irish-speaking friends: 'Any attempt to enter the conversation in English was rebuffed. I retired defeated and angry from my struggles with the language.' In time Hartnett went back to writing in English. No one doubted the genuine feeling behind his gesture, but it carried with it an air of futility and self-defeat. Another poet, Brendan Kennelly, delivered a diplomatic riposte to Hartnett's shift: 'Ideally, forget the idea of allegiance to one or other language, accept the gifts of both.' The use of Irish becomes an opposition for some people, prompting an adversarial relationship with its influential partner, English. Nuala Ní Dhomhnaill describes such people as 'professional Irish-eens', and recalled an event she attended alongside Seán Mac Réamoinn, a journalist and broadcaster, at an event in Limerick. At breakfast Mac Réamoinn and Ní Dhomhnaill chatted in Irish before boarding a train for Dublin: 'Suddenly the volume went up,' recalled Ní Dhomhnaill. 'He starts talking Irish in a much louder voice, and I wondered what the hell was going on. He was becoming the public voice of Irish. I've no time for any of that rubbish.'

Italian writer Italo Calvino once wrote that 'everything that forces us to give up a part of ourselves is negative'. Calvino was explaining how his membership of the Italian Communist Party never came into conflict with his professional life as a writer, but the analogy fits the topic of taking up languages and putting others down. The Irish language is constantly compared to and measured alongside English, as if one or other language had to be declared a winner in some form of linguistic Hunger Games. Times have changed, and in a globalised world bilingualism and multilinguism are the norm, monoglots the growing exception. This reality is easily overlooked as the sphere of Irish influence operates at its strongest in Britain, the US, Canada and Australia among English speakers. Even as I settle into this neat conclusion, a fragment of a poem arrives from Italy in an email from my friend Virginia, a linguist and native of Turin with an eagle eye for the disruptive quote. She speaks Italian, English and German, along with a dash of Hungarian, and is contemplating a dalliance with *an Ghaeilge*. Virginia felt like her brain was 'rewired in English' when she studied it, and she observed, 'because space is limited, it probably had to kick some Italian bits out'. She sent on a fragment of a poem by Afric McGlinchey, from the Italian–Irish collaboration, 'A Different Skin': 'when a foreign language percolates your own / until its idioms even permeate your dreams / that's not just acquisition, but erosion too'. The English language has put down roots within us, no longer a foreign tongue even if it lacks the deeper, ancestral connection to our past. As a nation we have put on a second coat.

I find myself making one small gesture over time, and that is my farewell to English language radio (providing Lyric FM's *Blue of the Night* is permitted as an exception, as no one really speaks during that show, and if they do, I promise not to listen). My connection with RnaG has grown over the past three years; it is an intimate part of my home life, a welcome friend each morning in my kitchen. My awareness and interest in the issues discussed on the station have grown. I want to know what's going on in the three main Gaeltachtaí, *na himeachtaí* (events), the conferences and gatherings, the news and scandals. I want to hear the children from schools in the Gaeltacht discussing music and drama and the old recordings from the archives. The turn to Irish coincides with a growing impatience at the commercialism of mainstream English language radio, the narrow range of topics discussed, the narrow range of pundits called in to offer their opinions and the sense of dull repetition around every issue, from economics to sport. It may not be entirely the fault of RTÉ Radio 1, Newstalk and Today FM, once my staple news diet – I may simply be growing old and grumpy. The old talk shows ran like sugar through my veins, a shot of Joe Duffy, an interview on *The Pat Kenny Show* or an investigative report on *Drivetime*. All that has gone, and like sugar leaving the body, within a few weeks the urge to listen has gone – I can hardly believe I ever listened to them at all. And, this being Ireland, people send me links if something important is heard, something regarded as vital listening for me and my research. That occasion has probably arisen half a dozen times in three years – *Oíche mhaith agus codladh sámh.*

My life is slowly becoming trilingual or, to be more precise, bilingual with a side order of competency in Irish. On any given morning I will begin the day with *Iris Aniar*, the RnaG chat show. I will then turn on the computer and read the newspapers from Latin America along with emails from Colombia and Argentina before working on my latest writing project in English. As the day progresses I will read some Irish and English, listen to more RnaG, write an email or two and make a phone call or two *as Gaeilge.* I might just as easily meet my neighbour Alba (Spanish- and Dutch-speaking) or Tony, a local walking guide who speaks Irish and Italian.

There is no hostility between the languages, no competition, just a growing cooperation and occasional overlap. I protect the fresh shoots of spoken Irish, the most fragile of the three languages, from its overweening companions. If there is any language that can accommodate a degree of erosion it is my

English, which enjoys hegemony in all areas. Spanish is topped up on annual visits to Latin America, whereas Irish is under cultivation, requiring tilling, watering and feeding.

Jhumpa Lahiri, a Bengali writer based in the US, performed a grand gesture that ranks alongside Hartnett's farewell, shifting the language of her writing from English to Italian. Lahiri, who speaks Bengali but lacks total fluency, wrote her first books in English, winning global recognition. Infatuated with the notion of speaking Italian, an ambition she nursed for over two decades, she finally decided to do something about it. Lahiri, with her husband and two children, moved to Rome. In preparation, six months prior to departure, she stopped reading in English, 'an official renunciation', and once she settled in Italy, she began writing in Italian. The result, *In Other Words*, published in 2016, is a bilingual treatise on her journey. Lahiri wrote the original Italian version of the book while the English version, presented side by side, is rendered by a translator. The journey was never easy for Lahiri, and soon after her arrival in Rome she was on the verge of giving up: 'everything seems impossible, indecipherable, impenetrable'.

I recognised this feeling.

The language goalposts keep moving. The ground shifts beneath me, good days and bad days. The breakthrough comes precisely when faced with this pain barrier, this Berlin Wall of word-otherness. When she arrived in Rome her Italian finally ceased to operate like a light switch 'to turn on occasionally and then switch off'. Now the language was all around her. This is the Irish language in my life, so far, a light switched on and off at will. Any time of the day or night I can tune in to the RTÉ player and with the click of a keyboard the sounds of native Irish fill up my bedroom, my mind suddenly alert to the extra effort required in understanding the sounds. But my language has not been put to the bigger test, to live inside this other world of words. Irish poet Nuala Ní Dhomhnaill memorably described her own bilingual life as a kind of civil war going on inside her between two warring factions that left her constantly exhausted.

However, the mystical stuff, the poetry and Durcan's bones are unconvincing arguments for many people. Is there anything a little more practical for the non-believer? Did you know that speaking Irish is a vital defence against the effects of a stroke? At this point I have the attention of the most cynical naysayers and I'm not letting go. I know that you may think that Irish has no practical use, but just wait until you have a stroke – you'll be grateful for the *cúpla focal.* A study of 608 patients in India, detailed in the scientific journal *Stroke,* revealed that people who suffer a stroke and speak more than one language are twice as likely to recover their cognitive abilities compared to those who speak only one language. These abilities are well worth recovering, as they include language, memory and attention. Dr Thomas Bak, a neuroscientist at the University of Edinburgh and co-author of the research, explained that while a second language may not help prevent a stroke, it certainly helps the patient recover faster. The patients all enjoyed comparable health and suffered the same level of stroke, but half the sample of patients had one language only. The 'brain fitness' involved in bilingual living apparently keeps the neurotransmitter networks on their toes. Better still, fluency in the second language is not a prerequisite, just competency, and many of the beneficiaries simply absorbed the second language passively through life experience.

It is tempting to follow up this persuasive argument with another one: Did you know that, district by district, crime rates are lower in Irish-speaking Gaeltachtaí than elsewhere? It probably helps that Irish-speaking towns and villages are located in remote western coastal areas, where suspicious activities stand out, but it remains a statistic of note. After all, there are many towns and villages, equally remote, where English is spoken, which end up further down the same list. At this point, I ask my impressed audience a third question: Did you know that couples who speak Irish at home are twice as likely to stay together than those speaking only English? (For scientific evidence turn to p. 399.)

Setting aside the arguments and theories, the reality is simple: I have fallen in love with the Irish language, so practical arguments hold no sway. I don't care if it has no practical purpose – indeed I derive a perverse satisfaction from that reality, in an era in which everything is counted and calculated in terms of profit and loss, even time itself. Neither am I exercised by rumours of its imminent demise. Isn't the planet itself on the way out? On the same afternoon I wrote that sentence, *The Guardian* newspaper reported that the Milky Way was disappearing from sight as light pollution made it invisible to more than a third of the world's population, prompting one scientist to observe that 'we've lost something, but how do we place value on it?'

Irish isn't even my first love, as that unique honour belongs to Spanish, the language of my adolescence and professional life, the language of Julio Cortázar and Eduardo Galeano, the language that opened up the possibilities of love and rebellion throughout Latin America. The experience of learning Irish could not be more different: I am making slow, steady progress in a relationship that blossoms gently over the years, coming to fruition with measured steps and lesser ambition. But like so many things that grow slowly over a long period, it feels as solid as the beech tree that protects my cabin from the autumn gales.

CHAPTER 6

Staying the Course

Stop apologising

The harshest judgements we make are about ourselves, and learning Irish is no exception. 'I'm sorry, my Irish is awful' – learners apologise well before they have had a chance to butcher the language, but Apologetic Speaker Syndrome extends all the way to the fluent. Reuben Ó hAnluain, an Irish teacher educated in the 'old' days, believes that much of the violence inflicted on pupils by teachers was a kind of defence mechanism, to cover up the insecurities of teachers uncertain of their own competence. 'They didn't want students to ask questions,' said Reuben, 'so they created an atmosphere of fear.'

If the default position of the non-learner is 'God, I'd love to speak Irish', then the equivalent for the competent speaker is 'My Irish is terrible', while the fluent frequently defer to the native speaker, who in turn remains cautious around the academics. In a less insecure world a good speaker might well inform the learner that yes, their Irish does sound pretty awful, more than terrible, a dark stain on humanity, but *coinnigh ort*, keep going, the beginner must practise, and the more fluent must bear with it, recalling if they can their own steps in learning something complex from scratch.

The apology syndrome goes beyond language, of course; just watch as the Irish wander the world, shuffling by people – sorry,

sorry – paying for something – sorry, sorry – opening a door for someone else – sorry, sorry – being punched in the head – sorry, sorry, sorry. Punch me again, *muna miste leat* (if you don't mind).

Stad anois é! (Stop now!)

We apologise long before we have done anything worth apologising for, a habit that carries with it echoes of the tug of the forelock and the cowed attitude before authority. Anyone who starts learning a language begins speaking in a style that resembles a child playing the first notes on a violin – a painful assault on the ear. With practice the scratchy beginnings eventually lead to smoother notes. A good speaker will recognise a weaker speaker within a few seconds and adjust their speech to help you understand them. Toner Quinn, a musician based in Connemara, was partially raised in An Cheathrú Rua but attended school in Dublin, and never fully grasped the language. His shame was heightened because his father, film-maker Bob Quinn, became a prominent public figure in the Gaeltacht in the 1970s, lending the impression that his children spoke Irish with ease. 'I would avoid people if I thought they were going to speak Irish to me,' Toner told me. Really, I wondered, you would actually walk away and hide?

'Absolutely, anywhere.'

Quinn was dispatched to the Gaeltacht as a teenager, but still he suffered a paralysing lack of confidence. He went to college and still couldn't kick that deep-rooted feeling of inadequacy. When I listened back to the recording of the interview, I was struck by how often Quinn described the learning of the language as a 'struggle'. He also explained why he felt people were so quick to declare their ignorance of the language, bragging about knowing no Irish despite all the years of study in school. 'It's a self-defence mechanism,' he said. 'It's a lot easier to say sorry I don't speak Irish than to try and speak Irish and go through that difficult process.'

I understood this feeling myself. When I began to speak Irish to friends I had to brace myself for the occasion, sensing I was about to make a fool of myself. I assumed that the person in front of me was thinking, Why do I have to speak to this moron and when can I make a rapid exit? I also realised, as soon as I could string some sentences together, that the journey was going to be far longer than I imagined. Like the layers of an onion, a hint of competence brings easy praise from the monoglot majority, but as soon as you engage with better speakers you notice how meagre your skills really are. 'Some days you would have a good experience of speaking Irish,' recalled Toner, 'because you would meet someone who was roughly around the same level as you. Other days you would have a conversation and come away feeling terrible.' Much of what we feel and think about language is simply constructed inside our head, amplified by our judgmental inner voice, hardening to conviction when we meet better speakers, assuming we are being condemned. 'I notice this all the time,' said Toner. 'People who are learning Irish go so far and no further. They won't speak Irish to you because they are "only learning". They don't want to start speaking until they are absolutely fluent, but the only way to get fluent is by practising it.'

On a visit to Belfast I pulled into a parking space behind the Cultúrlann, the Irish language centre in the city's Gaelic Quarter. A man in his 30s sporting a long beard ran over to the car and waited for me to wind down the window. He gestured towards the registration plate (County Clare), and then pointed to the County Clare sports jersey he was wearing. Colin was born in Ennis in County Clare, but his parents had 'taken me to this shithole' while still a small child. I addressed him in Irish, at which he quickly became apologetic. 'I want to learn Irish,' he said, with great enthusiasm, 'but not this year.' He explained that if he began lessons in 2016 people might think he was 'jumping on a bandwagon' because of the 1916 anniversary. Further, he said, 'I don't want to speak shit Irish like Gerry Adams. I want to be fluid in the language, not saying "agus, agus, agus" all the time.'

On a US television show, actor Saoirse Ronan was asked about the pronunciation of her name. 'It's a ridiculous name,' she said, apologising. 'It makes no sense.' Saoirse, meaning freedom, no sense? Ridiculous? Méabh Ní Choileáin, a visiting Irish teacher on the Fulbright scholar program, which sends Irish teachers to the US, lamented the lost opportunity: 'Explain that *aoi* in Irish sounds like ee … and like most other sounds in Irish, is actually very consistent and evident in many other popular Irish names, like Aoife, Caoimhe or Aoibhinn.' But Méabh also lamented her own tendency to apologise for the difficulties of Irish grammar. 'For the first few weeks, my instinct, whenever I thought the language might be too confusing for my students, was to apologise. I learned that, despite my love for Irish, I was terribly apologetic about it.'

The challenge: Spend a whole day without saying sorry to anyone.

The Doolin ferry: a fiver for your thoughts

I arrived into Doolin village in County Clare determined to speak Irish all the way to the annual Liam O'Flaherty gathering, which takes place at the end of August each year on the Irish-speaking island of Inis Mór. O'Flaherty lived a remarkable life, enlisting in the British Army during the First World War, suffering shellshock, returning to join the Irish rebellion, travelling the world, writing some excellent short stories. Best known for *The Informer*, adapted by director John Ford and turned into a major film, 31 August marks his birthday, and each year a committee organises a weekend of events, combining speakers, readings, drama and music.

The ferry to Inis Mór is about to leave.

'*Ticéad le do thoil*', I say to a young man who approaches me by the quay. He passes me on to his Polish colleague, who tries an approach he has clearly tested over time.

'T I C K E T?' he enunciates, V E R Y S L O W L Y.

I am not for the turning.

'*Ticéad don bhád go dtí an t-oileán.*'

An older man emerges from the ticket office and ushers me in, a smile on his face. '*Anseo, anseo*,' he says, cutting short any possibility of further embarrassment for either party.

'*Cé mhéad ar an ticéad?*' I ask, sensing victory, but momentarily cautious, aware that if I encounter a real-life fluent speaker, my Ladybird Irish will rapidly be unmasked as little more than a sham.

'*Fiche*,' he says, '*fiche.*'

He hands me the ticket.

'It should be 25,' he adds, somewhat sheepishly, 'but I couldn't remember how to say that.'

He shook my hand. '*Seosamh is ainm dom*,' he says. 'You know your Irish is very easy to understand, you have no dialect.'

'*Go raibh maith agat*,' I reply, thanking him for what ranks as one of the worst insults you can direct at an Irish speaker, even a mediocre one.

As I walk proudly onto the ferry boat, I realise this is the first time I have ever made any money from the Irish language. It may not be popular but it may be profitable.

How to win friends and influence people: the punk rock approach

An Irish language speaker, unlike speakers of any other language, is invariably defined as an 'enthusiast' or 'advocate' for the cause, and before you know it the enthusiast has been upgraded to the status of fanatic. Anyone caught red-handed speaking *an Ghaeilge* is a legitimate target for random inquiry and endless complaint. Why did I have to study Irish at school? Why do I have to pay for the translation of all those documents in Europe? What sort of a name is that for a child? There are variations on the theme, as in this response, directed at me outside the Róisín Dubh one night in Galway: 'Would you ever stop showing off?!'

The hostile attitudes alternate with fawning enthusiasm for the gift of the Gaeilge, as if you were overheard speaking in tongues rather than merely the Irish tongue. Joe Strummer, lead singer and chief ideologue with punk rock band The Clash, was once asked to define punk. The image portrayed by the media suggested it was about yobbos spitting on passersby or pampered stars smashing up hotel rooms: 'Exemplary manners,' responded Strummer.

The Irish speaker, whether they like it or not, is thrust into the role of linguistic ambassador, invariably called upon to defend, justify, serve or otherwise explain their strange habit. The native speakers have had this package thrown at them ever since they were old enough to mingle with their English-speaking peers, and can be excused for losing patience with it.

Give the native speaker a break and step up to the task. A new speaker of Irish is jokingly referred to as a *saighdiúir eile don teanga* (another soldier for the cause), although *siciteiripe eile don teanga* might be more appropriate these days, a psychotherapist who can absorb the anger directed at the language without taking it personally. It's in the nature of a minority language spoken alongside its majority partner that it stands out and draws attention to itself. English speakers are never called upon to justify their choice of language. Don't rise to the provocation, if you can possibly help it. If someone actively, truly hates the language, there is probably something else going on inside their head, entirely separate from the language issue.

Papa don't preach

In the confines of the H-Blocks, in Northern Ireland, prisoners established an Irish-speaking Jailtacht and carried on a hunger strike to the death, but even they could not abide the language zealot, dismissing them as 'culture vultures' and 'paddy Irishmen'. Gaelbores take note. Every person who speaks Irish is a potential goodwill ambassador, but if you complain and criticise others for their lack of competence or interest in the language, you damage confidence and reduce the possibility of a return to the language. There may be no second opportunity. If you use Irish in public with strangers, try not to insult them. I didn't think it needed to be said until I watched as a member of my *ciorcal comhrá*, on encountering a waitress with little Irish, made a disparaging comment. The woman had no choice but to attend our table as another member of staff with better Irish was busy elsewhere. This is precisely how not to give Irish a good name.

When it comes to correcting learners, there are ways and means. I exchanged a number of emails with Sorcha de Brún, a fluent speaker, who had a way of correcting my Irish that was so subtle it took me weeks to discover it. Rather than pick me up directly on my errors she would discreetly reuse a construction I had messed up, thus showing by example where I had gone wrong. There are also occasions when the pidgin Irish speaker is far better equipped to encourage the *glantosnaitheoir* (absolute beginner) than the more experienced *cainteoir* (speaker). I have regular, minimal chats in Irish with a couple of people who work in local shops. They have difficulty understanding anything more complex than greetings, but they clearly enjoy the exchange. I don't speak full sentences with them and sometimes drop *séimhiús* and *urús* that might cloud the meaning of the word that follows. One good exchange can act as encouragement to try another, and if interest grows the learner will see for themselves the importance of better grammar and syntax.

The living example of an Irish speaker happy in their skin with the language, not forcing it on anyone or needing to win an argument over its worth, is far more inspiring than the pushiness of age-old arguments about the intrinsic value of the language. This relaxed attitude should not extend to communication with government officials or attempts to access state services. Give them hell. It is widely assumed that a public defence of the language implies some sort of fascist tendency, but travel overseas and meet other minority languages and you will find no apology for a robust approach towards officialdom. Iceland has become a popular destination for holiday makers in recent years and one regular pastime among tourists is the removal of road signs with curious symbols written in native Icelandic. The issue reached crisis point in summer 2016 as signs warning of imminent danger disappeared at an alarming rate. It was suggested that road signs be rewritten in English, making them less collectable, but that idea was immediately ruled out. Viktor Arnar Ingolfsson of the Road and Coastal Administration, the body responsible for the signs, told reporters that most Icelandic people are fiercely protective of their language, which has changed little since the times of the Norse sagas. 'We use English as a second language on some road information boards, and get complaints,' he says. 'Besides, not everyone here understands English.' Rather than introduce English language road signs, they strengthened existing ones 'using bolts that can't be dismantled with an ordinary car toolkit'.[16]

Say her name

I know it's a risky business, saying her name out loud, but just swallow your pride and go for it at every opportunity, particularly those random and brief public encounters –

speak a few words of Irish. When I meet someone, anyone, I mention the Irish language, in Irish. It helps to have the pretext of writing a book, but I was doing it before that too. In four out of five cases, the person had something to say about the language, almost always a longing to learn more. '*An bhfuil Gaeilge agat?*' Do you speak Irish? If by some freak occurrence you find yourself dealing with a native speaker, don't panic and don't forget rule *uimhir a haon* – never apologise. *Táim just ag foghlaim*, the magic words, and the casual addition of 'just' into an Irish sentence makes it look like you're spending time in the Connemara Gaeltacht. The living example of spoken Irish, however hesitant, is the proof of life, the photo of the captive in the jungle with the day's newspaper in hand. Unfortunately, that newspaper won't be *Lá*, *Gaelscéal*, *Foinse* or *Nós*, as there is no printed newspaper in Irish left. *Is mór an trua é.*

Rónán Mac Aodha Bhuí abú a thaisce

We are back to RnaG once more and I'd apologise for going on and on about it only I'm trying to stay true to my own advice. This is public service at its best, up there with the health system and the fire brigade. Rónán Mac Aodha Bhuí is the supportive older sibling to a community of young musicians and Irish speakers from his position at the helm of an afternoon music and chat show. Every time I see him I want to give him a hug. *Rónán Beo* broadcasts from 3pm to 4pm, *Máirt go hAoine*, a dynamic show revealing a wealth of hidden Gaelic treasures, from contemporary *traidcheol* and *rapcheol* to heavy metal and reggae and, on one occasion, a lengthy interview with a man who had recently become homeless. This is the show where you will hear a young vegan from Donegal explain herself without fear of 'balance', as in some crank with a sheaf of scientific documents financed by some billionaire biotech company. It is also the place you will hear Linda Ervine and other people of a Unionist or Protestant background have their say despite Rónán's unabashed and occasionally tiresome from-the-heart Republicanism. I asked all my interviewees (over 40 of them) if there was any figure who inspired them and Rónán's name cropped up again and again. Éamonn Ó Donaill, director of Gaelchultúr language centre, was one such fan: 'He makes the language accessible, welcomes everybody; he is not precious in any way about it.'

Health Warning: Rónán belongs to Gaoth Dobhair, otherwise known as Mecca na nGael, the heart of the Gaeltacht. It takes time to tune into his accent and a few of his expressions. Watch out for lots of 'gujaymars' (*cad é mar atá*) and 'shart a hart a hart a nivnee' (seven, eight, eight, zero), as Donegal speakers use an 'r' in place of a 'ch' in numbers. Over time, you will be seduced by this superior lilt.

There are other radio stations, notably Raidió na Life (Dublin) and Raidió Fáilte (Belfast), but there are only so many hours in each day. If I lived in Baile Átha Cliath or Béal Feirste I would undoubtedly be paying attention to them.

Oideas Gael, know thyself

All roads lead to Gleann Cholm Cille, Donegal. Liam Ó Cuinneagáin and Oideas Gael are, without a doubt, the most common reference points for people returning to the language, unless you count Duolingo, an app which does not come with a nearby beach. I lost count of the times I asked someone how they got going with their Irish and received the answer – a trip to Oideas Gael. Liam Ó Cuinneagáin, director, is a psychologist as well as a linguist, and it shows. The atmosphere is relaxed and helpful, non-competitive and inviting. You won't speak Irish after a week in Gleann Cholm Cille but you will have the tools and the confidence to continue and you may even have some new friends to hook up with nearer to home. It is neither

cheap nor expensive; a week's tuition and accommodation can
be achieved for 400 euro, or almost half that amount if you
sleep in a tent and live on porridge and tea.

Bill Gates vs Antain Mac Lochlainn

All the Irish language hipsters swear by Duolingo, a language
app which has taken the world by storm. One after another,
almost all my interviewees, closely connected to the language
and its development, sang its praises. There are 2 million people
signed up to the Irish app, myself included. (I signed up but
never listened to it.) Manchán Magan is a huge enthusiast for
the system: 'It's phenomenal. It's a whole other way of learning,'
he says. The ultimate argument in its favour is that billionaire
Bill Gates has chosen it to learn Spanish. 'He's got like 24 billion
euros, he could have any tutor but he goes to Duolingo,' added
Magan, who is relearning Mandarin through the same system.
'It's all games. You hear the word twice, then you have to say it,
and if you don't get the pronunciation it scores you wrong and
you have to say it again until you get it right.'

Maybe it's me but when I think of Duolingo I see a character
from Aldous Huxley's *Brave New World* sitting alone in an
apartment tucking into a takeaway in front of the television.
And on a point of principle, I'm not sure I want to do anything
that Bill Gates is doing. It is fair to say that my reservations
about Duolingo have nothing to do with the app itself; I'm
just a technocrank. I am suspicious, however, of the numbers
signed up. The 2 million people supposedly learning Irish by
app bear a striking similarity to the numbers ticking the box
on the census form. I look forward to hearing from them *as
Gaeilge, amach anseo.*

If Duolingo doesn't do it for you, or even if it does, then
try *Speaking Irish: An Ghaeilge Bheo*, a combination DVD and
book by Siuán Ní Mhaonaigh and Antain Mac Lochlainn, two

of Ireland's leading linguists. The video sessions are divided into 20 sections, as speakers talk about different aspects of their lives. It's a great way to dip into dialect without getting lost in it.

If I were 10 years younger I would beg this couple to adopt me.

Siuán presides over the Teastas Eorpach na Gaeilge (TEG) scheme in Maynooth, the only centre in Ireland that certifies competency in Irish, spoken and written, without fear or favour, to a recognised European standard for all comers. The TEG system is also the only Irish language-testing organisation affiliated to the Association of Language Testers of Europe (ALTE). There are five levels in TEG, from the basic (A1) to the highest (C1), covering all speakers, from beginner to fluent. The system is designed in such a way that anyone can test their competency, no matter what their level. If you received a pass in Irish in the Leaving Cert you should be able to get a foot on the TEG ladder, encouraging greater efforts.

I had a go at the B2 *scrúdú cainte* in May 2016, the second-highest level. Each level comes with a syllabus and sample exam papers, outlining exactly what you need to know. I was going to write a funny aside about going to Maynooth to sit the B2 test but there was no funny side to it. As I approached the exam centre I had the same hollow feeling of despair that accompanied me to the oral Irish Leaving Cert exam in school. There was one major difference this time – this oral exam was undertaken of my own free will and the result was for me alone. I faced a far greater challenge when I travelled to Casla, Connemara, for my first full-length interview on RnaG. That was truly terrifying.

Before TEG there was no standardised system of assessment for adult learners of Irish. Criteria varied from course to course and teacher to teacher, 'so you couldn't look at somebody's qualification and know exactly what level of Irish they had,' explained a TEG examiner. Maynooth University spent years developing a syllabus for the different levels of Irish based on the Common European Framework of Reference for Languages (Council of Europe, 2001) This system is applied to all the main languages across Europe, a syllabus written for each level, learners planning their study step by step. If this system was applied to schools, no one would be left behind, as the TEG stages, from zero to fluency, offer a clear set of signposts every step of the way. This system opens up the possibility that even if your teacher doesn't happen to be an all-singing, all-dancing performance artist, you can still learn the language at school.

In previous times teachers could spend years ploughing away at the language, a *seanfhocal* here, a verb there, maybe an emphasis on grammar elsewhere. When it came to exams, personal criteria came into play. A confident speaker may have poor grammar but their fluency masks their inaccuracies. The examiner may like a particular student or feel they have made a special effort or find themselves under pressure to give good marks to encourage pupils or boost student numbers. The TEG system takes away that uncertainty and insures that anyone with a B2 grade, from Manchester to Melbourne or Dingle to Derry, has a similar level of competence. The TEG exams are held at exam centres in An Spidéal and Limerick but also New York, Sydney and elsewhere, giving overseas learners a chance to certify their proficiency. When I spoke to Rossa Ó Snodaigh of Kila, a keen language activist, he spoke enthusiastically of TEG, convinced that its systematic application, along with a redesign of teacher-training methods, would go a long way towards improving language competency. And Bill Gates has never even heard of it.

Meanwhile Antain Mac Lochlainn is the final court of appeal when it comes to accuracy in Irish. That opinion, I should say, is entirely personal. I have been grappling with several of his books, notably *Cruinneas* (accuracy – what else?) and a translation manual, *Cuir Gaeilge Air*, and listening to him on occasional interviews on the radio. As I returned to the Irish language, small details struck me as significant – languages are feminine nouns, apart from English, which is masculine. Why is English the only masculine language in the world? *Cén fáth, Antain, cén fáth?* I wonder is Mac Lochlainn's phone number listed in the directory?

Setting goals and targets

I found myself setting up targets to push myself a little further out of my comfort zone. I shifted from *An Ghealach Ghorm* to *Cormac ag a Cúig*, RnaG's main current affairs programme. I read articles on Tuairisc.ie, an Irish language website, bite-size updates from the Irish-speaking community. Despite having some very fine journalists and columnists on board, Tuairisc.ie is a dull news site that ruffles no feathers, lacking any sense of investigative purpose or conviction. It is unfair to single out Tuairisc.ie, however, as there is a notable lack of critical zeal amongst the Irish-speaking fraternity, across the board, unless you count off-the-record opinion, in which vicious personal critique replaces reasoned debate.

I am reading constantly, beginning with teenage fiction, gripped by *Tromluí*, a fast-moving adventure written by Áine Ní Ghlinn. I then tried *Aois Fir* (Liam Ó Muirthile), tough but rewarding, and after that I enjoyed *Rocky Ros Muc* (Seán Ó Mainnín), a highly accessible account of a boxer from Ros Muc who achieved considerable success in the US.

CHAPTER 7

Why We Didn't Learn Irish at School

idan Doyle, professor of Irish at Cork University, wrote an article for *The Irish Times* entitled 'The Irish language is not part of us, it has to be learned'. Doyle argued that 'no amount of campaigning or legislation can turn a weak language into the main means of communication for a country that is comfortably ensconced in the Anglophone world and global economy'.

There were 173 comments posted beneath the article, a boiling cauldron of feverish assertion and angry denial. E.V. McFinnity made a point about the vagaries of Irish grammar: 'Any language that can give us, *an bhean* – the woman (nominative), *hata na mná* – woman's hat (genitive), *ar an mbean* – on the woman (dative), *na mná* – the women (nom. plural) *cumann na mban* – women's association (genitive plural), deserves to die.' McFinnity had a point, but I couldn't help feeling that behind the frustration lay a genuine interest and *grá* for the language. Anyone capable of such a comical, forensic exploration must surely harbour a deep attachment to the language. Or maybe he simply did hate it. I notice a tendency among some of my Irish-speaking friends of throwing up their hands once in a while, wishing the language might simply disappear forever.

McFinnity took me back to the Flann O'Brien quote that opens this book, in which the satirist concludes that the language, with its deliberate ambiguities, takes us 'far from home', a sharp contrast to the widespread assumption that it takes us right back home, to a home that is more home than the one in which we currently reside. This ambivalent attitude seems built into our relationship with the language. While almost all the comments beneath the article were anonymous, one exception, Willeke, posted this pithy resumé: 'Born in Flanders, I grew up speaking Flemish with family and friends; Dutch in school; learning French at the age of 11; English at age 13 and a choice between German and Spanish at age 16.'

I had to count twice to be sure – Willeke had learned five languages by the time she left school. She seemed perplexed at the level of vitriol expressed in the comment thread. I found her email address on the Internet and wrote to her, asking her to explain how this multilingual feat was achieved: 'Learning languages in Belgium is one of the great things about a small country squeezed in between different linguistic areas,' she replied, citing the Indo-European and Germanic languages to the west, north and east (England, the Netherlands and Germany) and Roman languages to the south (Wallonia and France). 'What's even better is that the languages are taught at a young age.' She was born just 10 km from the French border in Kortrijk, 'so my dialect was laced with French words or sayings'. At home she spoke the Kortrijk dialect and learned Dutch from kindergarten onwards. 'Dutch is also spoken in official events and on Flemish television, although programmes spoken in different dialects are now broadcast also.'

My head was still reeling as I imagined the neuro-pathway dexterity required to speak and switch between so many languages. Yet Willeke made it all sound reasonably straightforward. 'Other ways I found it easy to learn languages was through subtitled programs on Flemish and Dutch television channels, whereas English-spoken television programs broadcasted in French-speaking regions are dubbed in French.' It came as no surprise to discover that Willeke was keen to get to grips with Irish: 'The love for the Irish language is still there ... I still watch TG4 programmes in awe and tell myself to finally get to grips with it. It's fair to say that my only real attempt of learning Irish was when I saw that my local library did an "Irish for beginners" class shortly after I moved to Ireland.'

Willeke didn't prosper in these lessons, however, as most of the class were parents who wanted to brush up on their Irish so they could help with their children's lessons. 'We were continuously holding up the class asking how it was pronounced, or written,' she said, 'after a few weeks, I thought it futile to continue the class as I wouldn't learn anything this way since the class was really for those who wanted to brush up their language instead of real beginners.' This is an important reminder, that despite the proud ignorance behind the all too common 'I haven't a word of Irish!', spoken as if it were a notable achievement, there is a distinct advantage to those who passed through the education system – we know more Irish than we care to admit.

As a *focal scoir* (final word) she added that 'as a teenager I would translate lyrics of English songs, so it's fair to say that the English dictionary in my house was rather used and abused'. Willeke didn't mention any inspiring teacher or method; her accumulation of language was a perfect if unplanned combination of dictionaries, school, kindergarten, dubbing, subtitles, television, music and porous borders.

I recently found some old report cards from school. I was a damn fine student in primary school, enjoying high marks in all subjects. In secondary school this pattern continued, but my grip on mathematics suddenly collapsed as we tackled new areas of the subject for which my brain was simply not wired. I couldn't get the hang of it at all. I went from confident As and Bs in primary school to a bare D in pass maths in the Leaving Cert. Almost everything I use in everyday life, my numbers and calculations, were learned in primary school. When it came to art I was completely lost. I left school unable to draw anything more complex than a stick figure after 12 years of classes. It is rare to find a school pupil who does not struggle with some subject. In May 2016, Tim Peake, floating 17,000 miles away from Earth inside the International Space Station, answered questions from school children about science. Emily, aged 13, asked a question: 'What would you say to anyone who finds science difficult?' Peake thought about it. 'Just keep trying,' he replied. 'Anything worthwhile is difficult.'

I had volumes of research, dozens of interviews and hundreds of casual encounters and opinions about the state of the Irish language. It was time to find out what was happening in the classroom, the first and often last point of contact with the language. What happens there shapes a lifelong attitude, an attitude that is then passed on by these future parents to their children, and the whole sorry cycle starts all over again.

I needed to find an Irish teacher who could explain the perennial problems in the classroom. I wanted to know more about the syllabus and the methods used in teaching Irish today. Why do we continue to march off the side of the language-learning cliff rather than start again with better tools? It is widely acknowledged that the classroom is a friendlier place than it used to be, but in my conversations with teenagers I got the feeling that the outcomes were depressingly similar to those of yesteryear. After all those years in school and all the reviews of the curriculum, spoken Irish still eluded this generation of school kids.

Cóisir sa Ghairdín

Was it the teacher or the syllabus, or both? Was anyone doing
anything about it? I hoped to find someone with a foot in the old
system and a hand in the new, actively involved in the shifting
debate on Irish in our schools. I managed to nurgle an invitation
to President Micheál D. Ó hUigínn's *Cóisir sa Ghairdín*, a party
at the presidential residence for the Irish language community
in June 2016. This garden party revived a tradition established
by former President Douglas Hyde by which the Irish language
fraternity enjoyed an official afternoon out in *ómós agus
aitheantas* of their role in maintaining the language.

There were hundreds of people gathered inside a marquee
at Áras an Uachtaráin, seated at tables where sandwiches and
cakes awaited. The Irish language community often talk about
how small the *linn* (pool) of speakers is, and how everyone
knows everyone else. I recognise a dozen people out of the
estimated 500 here, and half of them are in Kila. Most of the
others I met because I asked them for formal interviews for
this book. Despite attending public events for more than a year
involving music, comedy and books, travelling the country in
search of inspiration and energy, I am a total stranger here.

The music on stage passed smoothly through the generations
as Seo Linn, *an Ghaeilge*'s answer to One Direction, played a
brief set, before rushing off to perform for Joe Biden at the US
embassy. Michael D. arrived with his wife Sabina and Louki,
the family dog, who looked entirely at ease, mingling freely
with the crowds. It is on occasions like this that you realise how
lucky the country is to have someone of Michael D.'s stature as
president. A relaxed, fluent Irish speaker with a genuine *grá* for
the language and all that comes with it, Higgins's brief speech
touched on Hyde and the revival, the 'central role' language
played in the run-up to the 1916 Rising, before jumping to the
present and the successes of this generation, notably TG4 and

the gaelscoil movement. Higgins singled out the role played by Irish language schools in facilitating the rebirth of the spoken language and the campaigns underway to establish secondary schools, as a matter of urgency, to cope with the growing demand for Irish language education around the country.

In diplomatic fashion, Higgins told the audience that he had raised the issue with Taoiseach Enda Kenny, asking him if there might be ways to remove the obstacles to establishing Irish language schools. 'It would be a serious failing of the state if it was unable to provide education to children in the first language.' At the time of writing there are 302 *gaelscoileanna* (Irish language primary schools) across the 32 counties, but only 71 post-primary schools and *Aonaid*, the Irish language units housed within English schools, a stopgap measure in the absence of a dedicated *meánscoil* (secondary school).

There are long-standing campaigns underway for urgently required secondary schools in Portlaoise, Kildare, Cork, Galway and Sligo, while an estimated 650 parents await facilities in Irish for their kids in the Dublin 15 area. Higgins was followed by Cór Chúil Aodha, the choir established by Seán Ó Riada in West Cork and carried on by his son Peadar. Then came Kila, that whirlwind of positive energy combining traditional instruments with other musical inspirations from around the world. All around me bright young things spoke Irish while an occasional whispered confidence marked the arrival of celebrities, who seemed to be mostly weather forecasters. Higgins, in an off-the-cuff remark, contrasted the joyful and liberated mood of this gathering with the stereotype of the sombre Gaeilgeoir on the lookout for grammar errors and immodest behaviour. After the speeches and music I bumped into Reuben, a fellow student at Trinity College in the 1980s, who was a keen member of the Cumann Gaelach, or Irish language society back then. I had often stopped to chat to him as we crossed paths on the university cobblestones. We first met while I was on the campaign trail, seeking election as 'entertainment officer' in the student's union, organising gigs and services in college. I recall a brief, embarrassing *cúpla focal* at a Cumann Gaelach event on the campaign trail. I had met him a couple of times since then, in passing, but knew nothing about his life. He told me he was an Irish teacher and readily agreed to talk to me the following week.

On the night before the interview with Reuben and feeling a bit morally shabby I looked up his status on ratemyteacher.ie. My brother, a lifelong teacher, will probably never forgive me for this cheap shot. All over the country, vastly overprivileged teenagers publicly label and libel their teachers on evidence that makes the legal case against the Birmingham Six look convincing. 'Gaeilge has been a struggle and I feel that I will do very poorly in the exams,' wrote one pupil. 'omg i love this guy to pieces!!! he such a nice guy and really helpful as a teacher :) we luv u maistur,' wrote another pupil, who would do well to brush up on her English, while a third insisted 'He's great! I used to hate Irish now it's one of my favourite subjects!' Reuben greeted me at his home in Monkstown, County Dublin, which he shares with his wife and three kids. As a child, he moved around frequently, attending eight different schools across Ireland, from Donegal to Dundalk and Ennis to Dublin, not forgetting Galway and Sligo. He had a strong interest in Irish from an early age but still found it tough going: 'I remember crying over my homework at times, blotting the ink from the fountain pens.'

Reuben was ticking all the boxes for my ideal teacher, but a dash of violence would complete the picture. Sure enough, when he began secondary school, in the 1970s, his Irish teacher devised a punishment regime modelled on a restaurant takeaway menu. Each day at school the teacher would correct the homework and point out mistakes, which pupils had an opportunity to correct before class the following day. The teacher cast a fresh eye over the corrected homework and if any remaining errors were found, the pupil was ordered *amach* (out) to await punishment. 'He gave you a choice,' recalled Reuben, whose voice swelled with emotion at the memory as he adopted the body language of the teacher, poised and ready to strike. The 'choice' was between 'the Chinese, the Regular and the Daily Special'. The student who picked the Chinese would receive Chinese Burns, involving the pinching and twisting of ears or the flab at your belly. The 'Regular' was either the strap or a number of lines, or both, while the 'Daily Special' was a gamble on the mood of the teacher that day. 'It could be simply "*suigh síos*", or it might be a kick in the shin or the side of a ruler across your knuckles,' explained Reuben. 'It was violent.'

Reuben's school days also brought him into contact with kinder teachers, and he spent time in the Gaeltacht, developing a lasting love for the language. When he left school he became a teacher: 'I thought, Maybe I can get kids to like it, and not have a fear of it, and not hit them, show them the relevance of it, that you can have a bit of a laugh through Gaeilge.' He began teaching summer courses in the Gaeltacht, where he met highly motivated teachers using innovative teaching methods. Thirty years later Reuben is still in the classroom, working in Alexandra College, a private all-girls school in south county Dublin. He began teaching under the old Intermediate Certificate system, largely a rote learning system, which was swapped for the Junior Cycle in 1989. The Junior Cert syllabus remains 'a brilliant language course,' but the delivery and assessment fall short, offering too many opportunities for short cuts and the temptation to anticipate exam questions, hoisting pupils over the points threshold but leaving them with a 'shallow learning experience'.

The Junior Cert has been revised and a new specification will be taught from autumn 2017, turning the spotlight on the student, who must research topics and present their findings as oral skills finally take centre stage. The nouns and verbs still have to be learned, but they are applied more consistently to support and sustain the spoken word. Reuben will be watching closely – he took three years' leave in 2010 to join the National Council for Curriculum and Assessment (NCCA) and was a key participant in drawing up the new guidelines. He also participates in teacher-training modules in UCD, and with school kids of his own, he has a broad perspective on the issue of Irish in the classroom. One of the most important developments for the Irish language in schools is a long-awaited (as in 60 years or more) special syllabus for Irish speakers. The Leaving Cert Irish exam is far too easy for native speakers, lacking any sense of challenge, aimed at the majority monoglot population. It is rarely noted that in past times, native Irish speakers, who only learned English at school, were expected to take the same English exams as pupils raised entirely through English.

So much for the theory, but what happens when a pupil walks through the door of Reuben's classroom? 'I tell them they are now entering the Gaeltacht for the 40 minutes, on a free school trip.' The creation of an Irish language environment, however artificial, is a key aspect of building belief and credibility around the language. Reuben speaks only Irish to his pupils unless a difficult grammar point arises. In order to encourage the spoken word, he devised a glossary of classroom terms, which he has printed up in a handy pocket size, neatly fitting into the textbooks. If a pupil addresses him in English, he replies, in comic fashion, as if they had bumped into a stranger in France and addressed them in English, 'Mumbo Jumbo, *me no tuigim*,' and other pupils step in to help the 'monoglot' máistir. If a child from another class knocks at the door with a message they also know they are entering an Irish-only zone, and again his pupils will help the messenger get the message across.

'I don't force the Gaeilge down on them,' he says, 'I'm helping to bring their Gaeilge up and out of them; it's in there, they've been doing it for six or eight years in primary.' Reuben's classroom celebrates the language with posters and memes and jokes visible on the walls. ('How many Irish speakers fit into an ambulance?' *'Naonúr, naonúr, naonúr ...'*) There are short films and debating contests, as pupils are encouraged to bring their own passions into the classroom, making it a 'two-way open door', where One Direction, Ed Sheeran or rugby can be discussed.

The government decision to increase the value of the Leaving Certificate oral exam to 40 per cent, taken in 2007, has been an enormous boost to Reuben's approach. His students also avail of an optional oral exam available to Junior Cert students, which also counts for 40 per cent. I never knew there was a Junior Cert oral exam, but the option is catching on fast, and one in five students took it in 2016. Reuben's students are clearly benefitting from his personal enthusiasm, as he brings renowned writers in to talk to his pupils, notably Nuala Ní Dhomhnaill and Áine Ní Ghlinn.

The academic endgame – the vital points race – invariably intrudes when students begin their final year in school: 'You can have a great fifth year group,' explained Reuben, 'then you walk into the classroom in sixth year and the pupils are suddenly hungry for points; they are different animals.' And well they might be, as the final exams still determine access to third level education and other opportunities.

Pearse/St Enda's

In passing Reuben mentioned that Pádraig Pearse had taught in Alexandra College for four years (1903–7). During that time he had visited Belgium, to see the bilingual education system at work, developing ideas which would be published as 'The Murder Machine'. 'What is in those documents,' said Reuben, gesturing at his files from the National Council for Curriculum Assessment, 'is an attempt to catch up with Pearse's ideas of school as student-centred, inciting the imagination.'

I was struck by the confidence with which Reuben spoke of Pearse as an educator so far ahead of his time that the curriculum, more than 100 years later, was still trying to catch up. Pearse was familiar to me as one of the 1916 leaders, and his 'Murder Machine' essay had become a catch phrase for an education system turning out submissive individuals rather than critical thinkers. At school, Pearse's legacy had been reduced to two words – 'blood sacrifice', and he was easily written off as a deluded dreamer, a zealot harking back to a mythical Gaelic past. I had also assumed that Pearse was a conservative Catholic who had little in common with fellow rebel James Connolly, a labour agitator and equality advocate. It seemed hard to believe that Pearse's ideas could still hold so much relevance today.

Pearse was educated by the Christian Brothers following a simple but mind-numbing strategy: 'To gain results under the Intermediate system every subject had to be learned by heart, with the result that the majority of victims hated the sight of books for the rest of their days.' Pearse devoured English literature, reciting Shakespeare and Milton, enjoying Latin and French lessons at school. As a teenager he discovered the Irish language, which quickly acquired importance in his life: 'The turf fire was back and the dead voice was speaking to us again.' At 16 years of age, he was appointed a pupil-teacher of Irish at his school in Westland Row, and a year later he joined the Gaelic League. By 1908, before he had turned 30, Pearse raised funds and found both premises and pupils for St Enda's College, a progressive child-centred school combining manual and intellectual preparation, a system based on the freedom of its pupils and the inspiration of its teachers.

There were many critics, including future Minister for Education Eoin MacNeill, who warned against the futility of attempting to turn out Irish language speakers: 'Your school-taught language will never be more than a simulacrum of the living thing.' Pearse brought students on scholarships from the Gaeltacht, their presence intended to help the city kids learn Irish properly. The Gaeltacht kids didn't mix easily with the other boys and tended to keep to themselves. Seventy pupils were enrolled in the new boarding school, with Pearse's mother, sister and brother playing key roles in the teaching and administration. Thomas MacDonagh, future 1916 martyr, was Pearse's right-hand man, and before long the school was a thriving, noisy centre of activity in which visitors spoke disapprovingly of how the boys and girls ran wild and in which the teachers worked hard to meet the expectations of their demanding headmaster.

Pearse himself was exhausted by the tasks before him. There was dancing, music and athletics, art and theatre, with school shows performed on the stage of the Abbey Theatre, enjoying press reviews and winning international recognition. When year two began, pupil numbers had doubled, along with the size of the buildings, and students were offered the classics and science, with laboratories and a large library now in place. The school was victorious in the hurling and football championships of Dublin and Leinster and the school vision was one of an Irish-speaking Ireland rooted in the Gaelic society destroyed by the British occupation. Pearse relied on cooperation rather than coercion, and pupils helped draw up the syllabus and shared a loyalty system in which trust replaced surveillance and control. The only child ever expelled from the school was dispatched because of cruelty inflicted on a cat. Pearse fostered learning rather than lessons, initiative rather than rote learning. The educational model had its dark side, as the cult of boyhood and patriotism was elevated above all else, but that too had its own context, as the pre-Rising generation struggled to awaken crushed concepts of statehood and freedom which were common across Europe at that time. These days the struggle for LGBT rights inside the school system and the secularisation of school patronage are markers of another era, with new values and priorities, as personal freedom and individual opportunity move centre stage. In a 'true' education system, wrote Pearse, 'Love of beauty ... love of books ... love of knowledge and love of "heroic inspiration" would go hand in hand with grammar and mathematics.'

St Enda's offered European languages (French, German, Italian, Spanish), botany, zoology and geology, alongside vocational subjects like typewriting, bookkeeping and shorthand. Small wonder the Irish education system has yet to catch up. The pageantry and costume of the school also attracted attention, the adulation of the old myths and sagas, Cúchulainn and the values associated with ancient Ireland, its blend of violence, honour and chivalry.

After a feis in County Louth, Pearse's pupils arrived at the local train station dressed in the uniforms used for *The Boy Deeds of Cúchulainn*, a play they performed. They carried axes and 'tall gilded spears' accompanied by pipers and a banner of the Fianna, with gold sun disc. A crowd soon gathered, swelling 'to the dimensions of a riot', singing a rebel ballad about the 1798 Rising. The leap from pageant to rebellion, from the make believe to the make real, was easily glimpsed by the locals. 'Perhaps they expect us to lead them against the Castle,' speculated Thomas MacDonagh, who, along with Pearse, would undertake precisely that task in 1916.

Ontario

Ireland isn't the only country to grapple with language competence and bilingualism. In 1977 the Ontario Ministry of Education in Canada established three levels of desirable competence based on a certain number of hours spent teaching a language. The first level, 'basic', could be achieved in 1,200 hours, the next level, 'middle', would require 2,100 hours of instruction, while the most advanced level would require 5,000 hours to achieve.

How are we doing?

In the 1980s Irish primary school children spent 1,728 hours learning Irish, at a rate of 5.4 hours per school week. In the early 2000s the recommended minimum hours for Irish in the new curriculum was much lower, just 3.5 hours per week, for a total of 936 hours. This came as a surprise to me. I imagined we had spent far more time on it. Secondary school students endured just three hours of Irish per week, giving them a total average of 452 hours. The combined total of hours spent learning Irish added up to just 1,388 hours, or 1,450 when adjusted to include Transition Year hours.

Irish language learners can only reasonably be expected to achieve a basic level of competence, with greater fluency almost out of the question, as students receive just one third of the hours required to achieve such a standard. Irish schoolchildren should be able to hold a simple conversation, read simple texts and return to the language in later life. At the second level, learners should be able to read newspapers and books with the help of a dictionary, understand radio and TV and converse reasonably well. The highest level was close to fluency, the learner able to continue their education in the medium of that language, accept a job and converse easily.

If you compare the Irish language learner in an English language school to their counterpart in an all-Irish immersion system, the gap is stark. The all-Irish school tackles every subject through Irish (with the exception of English), giving a final total of 10,700 hours during the school cycle, putting every student in the highest category of language learner – able to converse in all situations, take up employment in Irish or continue their education in an all-Irish setting. No surprise there. My niece, despite no Irish at home and little in the way of a social life in Irish, achieved fluency during her school years.

When you subtract the time spent on general classroom wastage, crowd control, and the reliance on basic grammar and prescribed texts, the notion of a failed system takes on a different hue. According to a study carried out in the 1970s, teachers spoke for 70 per cent of class time, leaving less than a minute per pupil in my crowded class of 32. We may be expecting too much from a crowd of adolescents cooped up in a classroom all day with a teacher struggling to convert a points-based exam syllabus into some sort of playful Harry Potter-esque immersive adventure. It has also become widely accepted that teachers themselves frequently have poor spoken Irish skills, as teacher-training fails in the critical task of preparing them to teach Irish with a full understanding of the subject. This lack of language competence extends to Irish-medium education, and if you factor in some truly woeful textbooks *as Gaeilge*, it comes as no surprise that supposedly fluent students opt to take their Leaving Cert papers in English, in case they misunderstand the exam questions.

'What exists in Irish is goodwill, energy, enthusiasm, talent, hopes,' explains Diarmuid Johnson, linguist and teacher, 'all these virtues, so teaching Irish is a virtuous thing, but the methodology is still rough, so the results are very mixed.' Johnson insists that you can't learn a language at school. 'Languages at school are great, but when you leave school you need to go to France, Germany or the Gaeltacht ... nobody else can do it for you, you have to carry the load; like all the other important things in life, you have to take responsibility.'

You are probably your own best teacher.

CHAPTER 8

'There's a fecker on the phone looking for services in Irish'

J ust when I needed it most, Rosita Boland came to the rescue. 'Can anybody truthfully say that Irish is a necessary language?' she asked in a column in *The Irish Times*. Rosita vented her anger and disappointment at failing to learn the Irish language, sparking a national conversation. My personal reflections were suddenly cast into a wider pool, which rippled across the country. More than 300 comments were left in the wake of the column, mostly venomous outpourings from defenders or naysayers of the language. The column was accompanied by a photo of Peig Sayers, a clichéd symbol of the Irish language. Peig, a storyteller from the Blasket Islands in south-west Ireland, haunted a generation of school children, who struggled with her 200-page memoir, once required reading for Leaving Certificate students. Every household in Ireland had a copy of the bible, Mrs Beeton's cookbook, Dr Spock's advice on child-rearing, Leon Uris's *Exodus* and Peig. The book began with a grim portent, setting the scene for the story to come: 'I'm an old woman now, one foot in the grave and the other on its edge.' The photo on the cover showed an elderly woman with an amiable expression, hands clasped loosely on her lap, her head camouflaged beneath a large headscarf, a grim figure from another age, mercifully passed.

'I often found myself wishing the time I had spent trying to grapple with Peig had been spent in Spanish classes,' wrote Boland. As someone who has lived most of my professional life through the Spanish language I felt a bit smug recalling my dynamic teachers and conversation-driven textbooks. But I also recalled that while Boland was grappling with Peig in Irish class, I was engaged in word-by-word combat with *La Barraca*, a dry 19th-century Spanish novel, required reading for the Leaving Certificate course. I still have my school copy of the book, but had largely forgotten the subject matter. A quick search on the Internet informs me that 'the naturalistic ideal can clearly be seen in the narrative technique and in the reaffirmation of the influence of the environment on human beings' character and behaviour, as well as in the radical perversity of the "idyllic" nature of rural life.'

You can imagine how relevant that seemed to my life as I discovered The Clash and the Virgin Prunes and dreamed myself into the mosh pits of California to see the Dead Kennedys and Black Flag. *La Barraca* spoke of poverty and hardship, the mirror image of Peig's hardscrabble life on the edge of the Atlantic Ocean. I studied it with some difficulty and little enthusiasm. Both books have long since vanished from the curriculum.

It would be safe to assume that when faced with the question on the census, Do you speak Irish? Boland must surely answer No, or even *Hell no!*, yet she admitted that until the 2016 census she had always ticked the Yes box, an acknowledgement of the years spent studying the language. 'This is a disgrace,' concedes

Boland. 'I finished my school career with only the most shamefully tenuous grasp on a language I had studied for years.'

Gone is the tick on the box.

Boland explained that she got on perfectly well in all her other subjects, and that she tried at least as hard in Irish, if not harder. There was no pleasure in it and no possibility of putting an end to the torture, because it was compulsory. Rosita visited the Gaeltacht one summer and also took grinds, so Irish was clearly regarded as important in her home. For Boland the disgrace lay in being forced to study a language for which she had no aptitude, no interest and, critically, even if she could speak it, 'would be of exactly zero use to me in the wider world'. Boland visited Latin America and wished she had learned Spanish, 'something useful'. The catalogue of uselessness continued, Irish being a language about which 'nobody could describe ... as a useful way of communicating with local people'.

But languages are flexible instruments, and we don't know what role they will play in our lives. In Latin America I have often researched and written about indigenous people speaking languages other than Spanish. In January 2014 I attended La Escuelita, a 'little school' in south-east Mexico run by the Zapatistas, an indigenous rebel group that set up autonomous self-governing districts across an area larger than all the Irish Gaeltachts combined. The rebels launched an armed uprising against the Mexican state in January 1994, demanding land and freedom alongside the right to education in their own language. The Zapatista rebellion became a global cause célèbre, attracting thousands of young Europeans keen to meet a movement that embraced diversity and rejected old paradigms. Many of these young people traipsed into isolated jungle communities in search of inspiration, blissfully unaware of their disruptive impact on small, traditional communities.

After several years and thousands of casual callers the Zapatista locals put an end to the visits, but in late 2013 they invited all comers to stay, once off, for a week, pairing visitors with a local family to share their food and work. The cost of the five-day trip was €20, a sum that included textbooks, transport, food and lodgings. The experience felt like a return to my childhood Gaeltacht summer course in West Cork. We departed on special buses from San Cristobal de las Casas, a colonial town and tourist hub, where we met our fellow 'school' pupils heading into the jungle.

When we arrived at a regional Zapatista HQ our names were called out, one by one, and we paired off with our hosts. We were divided into small groups and spread across almost a hundred villages. I was bound for a place called Moises Gandhi. Upon arrival the locals held a small ceremony, with music, flags and speeches. I was brought to my lodgings, where I met my *bean an tí*, María, her husband Marcelo and their six children. Each morning María prepared tortillas, beans and rice, while Marcelo, the *fear an tí*, took us to the fields and handed us a machete. They lived in a small wooden shack with two bedrooms, a few chairs and an open fire, a home they shared with their children, aged from two months to 15 years. The house had a couple of light bulbs but not a single electronic device – no cooker, fridge, television, computer or phone. My host family spoke only Tzeltal, a local language, and the week was spent in theatrical fashion, lots of gestures and pointing, but also language-learning, as I picked up useful everyday phrases.

Is Tzeltal a difficult language? I have no idea. The everyday expressions were made up of sounds, which I listened to and repeated until familiar. Is Tzeltal a necessary language? If you want to get a university education, a job in a city or migrate elsewhere, it can't be of much use. If you remain in the area, as 95 per cent of locals do, alongside your parents and grandparents, involved with the farming, fiestas and religious celebrations that dominate the community calendar, then you cannot survive without it. Many villagers have a passive understanding of Spanish, especially those who sell their produce at regional markets. The kids learn Spanish at school. A couple of homes in each village have televisions and kids will gather to watch cartoons, always in Spanish. Tzeltal is spoken by about 300,000 people across the state of Chiapas. For them, it is useful, not for jobs or commerce, but as the thread that weaves the social fabric, the unbroken link to their ancestors.

The more you travel the more you realise that while trade is global and English is the language of trade most people in the world still live largely small, local lives, speaking 'minority' languages. The average citizen of the world, should that person exist, speaks two languages, and may passively understand others. Any traveller to Guatemala, Peru, Bolivia and Mexico will become aware of a swathe of the population chatting to each other in native languages. The culture they represent, the historical Maya sites, the markets, the clothes, the music and dignity, the sense of community, frequently defines the visitor's journey. I find myself wary of the term 'useful' when it comes to evaluating the world. The useful, for me, is what connects me to other people and to the natural world around me. Critically, that includes languages, and Irish is as important as any other. I don't demand anything of it. I find it difficult to relate to Rosita's perspective, as I have been meeting dozens of Irish language speakers who enjoy and relish the language, not as campaigning fanatics or compulsory neurotics. Irish comes as naturally to these people as the sun rising in the east, and they have no desire to inflict it on the unwilling.

Everything we study at school is compulsory, in that subjects are offered along a narrow range, from the core (Irish, English, Maths) to the optional (German/Biology, History/Chemistry), on the basis of providing a rounded education in a particular context – in this case Irish society. The term 'compulsory' means 'required by law', but it also means 'coercive', which, according to the Oxford Dictionary, signifies 'persuading an unwilling person to do something by using force or threats'.

The issue of compulsory Irish is constantly raised by people I talk to about the language, with widely differing opinions. 'I would be against any form of coercion,' said Diarmuid Lyng. 'I see the people who argue against it. I see their reasons. I can't assume I know what's best for people but deep down in me there is the God complex. I'm thinking, But if you only tried it, it's like your mother feeding you food when you're young – But you would like garlic, I'm like, I don't fucking like it.' Many people argued in favour of Irish as a compulsory subject but not in its current form. There is a strong case to be made for having a separate Irish syllabus for native speakers and students with a high level of Irish and another to teach basic conversation skills to all. There is also an urgent need for a subject that outlines the 'Why' behind learning Irish, including the history of the language, which remains a complete secret to most children.

Rosita's column prompted radio debate and commentary, forcing me back to the forgotten English-speaking channels, and I had a moment of strangeness when I heard English coming from the radio, my Irish-only zone. On one programme Rosita argued the toss with Bláthnaid Ní Chofaigh, a television and radio presenter. Rosita told presenter Sean O'Rourke that not only had she failed to pick up the language, she had also picked up resentment towards it. O'Rourke asked if she felt she shouldn't have been made to learn it. 'Yes,' she said, 'it is not and has never been necessary to me in my life.' 'What about the beauty of the language, the richness?' asked O'Rourke. Rosita acknowledged the passion other people had for the language but noted how quickly those people became emotive on the topic.

'It's not just about the language as a subject,' she said. 'There are many other layers to it.' Bláthnaid sounded genuinely hurt and afraid. 'We are a minority, the Irish language is in crisis, it's an attack on our identity, our origin and what is important to us … when you are a minority it is a constant battle and we are scared of losing it.'

The Irish language inhabits a largely invisible realm under the radar of everyday life and the majority experience on this island. 'I think I'm saying what a lot of people are thinking,' said Rosita. She might be right. I certainly don't believe a lot of people are thinking as I do about the Irish language. I am enjoying the learning process and have even reread Peig, that fateful memoir, finding it fascinating, moving and memorable.

The conversation returned to notions of usefulness and school: 'I don't use the theorems I learned,' noted Bláthnaid, adding that she had the disadvantage of having to learn a second language (English) to function after school. It's not the fault of native speakers, observed Bláthnaid, that the rest of the country doesn't speak Irish. She then added, and you could hear the tremble in her voice, 'it shakes me, it makes me nervous', the idea of putting an end to compulsory Irish at school.

Once the issue of compulsory Irish has been dealt with, the cost of translating official documents can never be far behind. 'What practical purpose does it serve?' Then came the special funding for the Gaeltacht and finally the 'bullying element' among the Irish language enthusiasts. 'I like even less having my national identity pinned to a language I never use and cannot speak,' said Boland. 'Am I any less an Irish citizen if I choose to disassociate myself from our ordained "national language", and state that the English language is actually the one in which I feel at home expressing myself?'

The notion that speaking Irish makes you more Irish exists largely in the imagination of people who imagine others are judging them. In all my travels and chats and interviews, I met just one person who, I suspected, felt that way, yet even they refused to say it out loud, such is the general anathema to the notion. Yet there is something in it. The British people who set up home in Spain, spending decades there without learning the language, are clearly missing out on some basic shared experience in the place where they have settled. The Irish language has been out of widespread everyday use for no more than three generations. It still represents a deeper connection to a relatively recent past, one that is genetically encoded in our bodies. This is hardly a radical concept, and only reflects what Seamus Heaney said in more poetic fashion, that a knowledge of Irish is a vital tool for connecting to the ground beneath our feet, the place where we live, the spirit of our ancestors.

If current research is to be believed, we may be asking the wrong questions. The issue is not whether we are more or less Irish if we speak the language, but that learning a second language is as fundamental as learning maths or history, maybe more so. These days it is clearly helpful to speak one of the 'super' languages (Chinese, English, Hindi, Spanish or Arabic) alongside another lesser-used language, usually linked to one's native land. However, even the 'super' languages have their limits. A Chinese tourist visiting Heidelberg, Germany, in August 2016, unwittingly signed asylum application forms when he went to report a stolen wallet. Mr L., as he was known, spent two weeks inside a holding centre for refugees, located 220 miles from Heidelberg. He spoke only Mandarin. 'The events, once set in motion, were hard to reverse,' reported one journalist. Without help Mr L. might have spent six months in the holding centre. The monolingual citizen is a disadvantaged minority, as between 60 and 75 per cent of people around the world speak two languages or more, and many countries have multiple official languages – 11 in South Africa and 24 in

India. The English and Irish languages are bilingual bedfellows, offering cultural enrichment and a dual seam of literary treasures.

In the confines of a single opinion column Rosita Boland laid out much of the debate, which simmers on, periodically surfacing in the media. I phoned Rosita, not knowing exactly what I wanted to ask her but wanting to probe beneath the column. I told her about the book I was writing and asked her how well she had fared with other languages at school. 'I've got no ability with languages,' she told me. 'I could be studying Irish until the cows come home and it wouldn't make any difference. I was almost as bad in French.' I was reminded of my own inability to learn maths and art at school, a very different issue to the usefulness of either subject.

Some months later the Rosita Boland column arose in a conversation with Manchán Magan, who recalled hearing the reaction to the article long before he got around to reading it. 'The hurt you saw in Gaeilgeoirí about that article, they were so wounded,' recalled Magan. 'So I went back to it, thinking, it must be scurrilous, I'm going to get angry.' Mánchan was underwhelmed. Apart from the argument about usefulness, 'loads of things aren't necessary, art isn't necessary'. Manchán largely agreed with Rosita. 'She says, "I feel bad, it shouldn't be forced down my throat." That makes sense. I can't see what's insulting about that.'

When I removed the Irish language from the mix and examined the feelings behind Boland's column, I returned to my battle with DIY, to the bookshelves, hammers, nails and saws. I still feel utterly useless in that realm. However, no one in their right mind has suggested that my lack of DIY skills makes me less of a human being, just as not speaking Irish is no cause for shame in this country. And yet something still rankles.

Inside the health food shop in Kinvara, County Galway, a

customer was speaking Irish to the woman behind the counter. A third person entered the shop. After he left the shop, he told his waiting companion that he felt 'insulted' by the two Irish speakers. His companion, an Irish speaker, told him to imagine two people speaking French inside the shop. Would that have caused offence? The offended individual thought about it and corrected his initial response: 'I feel bad that I can't speak Irish.' The people inside the shop didn't comment on his lack of Irish or question his identity, yet something within him sparked the thought. Rosita's rejection of Irish in her life seemed marked by the same unspoken assertion, 'I feel bad that I can't speak Irish.' The issue of teaching the Irish language, discussed elsewhere, is also relevant. Rosita was done an injustice in that Irish, a language anyone can learn, remains a mystery despite all the time and effort invested.

It may be a wild miscalculation, but I can see Rosita attending a week-long course in Oideas Gael and emerging with a completely different attitude. The word 'Oideas' means healing or cure, and it feels like Irish people need some sort of healing when it comes to the language. It may not erase the bad memories but it will surely suck some of the poison out of it.

On the same day that Boland's opinion piece appeared, another story involving the Irish language came to light. Caoimhe Ní Chatháil, a native speaker from Donegal, complained that mobile phone company Three Ireland refused to accept her name in Irish when she attempted to top up her credit online. 'You must provide a valid last name,' was the response, as the system 'doesn't recognise special characters.' Her name in Irish was invalid because it contained a *fada*, or accent, which the website was unable to process. I phoned Caoimhe and asked her what motivated her to go public with her complaint. 'I was particularly angry this morning,' said Caoimhe, 'after reading the Rosita Boland column.' That prompted her to take up the cudgels and challenge the missing *fada*. Ní Chatháil was raised through Irish, her mother tongue and primary language. When she was in England, she told me, no one ever asked her for an English version of her name. When she queried the company over their inability to process her name, Joolz in customer service responded, 'Hey Caoimhe, have you tried entering your name in English? Is the translation Caoimhe Cahill?'

Joolz clearly didn't understand why anyone would insist on a certain spelling of a name when an alternative option could get the transaction completed in double quick time. The objective is to top up your phone. 'It's another example of the disrespect and ignorance that people have of the Irish language,' said Caoimhe. Within a few days, the oversight had been rectified. For English speakers with familiar surnames who never have to consider such issues, Caoimhe's stand is easily dismissed as the mentality of a crank determined to find fault with something. She admitted that the issue of the *fada* arose each month as she went to top up her phone, and that up until then she had let it go, filling in her name incorrectly to get the job done.

I have yet to meet an Irish speaker who has not grown weary of this conflict and simply surrendered to it. Éamonn Ó Dónaill, director of Gaelchultúr, admitted he had reached a point where it had become too uncomfortable to attempt to access state services in Irish, and he could no longer be bothered. A colleague, however, had recently phoned up the revenue service (*coimisinéirí ioncaim*) and asked for service in Irish. The woman at the other end of the phone asked him to hold the line, pressed a button and (presumably) assumed the caller was on silent. She spoke to a colleague: 'There's a fecker on the phone looking for service in Irish. Anyone around?' Ó Dónaill himself once rang the Department of Education and requested the number of an office extension in Irish. 'Say that in English and you might get through,' was the response. The examples are endless. When I met Julian de Spáinn, general secretary of Conradh na Gaeilge, he had recently applied for a passport for his two-year-old daughter. His odyssey began inside Rathmines Garda station, where he was informed that they had no forms available in Irish. 'Would you not take the forms in English?' they asked him. He proceeded to Terenure Garda station, where he met the same obstacle. At that point he called into Terenure Library but had no luck, and the same again at Rathmines Library. Finally, he tracked down a passport application form in Irish at his local post office, only to discover that it was out of date and no one had sent out the new forms. 'For the ordinary person with an interest in the language, how many of them would actually refuse the English form and go to the next place and the next place and the next place and the next?' he asked. The irony is that the state will then say that Irish services are not being used. 'They've created it that way,' he said, insisting that once services are provided in Irish, the dynamic would shift. 'Then it is thrown over to us; we'll see what happens then.'

By chance, when I was invited onto a panel discussion on RnaG, Diarmaid Ó Cadhla was interviewed on the same show. That week Ó Cadhla, based in Cork City, had spent a night in prison after refusing to sign a release form in English, insisting the authorities provide it in Irish. Ó Cadhla, who stood as a candidate in the 2011 general election, was sentenced to five days in prison for refusing to pay a €300 fine after committing an electoral offence – he failed to file legal papers required by the Standards in Public Office Commission. I was immediately curious about Ó Cadhla, wondering what motivated him to make his grand gesture. I phoned him up and arranged to visit him in Cork City, in the offices of the People's Convention, an independent political grouping. Ó Cadhla ran as a candidate for the People's Convention that year, winning 500 votes.

Like all candidates he was legally required to account for all campaign donations, but when the paperwork arrived, he let it go. After several warnings he ended up in court, and was finally convicted of an offence.

I expected to meet a language fanatic with wild eyes and bushy eyebrows cast from the pages of *An Béal Bocht*. Instead I was greeted by a quiet-spoken businessman who made a cup of tea and rubbed constantly at his eyes, plagued by a painful allergy. Ó Cadhla was born in Rinn Ó gCuanach, the small Gaeltacht in County Waterford, and described himself as a 'semi-native' speaker, moving to Cork City at the age of eight. Jeremiah John Kiely was the name on his birth certificate, but he was always known as Diarmaid, and while in his teens he registered his name in Irish. His home was a magnet for storytellers and musicians, with visitors like Séamus Ennis and Nioclás Tóibín adding to the atmosphere. Ó Cadhla was politicised by events in Northern Ireland in the 1970s and has been active ever since. 'I got more interested in what it meant to be Irish,' he recalled. When he left school he studied business and computers and subsequently started his own IT company, writing and distributing accounting software. Ó Cadhla employed nine people over a period of almost 30 years, but was forced to take a break when diagnosed with cancer in 2006. 'It was almost inevitable given the lifestyle I had, the stress,' he explained. 'I have only one lung; I had lung cancer, heart problems, multiple surgeries on my eyes.' He spent almost a year on his back, giving him time to think about his life. 'Is this really what I want to be doing?' he asked himself. 'And the answer was, No it is not.' Out of that process the People's Convention was born, Comhdháil an Phobail. The Irish language has been a lifelong passion: 'for me it's everything … If I'm not that I don't know what in God's name I am.' Ó Cadhla is married with two children, both of them raised with Irish. 'For a while, when they were young, they spoke almost entirely in Irish. They'd wake up at night speaking Irish.'

When the day came and Ó Cadhla was due to go to prison he asked the Gardaí to bring someone who could speak Irish. 'They did, it was all very friendly,' he recalled. At Cork jail, Ó Cadhla was processed, again through Irish. After a few hours, he was offered immediate release, a common occurrence for this type of offence. He gathered up his belongings and was given a release form, in English, to sign. 'I couldn't sign it,' he said. 'It's my entitlement, it's our language. I want it in Irish.'

The governor sent word through the prison officers – sign the form or stay put. 'The only reason at that point that I was locked up was that I wanted to do my work in Irish.' He was also unable to contact his wife, as a phone call from the prison also required filling out a form that was only available in English. The next day, the appropriate forms appeared in Irish. He admitted to having doubts by then. 'I was thinking to myself, God Diarmaid, are you an idiot or what? How many issues do you want to take on?' Ó Cadhla, a polite, committed, intelligent and stubborn individual, ranks as a champion fecker when it comes to demanding services *as Gaeilge*. And yet …

At the turn of the 20th century all handcart owners in Ireland were legally obliged to paint their names in English upon their carts. In the wake of the language revival some cart owners painted their names *as Gaeilge*, resulting in fines and prosecution. Pádraig Pearse, recently qualified as a barrister, defended Niall Mac Giolla Bhrighde – Neil MacBride – in 1905, appealing a ruling made against him in a lower court. Pearse lost the case but called on his cart-owning compatriots to stand firm: 'We advise all Gaels to simply ignore the British Law that makes it penal for them to use their own language to the exclusion of English. If they are summoned and fined, let them refuse to pay; if they are sent to prison, let them go to prison. The question can be brought to a head no other way.'

The situations are hugely different but the principle much the same – the right to use Irish when dealing with the state. Was Ó Cadhla's gesture any different from the action taken by Pearse 111 years ago, regarded by many at the time as a futile gesture? Today FM presenter Matt Cooper, on hearing Caoimhe Ní Chathail's tale, soon discovered that a member of his production team had tried to buy an air ticket online but found the airline refused to acknowledge the *fada* in her name. She bought the ticket, but when she got to the boarding area and presented the *fada*-less ticket, the staff refused permission to board the plane as the spelling of the name was different to that on the passport. No damn *fada*.

In the case of Ó Dónaill and his language business Gaelchultúr, rather than get mad, he got even, establishing a special course for frontline staff in the public sector, giving them the tools for communicating with the public in Irish. The take-up has been good, he says, the impact highly positive. Once members of staff experience even a brief return to Irish, they acquire the confidence to respond in kind. The issue with all the above is that it reinforces the notion of the Irish language as a 'problem' rather than simply a spoken language. In her essay on writing in Irish, Nuala Ní Dhomhnaill writes that 'Languages, such as Irish, with their unique and unrepeatable way of looking at the world, are as important for human beings as the preservation of the remaining tropical rainforests are for biological diversity.'

CHAPTER 9

Gaeltacht Reflections

I am off to the Gaeltacht for a week, but judging by the reaction of my friends you'd think I was off to volunteer in the orphanages of Kolkata. 'You are so brave,' says one. 'I wish I had the nerve,' ventures another. Memories of childhood trips to the Gaeltacht prompt different queries. 'Will you be sent home if you're caught speaking English?' I doubt it. 'Will there be any snogging?' I hope so. I recently discovered that one of the Irish language summer schools for teenagers has installed a *balla póige*, or kissing wall, where youngsters can come together and smooch during the nightly céilís. My informant then told me that not only was there a *balla póige*, there was also the elite *grúpa pógála*, or kissing group, the kids allowed to stay behind after the *céilí* for a spot of more serious smooching. It's a far cry from the summer college in Baile Bhuirne 1976, the high point of my previous fling with the Irish language. Back then there was a girl I fancied, Aisling. Her Irish was far better than mine, and I recall giving up all hope one morning when the teacher gave me a dressing-down over a botched *modh coinníollach*, the complex, conditional tense. My confidence was shattered.

Back in the present, however, my confidence was up. I was listening to nothing but RnaG, reading 'old books' to keep Peadar Ó Riada happy and engaging in occasional chats and a weekly *ciorcal comhrá*. I had got myself off to a *tús maith*, or good start, but it was time for decisive action: a return to *Tobar na Gaeilge*, the source, the Gaeltacht, those Irish-speaking redoubts scattered along the western seaboard, the remaining holdouts of everyday Irish.

There was of course a smidgeon of fear in the gut, as the *cainteoirí dúchais* (native speakers) have a reputation as cranky perfectionists who would rather see the language die a slow death than hear it spoken sloppily by hobbyists engaging at a basic level. And then there's the other problem – they can't seem to be arsed speaking Irish anyway. The Gaeltacht has been suffering fools on a regular basis since the Gaelic League announced that the most impoverished, damp, remote regions of the country were in fact the cradle and repository of a pure Gaelic civilisation. Every summer the movers and shakers and foot soldiers of the revival decamped to spend time amongst the peasants. These citizens of the Pale extolled the virtues of the simple life and vowed to keep it that way for now and forever more before heading home to the tea rooms of Stephen's Green and the reassuring pages of *An Claidheamh Soluis*, the newspaper of the revival movement, written almost entirely in English.

The Gaeltacht was created and defined by outsiders projecting their utopian visions upon a largely illiterate population who used Irish in the same way miners in Asturias use Spanish – for communication. When the Gaelic Leaguers came they were unable to understand the locals, who spoke their own dialect at their usual speed. Some observers lamented that instead of soaking up and preserving the Irish tongue the visitors inadvertently spread English among the natives. But that didn't deter the evangelists for this brave new world: 'Behind me I was leaving Anglicisation with all its hideousness and soulless materialism,' wrote one visitor. 'Before me lay the Gaeltacht where the spiritual passionate Gael with his simple beautiful customs, speaking his own language and singing his own sweet songs, lived as God intended he should.'

The reality was that as soon as the children of these windswept, barren regions came of age most of them left the country on boats bound for Liverpool and New York. The most important thing for their future was a sound knowledge of English. 'They were being reared for export,' explained Seosamh Ó Cuaig, a lifelong socialist and activist based in Connemara. Many still leave today, yet these coastal regions of Kerry, Galway and Donegal now find themselves at the heart of the country's fastest-growing tourist brand – the Wild Atlantic Way. They are also host to a new wave of language enthusiasts keen to listen and learn, no longer burdening the locals with notions of an authentic peasantry. TG4 and RnaG are based there, factories and local authority offices have moved in. These far-flung corners of the country are not so far removed from the urban centres. You can leave New York in the morning and arrive in Carraroe in time for dinner.

Over the past 30 years, discussions about preserving and expanding the Gaeltacht have become hand-wringing exercises in how to stave off outright collapse. In July 2014, the government appointed a Minister for the Department of Arts, Heritage and the Gaeltacht who does not speak Irish – Heather Humphreys. The appointment of Joe McHugh TD as Minister of State with responsibility for Gaeltacht Affairs in the same month was greeted with disbelief. At the time of his appointment, McHugh had only the most basic of Irish, probably on a par with my own. He needed an interpreter to carry out his job. For many in the Gaeltacht, this appointment summed up the dwindling enthusiasm for the language in government circles. I asked Julian de Spáinn to outline McHugh's main achievements on the job. 'Learning Irish I suppose is number one, that's essentially his main achievement.' McHugh's Irish improved on the job but nothing else appears to have been achieved during his brief reign.

McHugh seemed to view the job as a personal development course rather than the urgent defence of an endangered language, requiring ideas and initiative. The Irish language media gave McHugh an exceedingly easy ride, constantly reminding him of what a good job he was doing – not as a minister, but as a language learner. It has proved the most expensive individual language-learning programme in the history of the state. There was some good news though – after he left office, RnaG announced that McHugh had made the *ardrang* in Oideas Gael in August 2016 – *tiocfaidh ár lá!* Meanwhile, Humphreys, at the time of writing (October 2016), has refused all attempts by Cormac Ó hEadra, presenter of flagship RnaG news programme *Cormac ag a Cúig*, to interview her at the time and place of her choice, in English.

The mythical fussiness of the native speaker is taken as a pretext to excuse oneself from bothering with the language at all – why try when your best efforts will be mocked and corrected? I hear this refrain from people who aren't learning the language, merely trying out the occasional word or phrase, expecting a grateful response. 'I told a mate of mine I was going out to Tigh Mhollys,' a friend told me, referring to a pub near Spiddal, 'and he immediately corrected me', the Molly becoming 'Wally' because of the added 'h' demanded by the *tuiseal ginideach* – the house of Molly.

My friend appeared genuinely hurt by this correction of his pronunciation. I recalled the many times I spoke my damn fine French to the natives in Paris only to be dismissed with a haughty shrug. It wasn't a manifestation of the legendary French ennui; I was simply making a hash of the pronunciation. 'Come onnnnnn,' said my friend, noting my lack of sympathy, 'throw me a bone.' A week later we met up in Dublin, where I asked him if he was interested in going to a gig at Wellan's that night.

'Where?' he asked. 'You know, Wellan's?' 'No,' he said. 'Of course you do. Wellan's on Camden Street, the gig place, you've been there a million times.' 'You mean Whelan's?' he said, correcting me. Indeed.

Immersion: Corca Dhuibhne (West Kerry)

I signed up for a *dianchúrsa*, or tough course, in Kerry, Galway and Donegal. I travelled to Kerry first to join a class at the local adult learning centre, an Oidhreacht, in Baile an Fheirtéaraigh. When I arrived there on a gorgeous summer morning I fairly leapt out of the car with enthusiasm and flagged down the first native who came into sight. 'Hey, *a thaisce, cá bhfuil an t-Ionad Gaeilge?*' – Hey you there, darling (it's ok, it's a Donegal thing) where's the Irish Centre? 'Go down the road and turn right,' came the reply *as Béarla.* The phrase was simple, the response easier. There were only two options, down the road, *síos an bóthar,* go left or right, *cas ar chlé nó ar dheis,* and mind your *séimhiú*s as you go. The guy in question was loading boxes into the nearby shop; he had to be a local, and presumably spoke Irish. *Póg mo thóin, cabrón,* I muttered, under my breath. It felt like a punch in the stomach. Surely it wasn't too much to expect a response in Irish and perhaps a little good cheer thrown in. 'Fair play to you, *mo chara,* are you back with the language?' That would have been a bit more encouraging.

Inside the brand new Ionad Gaeilge, a custom-built language centre formally opened the previous week (July 2015), teacher Bernie Pháid awaited. I was assigned to a *meánleibhéal* course, where reasonable competence is assumed. Bernie soon had the 18 of us on our feet and chatting in what might charitably be described as pidgin Irish. I was curious as to why others had signed up. There were as many motives as learners: '*Bhí ocras don teanga orm*' (the hunger of the language was upon me), said the guy beside me. 'That's pure poetry,' I said. 'I'm a poet,' replied Paul O'Casey. His phrase explained everything. My return to Irish felt like the satisfaction of a mysterious craving, an empty room awaiting the return of missing furniture, or a record player longing for the return of an old, forgotten, yet familiar album. The size of the class and the poor acoustics made it tough for the *múinteoir* but Bernie, an accomplished singer, brought the language to life with snatches of local songs and *scéalta*. Her passion was contagious.

The week was useful but the locals kept to themselves. I shopped in Irish, checking out the dictionary for useful words. When I asked for *beacáin*, the shop owner looked at me strangely. 'No idea what you're talking about,' he said. I pointed at the mushrooms. 'Ah, *na muisiriúiní*,' he said, pronouncing it almost exactly like the English word. I was learning another lesson – spoken Irish and book Irish are two different things. It probably didn't help that I was staying in the tourist hostel in Dún Chaoin, where I played Scrabble with visitors from Switzerland and hung out in the kitchen, chatting to an Italian couple as they cooked a delicious meal. I had tried to find lodgings with other learners or locals but failed to find anything, as I had booked the course late.

An Cheathrú Rua

I moved on to Connemara for my next *dianchúrsa*, which took place at the Acadamh (academy) at An Cheathrú Rua, one of several language-learning units located in Gaeltacht areas. The Acadamh serves third-level students at NUIG, adult learners and specialised courses in digital media, with a fully equipped studio on site. While the Kerry course relied on the ingenuity of the teacher, this time *an múinteoir* arrived into class heavily armed with handouts, exercises and Power Point presentations. But the first class began with a speed dating-style session as we got to know each other. There were eight of us in the class, including a Dutch woman. It shouldn't come as a surprise to find people from other countries speaking Irish, and yet the habit is ingrained. Dutch? Really, how come you're learning Irish? Try as we might to discard it, somewhere deep inside the old notion lingers – Irish has no serious purpose, and the best it can hope for is starry-eyed natives clinging to lost roots and notions of authenticity. 'What's your favourite word in Irish,' I asked the teacher, who sat opposite me. '*Amanathar*,' she replied, a local word for the day after tomorrow, 'and you?' '*Drogall*,' I said without hesitation, rolling the word around the roof of my mouth. I had been listening to Donncha Mac Con Iomaire all summer on *Iris Aniar*, the morning show from Connemara. Within seconds of starting the show each day Donncha invited listeners not to have any '*drogall*', or reluctance, upon them should they wish to contact the station. The sound of the word, dragged out to its fullest, fairly reeked of reluctance.

The course seemed a bit too academic at first (almost every class was governed by handouts and grammar), but as the week advanced the approach made more sense. If you don't know the rules and regulations, the *séimhiús* and *urús* and *ginideach*, you are missing out on critical *cruinneas*, and cannot make yourself properly understood. I cried out loud on day three when I finally worked out masculine and feminine rules under the bemused gaze of teacher Cormac. Up until then, I hadn't even realised there were masculine and feminine forms in Irish. That seemed downright weird. After a week I had learned a lot but spoken far too little. The course offered one unique advantage: a host family to stay with and all meals included.

It felt like a return to childhood, as I rose each morning with no greater purpose than to turn up for *bricfeasta* on time and make my way to class. My very own *bean a' tí* prepared all the meals for myself and two other classmates lodging in the same house. Both of them had good Irish, one of them a teacher in a gaelscoil. Mairéad and Pádraig were excellent hosts, keeping a close eye on our needs, giving us the run of their home. Late one evening Mairéad arrived into the kitchen as we three lodgers drank tea, and a long chat ensued. We were thrilled at the opportunity for a relaxed chat with a native speaker. She had a quick sense of humour, making it all the easier to banter together. It felt like progress but also reminded me how little Irish we were speaking compared to, say, a learner of Spanish visiting Spain, who faces the language every time they want to order food or communicate with another person. We chatted briefly to Mairéad each morning, but on one of the days the breakfast run was left to Pádraig, who directed a question our way. None of us understood. It sounded something like 'Hurahasho' – incomprehensible. Pádraig repeated it a few times to no avail. Finally, he asked in English, 'Where are you from?' The most basic phrase in the book, uttered in a natural, fluent way, and we were lost. We'd heard this question many times before, but when it came inside the flow of a normal chat with a native speaker it proved unintelligible. We were in the lion's den. This was why we had come to the Gaeltacht, for those phrases and that understanding that comes with everyday interaction. Pass the sugar, fetch the tea, is there any more bread? Anything on later? What time will you be back? Are you having a shower before you leave? These small phrases are the bread and butter of the language, and they were still beyond us. This is where a longer time spent with better speakers in an atmosphere of immersion pays dividends. I still felt like I was on the sidelines watching the match rather than on the field playing. Months later, when I interviewed musician and native Irish speaker Marcus Ó hIarnáin, I asked him what he considered the most effective way for a learner to grasp the language. 'You have to move in with the people of an area that you want to learn the Irish from,' he told me. 'You have to live there. I'm not saying live for three weeks there – it means nothing to be in a place for three weeks. You have to live with them, mingle with them, work with them, drink with them, have meals with them, whatever. It's the only way.' I stopped asking after that. The answer was always the same.

The struggle to understand and be understood is a wonderful lesson in humility. The problem remained, though – we spent almost all our time outside class with our fellow learners rather than with locals. An unexpected highlight occurred when a friend of mine with an aunt living in the area invited me over for dinner. This was the stiffest test yet, as Róisín, Donncha, Sinéad and Máirín treated me like a fellow speaker over the course of a long evening covering politics, religion and the fate of the language. I arrived home and collapsed into bed. As I gazed out the window at the Connemara night I realised that for the first time I had ceased worrying about the language and simply enjoyed speaking it. 'You'll have to find a woman for yourself who speaks Irish,' said Sinéad, and I recalled my own total immersion into Mexican life, when I went out with a local woman, falling in with the habits and rituals, the conversational shortcuts that become as natural as my English language originals. There are variations on this theme of embedding with the locals. 'Go to west Kerry, off season, and stay with an old bachelor,' advised poet and lecturer Ailbhe Ní Ghearbhuigh.

Oideas Gael

After Galway and Kerry, the very hungry learner has no choice but to head to Donegal for the main course at Oideas Gael, a language centre in Gleann Cholm Cille, a village on the north-west coast. Director Liam Ó Cuinneagáin has spent his life pondering ways to help people learn Irish, and wherever I go, people talk about him in reverential tones. Ó Cuinneagáin qualified as a teacher in 1982, swapping the *ciúnas* of a small village in Donegal for the hubbub of inner-city Dublin. He soon felt guilty about teaching kids a language that had no relevance to their everyday lives. Ó Cuinneagáin created his own syllabus, visiting Moore Street, Dublin Zoo and Kilmainham Goal, designing lessons around local places known to the kids. The impact was immediate, as the children soaked up Irish while discussing places and people connected to their lives. By the end of the year Ó Cuinneagáin had secured scholarships to the Gaeltacht for enthusiastic students and watched as parents came forward and asked if they too could get back to the language. Just as positive parental attitudes play a key role in fostering a healthy attitude to Irish, the enthusiasm of the kids can have the same effect on their parents. He returned to Donegal in 1984 and established Oideas Gael, a language school for adults. In its first year 32 pupils signed up, but by 2014 that figure had increased to 1,200 learners. It seems extraordinary that the Department of Education has never troubled him for a teaching tip or two. Ó Cuinneagáin has one other skill that seems essential for cracking the mysteries of teaching and learning Irish – he is a psychologist. Oideas Gael has no methods and no textbooks. You can learn the harp through Irish, go hillwalking through Irish or simply enjoy the activities and ignore the language altogether. Irish is all around you, but it is the art of seduction rather than the heft of grammar handouts. Ó Cuinneagáin doesn't teach, opting instead to profile everyone who walks through the door (up to 120 on a week-long summer course) and help them settle in. He has gathered a coterie of facilitators around him, linguists with a friendly manner and a playful approach to learning. It probably helps that most of them are not full-time teachers, devoting only part of their energy to the demands of the classroom.

The system matches individuals of mixed Irish language abilities into shared accommodation so that we learn from each other as we go along. I found myself in a spacious, warm house with a young American, Jack, who had completed two years of an Irish degree course at the University of Notre Dame. His grammar was irritatingly perfect, and when he spoke he sounded like a *seanfhear* from Connemara. Then there was Sean, a quiet, older man from Monaghan, who read books about meditation and mountains, while Brendan, from Cavan, refused to speak any Irish. He seemed paralysed by the language. And yet he was there. I had already made a decision that I was not going to speak a word of English, even if it killed me. After a tetchy skirmish in the kitchen on the first night, I wondered whether that might yet come to pass. Sean and Brendan had opted for the hillwalking course and took off each morning with a packed lunch, returning at dinnertime all too often weary and wet. On Tuesday evening I caved in to Brendan's English as he recounted his fraught relationship with the language. I felt guilty for my relentless insistence on Irish. Remarkably, the next day, Brendan was using every Irish word he could find. By the weekend he had decided he was coming back for the Irish language course next time. The seven-day shift from unhappy and defeated learner to a more confident and determined outlook was particularly impressive. It felt like watching someone emerge from a car crash, undergo physiotherapy and then take their first steps on their own feet. The learning formula is such that Ó Cuinneagáin can calculate, almost to the hour, when the 'speech barrier' will be broken – usually Wednesday afternoon by 2pm. There are beginners from the US and Dubai and advanced learners from New York and Belgium. 'Irish people perk up when they see a Belgian or Russian in the same class as them learning the language, making mistakes,' he explained. 'It gives us the determination to get over the learning block.'

The classes started on Monday morning at 10am. Teacher

Diarmuid Johnson arrived empty handed and spent the first five minutes in silence, staring out the window. He had a confident, if somewhat aloof, scholarly air. There were eight of us in the class – the *ardrang*, level *a cúig*, the highest available, the vanguard. The first surprise: Johnson was from Connemara, not Donegal. The next surprise, we spent the first two hours savouring and polishing half a dozen Irish phrases with forensic precision. We picked them apart, ungluing the sounds, listening and repeating. We learned where the sounds were produced in the mouth and throat. More than a class, it felt like a meditation, a glimpse into the heart of the language. Try saying '*dhá dhath dheasa*' or '*tá teach na ngealt i nGleann Cholm Cille i nDún na nGall*'. The effect is magical, as the mysteries of the spoken tongue are revealed. We learned how to recognise and pronounce seven different Ls and added vital phrases to our vocabulary, notably '*Is mó bealach le cat a mharú ná a thachtadh le him*' – there are more ways to kill a cat than by choking it with butter.

Some of the most basic words are the most abused. The word for Irish itself, *an Ghaeilge*, is almost always mispronounced as 'Gayle-Geh'. You need to open your mouth and shut your teeth to say it properly. There is a phrase used by Irish language enthusiasts to encourage beginners to have a go – '*Is fearr Gaeilge bhriste ná Béarla cliste*', 'better broken Irish than clever English'. I've never seen anyone from the Gaeltacht wearing that particular T-shirt. *Cruinneas* in speech is critical, the difference between being understood and being humoured. Then there's the thorny issue of dialect, bubbling under the surface of any discussion about Irish. The Irish spoken in Kerry differs from that of Donegal or Galway, but just how different is it, and do the differences matter? If you can follow an everyday conversation in one dialect, then you are almost certainly capable of tuning in to other dialects. If you struggle with the drift of a conversation in Irish, then it's premature to be concerned about dialect. What matters are the sounds of the language, common to all speakers everywhere, even if accent and emphasis temporarily disguise their meaning.

On day three a new student arrived into class, moving up from a lower level. She struggled in the class, blaming dialect for her difficulties. 'It's my dialect,' she insisted, 'I want to speak my own dialect.' Johnson was patient but after repeated refusals to try out the phrases passed from student to student he looked irritated. 'You don't have enough Irish to have a dialect,' he said, outlining basic mistakes that had nothing to do with dialect. She flat out refused to try. 'Do you want to speak English Irish or Irish Irish?' Johnson asked, now sounding a bit edgier. 'I'm not speaking your fucking Connemara shite,' she said, picking up her things and banging the door behind her. We gasped at her nerve. Johnson laughed. He worked us like pack mules and by Wednesday afternoon the best pupil in the class (not me) was fast asleep, another drifting in and out of wakefulness. A truce was declared. '*Fág é ina chodladh*' – let him sleep!

Johnson is a poet, flute player and linguist who speaks Welsh, Breton, Irish, English, Scots Gaelic, French, Polish, German and Romanian. In class he is part performance artist, part *múinteoir*. One class was built around an attempt to sell us his coat, which, I discovered to my satisfaction, he subsequently lost during a visit to Dundalk. Another lesson leaves two women weeping with laughter. The topic? *An modh coinníollach*, the infamous conditional tense, which has driven millions to emigration and self-loathing and cost me my Aisling *deas óg i mBaile Bhuirne*, 1976.

When I left Gleann Cholm Cille I felt like a boxer, fit and ready for the big fight. I had been given a glimpse of future possibility. I sensed the improvement. I couldn't speak fluently but I took home an energy that pushed me to greater efforts;

a door had edged open and I needed to keep pushing at it. Meanwhile the Dutch, US and Belgian learners set me thinking – What motivates people from elsewhere to learn Irish?

Aki, Lena, Rachel and Matthew

A year after I completed my course in Connemara I was back in a classroom in the Acadamh, on the last day of a month-long intensive Irish learning course aimed at foreigners. Four weary souls were sitting opposite me, having been drilled by Diarmuid Johnson, my former teacher and guru. I expected great things. They came from Japan, the US, Germany and Canada. Aki, Matthew, Lena and Rachel carried no baggage from the Irish education system, no grievance when it came to compulsory Irish, and for two of the four learners, no inherited connection to the language, no distant drums beating out the rhythm of the ancient Gael.

We began chatting in Irish but switched to English when the issues demanded greater depth of expression. '*Is seanchaí mé*,' said Aki Yoshio, from Tokyo, Japan. Aki was a storyteller who taught Irish fairytales in the University of Japan, and while he had ample material available in English, he wanted to learn Irish, 'because the language is the country and the people's spirit'. Matthew Doyle was a student at Columbia University in New York who took up a beginner level Irish course, liked what he heard and decided to stick with it. Rachel Hoffman from Montreal, Canada, had set herself a target in life – to learn all the languages in her family background. These consisted of Spanish, Russian, French, Yiddish, Polish and Irish. She had French, Russian and Spanish under her belt, and Irish in her sights. Lena Schulte, from Paderborn, Germany, came to Ireland several years ago to improve her English but fell in love with the Irish language instead. English is a compulsory subject in most German schools and mandatory in most jobs, from office work to car mechanic to 'anything which needs a university degree'. Were there any exceptions to the rule? 'Maybe a hairdresser,' she said. Aki began studying Irish in Tokyo three years ago, alone. 'Only two books,' he said, 'I don't speak English.' He discovered Micheál Ó Siadhail's *Learning Irish*, translated into Japanese. Aki told me there were maybe 10 people in Japan who speak Irish, but no native speakers. 'I had a Japanese Irish teacher,' he said, 'but their pronunciation is a little bit no good.' Aki had another teacher who spoke Donegal Irish, but he axed her because he couldn't understand her accent. Yes, word has reached Tokyo – stay away from the demon Donegal dialect.

I assumed that the Japanese, like many Europeans, learned English as a matter of course, but Aki disabused me of that notion. 'I learned English but I was not a good student. I hate English, just grammar, grammar, grammar, methods no exciting, just test, to write exam.' There were 40 others in his class at school – did they pick up English? 'No,' he said emphatically, 'because we don't need speak English in Japan.' What about films? 'We have subtitles.' The Internet? 'It's all in Japanese.'

Matthew learned Spanish at school but mastered it at work in a restaurant alongside Salvadoran work colleagues. 'I would speak Spanish non-stop at work, sometimes even more than I would speak English,' he said. He learned the language without ever leaving New York. His school lessons took place alongside 30 other kids. Did any of them learn to speak Spanish in class? 'Not at all,' he replied. Was the standard of teaching poor? 'No, the teaching wasn't bad at all,' he said, 'the students just weren't interested in the language. It was forced upon us, compulsory.' The experience of not learning to speak a language at school was uniform among this group. Rachel from Canada studied Spanish and Italian at school, but she and her fellow pupils only ever managed to speak a few sentences. Lena's experience with

English at school in Germany was similar: 'I struggled with it almost from the beginning. I took extra classes, private classes, to catch up because it's so important.' She told me she would have given it up if it hadn't been so vital for her job prospects. 'When I left high school I couldn't have a proper conversation; classroom conversations are somewhat artificial.'

Lena's three-month stay in Ireland switched her on to Irish: 'I started to really like the people, the music, the landscape and that brought me to the language.' The learning proved difficult – 'I don't have a talent for languages, really' – but she persisted, moved by the story of language loss in Ireland in the 19th century. 'I find that very dramatic. It really touched my heart when I learned that parents would prevent their children with violence from speaking their own mother tongue. It was this sentence, really, that kind of inspired me to give it a go.'

Matthew studied Irish for two semesters. His teacher was Padraig O'Carroll, borrowed from Glucksmann House, an Irish studies centre in New York. The immersion period in Connemara, his second, had been critical in improving his language skills. 'My progress has been exponential and I saw huge gains in my language. I can hold basic conversations now.'

In Montreal, Rachel signed up for an Irish language course that included conversation classes with visiting teachers from Ireland, three hours of instruction per week. Irish is also available off campus at regular social gatherings, while a 62-acre plot outside Kingston, Ontario, has been declared 'Gaeltacht Thuaisceart an Oileáin Úir', and runs a week-long immersion camp each year. The Canadian Gaeltacht is the brainchild of Aralt Tadhg Mac Giolla Chainnigh, born Harold Timothy Kenny in Ontario, who taught himself Irish as an adult. Rachel's first immersion course in Connemara, in 2015, permitted the language to flourish: 'I definitely learned more in the three weeks than in the entire year at school.'

Aki's goal was to become fluent in Irish. He planned to return every year and 'if I have a lot of money I will buy a house in Connemara'. The attitudes of some Irish people surprised them all. A taxi driver in Dublin laughed out loud when Matthew informed him he was on his way to an Irish language programme in Connemara. 'Why would you want to do that?' he said, incredulous. 'Why not learn a worthwhile language?'

CHAPTER 10

Inside the Gaeltacht – 'Do you do this on purpose?'

They start young when it comes to correcting *droch-Ghaeilge* (crap Irish) in the Gaeltacht. At five years of age Tadhg Mac Dhonnagáin's younger son was 'a full-on Connemara man' living in An Spidéal. His older boy was born in Dublin, spoke Irish at home and attended a gaelscoil until moving west. One morning, as Tadhg drove the two boys into town, a discussion began in the back seat of the car. The older boy was saying something about playing music, *ag imirt ceoil*, using the verb for playing a sport rather than *ag casadh ceoil*, used for playing an instrument. 'The guy in the back said "*Ag imirt ceoil? Ní bhíonn tú ag imirt ceoil, ag casadh ceoil, a bhíonns tú*"', recalled Tadhg. The correction was delivered in a tone of righteous indignation, with perhaps a hint of superiority thrown in for good measure. As someone who grew up with an always-older, always-brighter brother, I grasp the significance of these small but significant victories. The older boy got annoyed and switched to English: 'Maybe I'm not good enough for you, maybe, with your fancy Connemara accent. Maybe I shouldn't talk Irish at all' – the riposte delivered, of course, with an equal measure of dripping sarcasm. The younger boy summoned all the contempt that a five-year-old Connemara man might muster, and summarily dismissed his brother thus: 'ahh *dún do chlab, a chunt*' (shut up).

Gaeltacht Irish is a linguistic frontier that few outsiders manage to cross, a stark dividing line not just between Irish speaker and English speaker but between Irish speaker and native speaker. And there are other hidden depths within. Máirtín Ó Direáin, a renowned poet from Aran with a lifelong attachment to *saibhreas na teanga*, the richness of language, lamented his own lack of Irish in one small corner of life. His father had died when he was still a young child and he was not allowed out to sea with the other men. In interviews he expressed regret that he never had the opportunity to learn 'the language of the sea', regarding this gap in his knowledge of Irish as a wound upon his soul. Ó Direáin could have found the words but he would never experience the context in which they came alive.

This richness of expression is the secret of the Gaeltacht, hiding in plain sight. Diarmuid Johnson attended secondary school in Galway in the 1970s where the Jesuits had a Gaelic stream for students doing all their subjects through Irish. A third of the pupils came from Cois Fharraige, an Irish-speaking area in nearby Connemara. Part of the reason they were sent to the school was to learn more English. Johnson recalled his first day at the school, seeing two of the native Irish speakers standing beside a window, chatting together. 'I noticed that it wasn't the way the teachers spoke Irish,' said Johnson. 'I realised in that moment that Gaeltacht Irish, native Irish, was something else.'

It is rare if not unheard of for someone to comment on another person's standard of English unless they have learned

it as a foreign language. Irish speakers are different, as the
language, primarily an oral instrument, has traditionally been
a language of storytelling and song. The richer the language,
the more compelling the story and the greater the respect for
the speaker. Gaeltacht culture reflects this tradition of higher
and lower register, the everyday speech as a language of
communication and the 'higher' speech, a form of literature,
an art form, known as *dea-chaint*, or right speech. It reminds
me of the Buddhist principle of Right Speech, what you say and
how you say it as a reflection of a deeper truth.

Some villages were known for having a high concentration
of erudite speakers, the singers and storytellers who attracted
an audience for many miles around. Éamon a Búrc (1866–
1942), from Connemara, was one such storyteller, regarded as
the finest of his generation. One of his tales, 'Eochair Mac Rí
in Éirinn' (a king's son in Éirinn), ran to 30,000 words. It was
recorded by the Irish Folklore Commission in October 1938
and is believed to be the longest tale ever recorded from oral
narration anywhere in the world.

As I was preparing this book, a row broke out on RnaG (I
could start every chapter with that phrase; there is perpetual
warfare in linguistic matters on RnaG) after journalist Cian Ó
hÉagartaigh announced that the *droch-Ghaeilge* (see five-year-
old boy in back of car above) to be heard on the station gave
him a *tinneas cinn* (headache). On another occasion someone
pointed out a guest on RnaG who produced the harder 'English
T' (think 'TTROHnóna' for *tráthnóna*, instead of the softer
'tRAH-nóna'). That tendency, dear readers, is spreading among
the under 40s in Munster. Don't say I didn't warn you. Like
that painful advertisement about the half-price mattresses and
candles, when that Irish TR is gone, it's gone for good. My Irish
is not good enough to catch such nuances, but most people
I consulted on the matter agreed with Ó hÉagartaigh. As the

national broadcaster in Irish, they say, RnaG has a responsibility to maintain the highest possible standard of Irish.

People in the Gaeltacht often refer to the language as a private thing, part of an intimate home life and not for sharing with strangers, while teenagers use it in reverse – a public language closely associated with school and parental authority. When teenagers come together, they speak English. There are people with jobs in which they speak Irish who speak English at home, people who speak Irish to their kids only to receive a response in English, and all the other variations that come with the diversity of lives, jobs and families in a fluid, globalised environment. The only certainty is the lack of certainty when it comes to speaking and using the language.

The Gaeltacht also suffers the legacy of an older generation of native speakers, mocked as children when they arrived into Galway or Dingle or Letterkenny, speaking a pidgin English learned as a second language. These kids, now parents, may be tempted to put extra emphasis on English as their kids grow up, determined they will not suffer the same slings and arrows as they did. 'They got a fierce rough time,' I was told, 'like natives coming out of the jungle.' At school their fellow pupils would get them to pronounce certain words, knowing they would sound odd. The same rebuff and mockery came with efforts to access state services in Irish. The message was clear – use the language, it's part of us, but don't expect us to speak it back to you.

The Gaeltacht has a set of rules and rituals, informal yet consistent, acquired over the years. If you meet an Irish speaker in an English-speaking environment, you will probably continue speaking English to them. And it takes just one monoglot English speaker in company to shift the conversation to *Béarla*. I have heard the legend of the Gaelbores who mercilessly – no, gleefully – ice the Anglophile from the conversation; I have never met one. But they are out there, fingers in the dike, confusing love of language with some iron-fisted attachment to speaking it at all costs and in all company.

This act of exclusion probably does more to harm the language than even the *modh coinníollach*, and that's saying something. While the repeal of the grammar laws is an unlikely prospect in the near future, the Gaelbores can alter their approach should they decide to, encouraging rather than imposing the language. Ironically then, as a learner with limited opportunity for Irish-speaking encounters, I find myself taking advantage of all opportunities, insisting on Irish even if others in company cannot understand it. How else am I supposed to practise? There are ways of doing it without causing offence and without dragging it beyond the barriers of everyday patience. It takes a mindful approach to figure out that balance. And *drogallach* as I am to admit it, I am guilty of a crime that rightly irritates Irish speakers – engaging someone simply to practise the language, at times a mercenary exchange, as I might not approach the person otherwise.

Still, I wondered what life was *really* like inside the Gaeltacht, after the tourists and the summer students went home. On my trips to the various summer colleges, it felt like I was barely scratching the surface, gazing into a polished reflection that returned some predetermined idea of an Irish-speaking world. I had glimpses during my interviews with native speakers of the attitudes and habits and ways of being. There were differences in Gaeltacht life but it was hard to put my finger on them. The increasing mobility of the job market, the sameness of social media and the rapid liberalisation of Irish society have flattened out cultural differences inside and outside the Gaeltacht. When you travel through the Gaeltachtaí today it is only the signs that alert you to the difference between An Spidéal and Ballinrobe, between Gaoth Dobhair and Ballyshannon. And yet …

Nuala Ní Dhomhnaill, a poet who once lived in the Corca Dhuibhne Gaeltacht, told me she was packing up books into boxes and considering leaving Dublin. Would you go back to west Kerry, I asked her. She said she would love to, but couldn't stand the wind in winter. But surely with modern insulation and good heating, you'd hardly feel it these days? No, she said, in resigned fashion, 'my family suffers a *dúchas*'. A what? Her aunt told her long ago that the family suffers from a *dúchas* with regard to wind, *eagla na gaoithe*, a fear of wind. 'I can't sleep because of it,' this wind like no other wind. 'It's the door being pulled off the hinges and the howling at night.' I suspected that Ní Dhomhnaill had been influenced by the old manuscripts she was reading at UCD, but then I listened back to Peadar Ó Riada's interview and heard him mention the *dúchas* also. Peadar was talking about his own frustrations at learning Latin as he became an altar boy, and how he was reciting his lessons for his father on the night J.F.K. was killed, in November 1963. The day was memorable, not just for the obvious but also because his father was in bed with jaundice, an illness he had suffered since he himself was a boy. 'It nearly killed him as a teenager,' he told me. In passing he added, 'It's something particular to our family, a *dúchas*, weak livers.'

I checked out Dinneen and he had a few examples in his dictionary, notably the O Aodhs, or O'Hayes, who inherited 'a natural tendency towards warfare' from their ancestors. This might explain the onstage transformation of fiddle maestro Martin Hayes, a mild-mannered individual who turns into a wild marionette during his electrifying shows, looking like he is about to explode. It's in his blood. Dinneen included other examples, such as 'an inherited tendency to bad teeth' or 'a natural bent for magic practices.' I fancied I might find my own 'Dúchas an DIY', which would explain and justify my inability to knock two pieces of wood together without risking serious injury. Ó Riada explained that in older times this information was critically important to the balance and harmony of life in the community, and accounts for the extended surnames I heard repeatedly on the death notices on RnaG, revealing information about families. 'When we give someone's name,' explained Ó Riada, 'you know instantly the route of that person's lineage, so you had an idea if they were hot-tempered or they were creative or medical people.' The same applies to a tune, which is why airs and jigs are frequently prefaced by an explanation as to their origin. This serves the double function of acknowledging the source of an idea or tune and ensuring that it remains true to the original.

One major difference between life inside and outside the Gaeltacht is the casual disdain with which Irish speakers may be treated by officialdom. Marcus Ó hIarnáin, a musician from Carna, west Galway, recalled what happened when he took his four-year-old boy, who spoke only Irish, to Galway hospital for treatment. The doctor wanted to talk to the child to find out what was happening with his sore throat. He addressed the child in English, leaving the child speechless, unable to respond. 'Does this child speak?' asked the doctor. 'Yes, he speaks Irish,' replied Marcus. The doctor appeared horrified. 'Do you do this on purpose?' he asked. 'Do we do what on purpose?' replied Marcus, his temperature rising, his cheeks flushed. At that point his wife Mary ordered him out of the room, fearing open combat. 'I am not saying that our Irish is right,' reflected Ó hIarnáin, 'but it is what we had as children, whatever it is. It was what our parents before us had. We're proud of it and we don't care who thinks it is right or wrong.' The incident occurred more than 20 years previously, yet even as he retold the incident he was visibly upset.

When it came to schoolwork I assumed that native speakers enjoyed the support of appreciative teachers dealing with fluent pupils. Not so. 'The minute we put pen to paper there was *míle murder*,' said Marcus. The nuns, imported from elsewhere, 'beat us under the tables with rulers and fists,' he recalled. On one occasion in secondary school a nun told him 'You'll be fine for trotting behind a donkey', words etched in his memory, eroding all confidence in his studies. While three of Ó hIarnáin's sisters became teachers and two of his brothers followed the same path, Marcus was turned off 'book learning' for life: 'it broke us down completely … I can introduce you to 10 other people that were murdered in our school because of all this.'

What about his parents, I asked, naively, couldn't they do anything about it? 'My parents were terrified of nuns and priests. I'd get more beatings at home for saying anything against those people. My parents thought that priests and nuns were somewhere up there,' he said, gesturing towards the roof of the café where we sat. 'We all know that they weren't,' he concluded. 'I vowed when I left school that I would never open a book again as long as I live, and I've broken that law only once.' O hIarnáin has a beloved 1965 David Browne tractor that came to a sudden halt some years ago; he found the manual, read it and fixed up the engine. Marcus was born with the gift of making music and boats, a family trait, *dúchas an cheoil*. His mother told him that when she was pregnant with him, every time she would hear a tune, 'I'd be kicking, so she knew I'd be a singer, a dancer or a musician.' Ó hIarnáin not only plays the flute but also makes his own, along with the wooden cases that hold them. His latest project is a handmade *gleoiteog*, a traditional sailing boat similar to a Galway hooker but 22 feet in length. 'I'm building that with no knowledge, no books whatsoever, out of my hands and out of my head.'

Ó hIarnáin came to my attention when he announced on RnaG that the sleeve notes accompanying his new CD were written in English because of a dispute over the correct Irish spelling of words. Comhaltas Ceoltóirí Éireann and Gael Linn, key Irish language music institutions, were due to produce a book and CD, but the collaboration was cancelled. 'Both of the organisations refused to publish the book because I used Connemara Irish,' he wrote in the leaflet accompanying his latest album, *Coigil an Tine*. The statement sparked a heated debate on RnaG (yes, another one) about the *caighdeán*, the official guidelines for standard written Irish across all dialects. The concept behind the guidelines is to create a uniform, recognisable written language. However, the ironing out of local differences is seen by many as an attack on the purity of the language.

Antoine Ó Coileáin, an executive with Gael Linn, explained the issue: 'Marcus Ó hIarnáin is a fantastic musician and composer, I'm delighted to say we have several of his albums on the Gael Linn label. He's a real dynamo in Connemara. If the Ó hIarnáins are playing at a gig, you know they'll lift the roof.' Gael Linn was due to publish a book and CD featuring verse and descriptions of the natural world, as written by Marcus. 'Our job is to communicate with the widest possible audience,' said Antoine. 'This was something which was going to be published in Dublin, whether you like it or not ... People would have said it didn't read well and we'd end up having to defend the thing.' Ó Coileáin had no argument with Ó Iarnáin's insistence that the words appear as he wrote them, 'but the moment you try and promulgate something to a worldwide audience ... that's why there's such a thing as standard English'. It seemed a strange conclusion to reach when the text and songs in question clearly belonged to a local creative endeavour, with no aspiration to being recognised as a standard text.

It has been said that you can tell a Dublin Irish speaker from a Connemara native because the Dubs have an Irish word for everything. Speakers in the Gaeltacht have a more relaxed attitude. When, at the start of a radio interview, a presenter asked a native speaker the usual question, 'Conas atá tú?', the reply sounded utterly natural – 'Táim all right.' The Irish language enjoys a central role in the lives of Gaeltacht locals, but the shadow of its dominant partner hovers nearby, weaving in and out, borrowing words and phrases. The jargon-makers call this 'code-switching', and it occurs in a natural way among active bilinguals anywhere, switching from one language to another. Irish speakers use English words for many reasons, often out of habit but also because certain words came into the language before the Irish term was minted. The fridge was in the house before the cuisneoir, and bicycles came before rothars were named. The same applies to showers, microwaves and garden hoses.

The notion of either/or in relation to Irish and English has been superseded by both/and, the lived reality of two languages cohabiting side by side. That age-old question has given way to another one – which matters most? – the everyday conversations of a declining number of Gaeltacht speakers or the casual but growing interactions between learners and nua-chainteoirí, 'new speakers', from Galway to Belfast, the greetings and exchanges in cafés and shops? Does either one better stimulate the survival of the language? The new learners bring a wear and tear to the language that annoys some purists but also a fresh energy that raises spirits. There is no doubt, however, that the structures of English are creeping steadily into spoken and written Irish, undermining a wealth of expression that has developed over almost 2,000 years.

The gap between learned Irish and native Irish is as vast as the gap between any two speakers, one having lived and breathed a language from birth, the other having eased their way into it, without the foundations of total lived immersion. The second language learner invariably suffers the lack of natural flow and rhythm, the absence of *nathanna cainte* (local phrases), the dry accent and general inability to 'shoot from the hip', all making difficult the one basic function of language: communication. So how the hell do you learn them if no one takes the time to express them to you?

There are sound reasons why a Gaeltacht local might switch to English with you as you limp along, trying to complete a sentence. 'This poor fool is struggling with his *cúpla focal*, I'll put him out of his misery', while the visitor might be thinking, 'Jesus, I came all the way here to practise some real Irish, do me a favour.' The locals may feel that you are trying out the *cúpla focal* as some sort of favour to them – a favour, frankly, they don't need. For every enthusiast seeking a conversation in Irish, there are probably five more outsiders relieved and happy to do their business through *Béarla*. But the balance remains uncertain and can be a source of tension. One of Tadhg Mac Dhonnagáin's daughters began a part-time job in a local shop. She would happily speak to anyone in Irish but nine times out of 10 the visitor had no Irish, so the issue hardly arose. One woman arrived in, gathered up a few things and came to the till, without saying a word. The young woman told her the amount due, in English. 'What's wrong with you?' said the woman, '*nach bhfuilimid sa Ghaeltacht anseo?*' (aren't we in the Gaeltacht here?). Irish is always a sensitive subject, a thorn waiting to prick someone's carefully nurtured sense of hurt. 'The woman was keen to be insulted,' concluded Tadhg.

The expectations and projections we cast upon the language can have a powerful and at times numbing effect on our ability to learn and speak. We are already primed and ready for whatever it is we have decided is going to happen. In some strange way we almost invite what happens next. Diarmuid Lyng, an Irish learner turned speaker who moved to the Gaeltacht, recalled an early encounter with Dara Ó Cinnéide. 'It's hard to stand in

INSIDE THE GAELTACHT – 'DO YOU DO THIS ON PURPOSE?'   145

front of another adult and show a vulnerability in yourself,' he said. 'It's like he's [Dara] speaking out of the mountain. He's speaking this glorious Irish, and all I have to offer is my fucking school Irish.' Diarmuid knows he was projecting his own fears onto Dara, who may have been thinking something entirely different. 'Here am I thinking, Oh Dara probably thinks I'm a fucking eejit, but I'm sure he is sitting and looking at me and listening to me and saying, Fuck, isn't it great, there's somebody else pushing the language on and keeping the language alive, and it's someone involved in sport, he's exploring.'

The difficulty lies in recognising this dynamic and letting go of preconceptions: 'Once you can accept that, it doesn't matter what Dara thinks, you're just exploring something for the beauty of it itself.' Lyng can see both sides of the coin in the Gaeltacht. 'People give you the cold shoulder if you create it,' he said. As a student he arrived into the Gaeltacht and spent his time drinking, struggling to make it to the lectures. 'I was half there, half not there. People were thinking, Well, here's another student down who doesn't really give a shit. Am I going to invest time in someone like that?'

When he returned in a different frame of mind, he was greeted in a different manner. 'They met me with open arms and tried to help me as best they could ... with such goodness and beauty.' Lyng set up home in Baile an Chalaidh, beyond Ballyferriter in Kerry, in 2015. 'I was living at a small crossroads. The locals only really spoke Irish. They would invite you in and give you tea and sandwiches until all hours, and just speak and tell you stories, infinitely hospitable to any form of exploration in yourself.' This time round, Diarmuid believes, he was open to this. He brought that down with him and they met it halfway.

On brief trips to the Gaeltacht, the only option is to persist. My brother spent time in Carna and other Gaeltacht towns, speaking Irish to the locals. He had no complaint with the reception he got. It has something to do with his character, his patience and persistence and lack of judgement. If someone spoke English back to him, he carried on speaking Irish. It simply didn't bother him. In case you think it's only the vaguely competent speakers who suffer this complex, Toner Quinn, with *fiche bliain sa Ghaeltacht* (twenty years in the Gaeltacht), still gets it on occasion. 'I hear it all the time. People speak English to me, I speak Irish back to them, they continue to speak English. Then, once they get to know me, they'll speak Irish to me. I've no problem with that.'

While musicians, hurlers and priests have enjoyed a special status in the Gaeltacht, as in broader Irish society, what is it like to be an outsider in the Gaeltacht, someone cut off from church, sport and pub scene? Would a gay man or woman find the Gaeltacht a warm place to be? Colm de Bhaldraithe describes himself as coming from Planet Zog, more than an outsider, an alien. In the mid-1990s, he agreed to speak to Máirtín Tom Sheáinín on Raidió Na Gaeltachta about his life as a gay man in west Connemara. The interview came at a time when the social atmosphere all over Ireland was unrecognisable from today, whether you lived in Bray or Bearna. A fortnight after speaking out on Gaeltacht radio, de Bhaldraithe had his windows broken and received obscene phone calls, and an anonymous note was pinned to the communal notice board at his workplace in Ros Muc. Then his windows were smashed once more. De Bhaldraithe knew who was breaking his windows, and yes, they lived little more than a stone's throw away. De Bhaldraithe, living alone on a remote boreen, hesitated to call the experience frightening, but admitted he wouldn't want to repeat it. He responded by throwing a fancy dress party on Oíche Shamhna, Hallowe'en. 'It was a statement – I wanted to transform negative energy into positive energy,' he said. Reggae band Bréag came down from Belfast, while Galway supplied a salsa band, as 300 people turned up, dancing through the night. Two figures were built and burned on a bonfire – a 50-foot angel and a 50-foot devil. His work colleagues were supportive and the incident is all but forgotten, 'but it shows you how things were around here,' he says. De Bhaldraithe holds drumming workshops in schools and summer colleges throughout the year, an openly gay man combining Irish with music and costume in a vastly altered social landscape. 'The whole of Ireland has changed,' he added. At Coláiste Uisce, an Irish college in Mayo, de Bhaldraithe held workshops for visiting teenagers in summer 2016. 'They had never associated Irish with fun before,' he said. 'There was a lot of laughing, someone gets into a crazy costume and off they go. They're not thinking, they're laughing. It's a great release of fear, and they're using their bit of Irish.'

The annual influx of teenagers to the various Gaeltachtaí, 20,000 or more, attending summer colleges, staying with local families, is not just a boost to the local economy but a meeting of minds and hearts, one part of the country getting to know another. The days of compulsory mass and flag-raising ceremonies are in decline, but food remains an issue, largely the same old unhealthy fare I faced in the 1970s – this at least according to my teenage sources, who attended a range of Irish colleges. It should be noted that these teenagers, too cool for rules, returned to Irish college of their own will, and at considerable cost to their parents, year after year after year, until now, at 18, they had run out of summers. The standard of Irish varies from college to college, they say, but the experience of the Gaeltacht – the rituals, the language, the craic – are invaluable additions to the growing curve of life.

The local Gaeltacht teenagers are no longer the aliens of yesteryear, wearing old-fashioned clothes, and God forbid helping their families with work on the farm. The current crop of Gael teens are, sadly, gazing as intently at screens as teenagers everywhere else. A generation ago, parents harassed their indifferent teenagers into going to mass; nowadays some parents need to push and prod their sullen teenagers into speaking the damn language they worked so hard to defend and maintain and revive. Is it too much to ask? The answer is yes, in many cases, for a few years at least, but almost everyone I met agreed on this: that once the teenage blip is done, the weird zombies in your kitchen eventually settle down, and by the time they have their own kids, watch them go, they turn into little fíor Ghaels, fiercely protective of their language. Other teenagers, sensitive to the importance of Irish in their families, go to their bedrooms and speak discreetly to friends on the phone, not wanting to disappoint their parents.

However, adult speakers also lapse, weary perhaps at the double standards of a society in which Irish is lauded by one arm of officialdom but dismissed by another, when you actually attempt to use it in going about your business. 'There is a cynicism there,' said Éamonn Ó Dónaill, a Gweedore native. 'The lack of commitment from the government affects people's perceptions of the language; they get the feeling that it's not worth the effort.' He recalled a time when his nephew, at the age of five and with no English at all, needed speech therapy. The young child attended a therapist who was unable to communicate in Irish. 'What kind of message does that give a young person, this language that is not considered worthwhile?' Ó Dónaill believes that organisations bringing jobs and people into a Gaeltacht area should have a rapid learning programme for new arrivals, particularly their children, who attend local schools but only speak English.

Meanwhile the Gaeltacht remains the Tobar, the well, the source, the connection that ties the language to its ancestral roots. It is not an exclusive members-only club but an ocean awaiting any intrepid swimmers. 'There's an invitation, and we don't realise there's an invitation, to something other than the world we're coming from,' observed Diarmuid Lyng. 'When you take the leap, when you step off the ledge, you are held, surprisingly, by something you didn't realise was there.'

CHAPTER 11

A Fitzcarraldo in West Belfast

D ouglas Hyde once said, 'The Gaelic race was expelled and the land planted with aliens.' The border that separates north and south of Ireland is an unremarkable stretch of fields, houses and silence, marked only by currency exchange offers, a shift from kilometres to miles on the road signs and the disappearance of the Irish language. This 'soft' border may yet undergo a radical change once Brexit is implemented. My experience of border crossings in Latin America involved passport checks, the filling out of documents, explaining one's intentions and itinerary, extensive bag searches, some food stalls, noise and bustle and lots of people anxiously awaiting permissions. I am only vaguely aware that I am officially crossing from one country to another, yet I am gripped by feelings of reluctance and dread, a tightening of the stomach, some ill-defined but palpable unease. I have been coming to the north ever since I was a small child on family holidays to Cushendall, County Antrim, visiting my godmother Kathleen McCaughan, who owned the sweet shop at 19 Main Street.

My father was born in Drumlee, a remote rural outpost near Ballymoney in Co. Antrim. A Union Jack flies over the farm where he was raised. He never spoke about his childhood. More silence. Those regular trips to Cushendall form a key chapter in family lore, between the sweet shop, Cushendun beach, which lay within walking distance and the nearby cinema, which hosted late-night double features each weekend. We had the run of the place. Kathleen was an easy-going, generous woman who seemed totally relaxed around the small gang of children who came her way once a year. We siblings took turns working in the shop or huddled in a group around the counter, selling single cigarettes, sliders and penny sweets. The local singsong accents delighted us so much that on occasion we were forced to retreat in hysterics at some unexpected turn of phrase.

Kathleen invited us to take whatever we wanted from the shop. I didn't need to be told twice, and a familiar ritual was enacted at the start of each visit. I would take a jar of pear drops to bed and eat as many as I could. Then, sick and spent, I waited an eternity for the pain in my tummy to pass and for sleep to overwhelm me. That was it for the sweets and me until another year passed, and with it all memory of previous pear drop excess.

It was the early 1970s and the northern conflict was gathering pace but Cushendall was a safe haven, detached from the Troubles apart from the unusual sight of barbed wire wrapped around a quiet police station. I never saw anyone appear from inside, but we were told there were officers on duty. A phone attached to the wall outside was the preferred means of communication to those within. Late at night the young bucks revved up their cars, tearing up and down the main street, executing handbrake turns with impunity. It was years before I realised that this antisocial behaviour was probably part of a campaign to taunt the police or highlight their inability to function. There was an air of lawlessness about the place, combined with a sleepy rural charm. One morning I woke to hear sheep outside. They filled up the street, crowding road and pavement alike, on their way to the nearby mart.

On a couple of rare occasions I travelled up alone or with my father. In summer 1975 I woke each morning to the sound of Blue Oyster Cult's 'Don't Fear the Reaper', a dreamy summer hit played repeatedly on a turntable in a neighbour's house. The weather was balmy, windows open and the volume turned up so high I could hear the crackle from the needle when it reached the end of the record. In my late teens the visits dropped off as I travelled further afield, returning only for rare weekend stopovers before Kathleen died in 2003. The sweet shop closed long before that, after flooding destroyed the ground floor of the house on main street, forcing her into a nearby apartment earmarked for the elderly.

Meanwhile the war in the north had come into sharp focus in all its bloody chaos. The grim daily toll of shootings, bombings and destruction interrupted older, sweeter memories. A campaign for civil rights for the minority Nationalist population, launched in 1968, was beaten off the streets, and a guerrilla war evolved in its wake, leaving 3,500 casualties. The Good Friday Agreement in 1998 marked a formal end to hostilities, but as I drove across the border in 2016 I still felt I was entering a zone of uncertainty. There was no avoiding the implacable divisions – they were painted on the kerbstones and blowing in the wind – tricolour and Union Jack.

The rival factions clamoured for attention, Bobby Sands and the Battle of the Somme, two competing and bitterly opposed tribes that would never let go of their grievances. The very names of the towns and villages across the border struck me as chilling – Black Skull, Tandragee, Lough Brickland, Gowdystown, Corlust and Bleary. What must it be like to live all the time with that sense of something pressing down, of a question hovering in the background – Are you with us or against us? Loyal or disloyal? Green or Orange? Catholic or Protestant? Rangers or Celtic? Ireland or Northern Ireland? Stewart or Murphy? Holy Cross School or Belfast Model School for Girls? Everything on one side had its mirror image in the other. Even the government was weighted to insure the cooperation of Sinn Féin with the Democratic Unionist Party, implacable foes sharing the spoils of a dysfunctional state.

In Northern Ireland the Irish language has historically been viewed as a suspect device aimed at disrupting and destroying British rule. In the 1930s grants for Irish were removed, while in the 1940s the erection of street signs in Irish was outlawed. The Northern Ireland government decreed that the maximum amount of time to be devoted to Irish in school was one-and-a-half hours per week, and it could not be taught to children below third class. (Stop cheering you lot at the back of the class down south.) Interestingly, the British government offered one exception to the weekly 90-minute Irish language limit: the teaching of history could be omitted and Irish taught in its place. The authorities viewed a knowledge of history as potentially more dangerous than a grasp of the Irish language.

'The kind of history that would be taught in schools where it is desired to foster the study of Irish would be likely to have a bias of a very undesirable character,' announced the Northern government in September 1922, soon after the state formally came into existence. When it came to the Irish language the Northern prime minister made no apology: 'What use is it, in this busy part of the Empire, to teach our children the Irish language?' before concluding, 'We do not see that these boys being taught Irish would be any better citizens.' Long before the Republican movement would be accused of using the language for their own ends the Northern government had mastered the same trick. James Craig, Prime Minister for Northern Ireland from 1921 to 1940, presided over sectarian massacres and pogroms against the Catholic citizenry, the death toll rising to over 200 in 1922 alone. I never read anything about this bloody period of northern history at school in Dublin. The north slipped out of view after the War of Independence, and the south no longer seemed to care.

I had long assumed that Ulster, the heart of the British plantation project, was the place where Irish first disappeared from daily life, but the province proved resilient. There were pockets of native speakers in Tyrone, Armagh, Antrim and Derry in the early 20th century, and a dimly lit torch was passed on by a generation of enthusiasts who maintained a foothold in Belfast. In the period following the declaration of the Orange State, the Irish language community relied largely on Ard Scoil Ultach (Ulster College) near the city centre for language classes, céilís and lectures. The work of Cumann Chluain Ard, a branch of the Gaelic League set up in 1936, was critical in everything that followed, a hub where enthusiasts met and occasionally fell in love and married, sowing the seeds of future language developments. The odd parish hall offered classes, but opportunities to master the language were severely limited.

In 1965 there were an estimated 36 Irish-speaking families scattered around Belfast. A group of language enthusiasts began meeting, making plans to establish a small Gaeltacht in west Belfast. Discussions began among 19 families, a figure whittled down to five when it came to building the first homes. The young couples who signed up to the Bóthar Seoighe/Shaw's Road Gaeltacht project had youth, energy, dedication and resilience on their side. In the 1960s and 1970s the ghettoization of Belfast also proved helpful in setting up a tightknit Irish-speaking community with broad community support. The 2.5-acre site was bought from the Christian Brothers with a loan of £2,500 from Comhaltas Uladh, the Ulster council of the Gaelic League. The local architect and lawyer who took care of planning and legal issues were Irish speakers who gave their services for free. This spirit of active goodwill distinguishes the Irish language fraternity in Ulster from elsewhere in the country, a keen sense of volunteerism, of teaching, learning and bringing the language forward with a selfless attitude. This concept manifested itself once more even before the Shaw's Road homes were complete. In August 1969, as work began on the five homes, the nearby community of Bombay Street was burned out by Loyalists. Work on the new homes along Shaw's Road was put on hold while workers helped those families rebuild their lives.

The first house on Shaw's Road was completed in 1969, with three more added in 1970 and three more again between 1974 and 1976. The launch of an Irish-medium primary school, or *bunscoil*, in a small prefab beside the housing project, was critical to the success of the project. Up until then the language had only been available as a school subject or an adult conversation class. Several of the Shaw's Road residents had abandoned Irish at school, uninspired by a teaching programme more appropriate to Latin and Greek studies, as if picking over the bones of a dead language. When it came to establishing the local school, the community acted swiftly: a portable hut was purchased for £100 on a Friday, assembled over the weekend and classes started on the Monday. This is the second pillar of the Irish language boom in Northern Ireland – no one is hanging around waiting for funds to make things happen. If it needs to be done it will be done. A native Irish speaker from Donegal was hired as the sole teacher but left two years later. The job was then handed to a local person raised with Irish.

In September 1971 Bunscoil Phobal Feirste opened with nine pupils, seven of them from the Shaw's Road Gaeltacht, which lay on its doorstep. The parents of the pupils built and maintained the school, cleaned the classrooms and scrubbed down the school toilets. The Shaw's Road residents received a letter from the educational authorities ordering them to cease and desist, but they carried on despite the lack of funds and state recognition. This is lesson three of the Irish language renaissance in the North – don't ask for permission and don't take no for an answer. Just do it. The community fundraised all costs, rattling boxes inside pubs each weekend to pay the teacher's salary. In 1978, the Shaw's Road school opened its doors to pupils from non-Irish-speaking homes, allowing it to expand.

The school and home project quickly became a source of great pride to non-speakers in the area. By the beginning of the school year in 1984 there were 162 children enrolled, and a second *bunscoil* opened in the area in 1987. As the second primary school searched for premises the Shaw's Road community disassembled its first premises and offered it to the new school located nearby. Lesson four from the North – Shaw's Road, the mother ship, constantly facilitated the expansion of Irish language services elsewhere.

The chaos and disruption of daily life during the conflict and the proximity of the Donegal Gaeltacht prompted families to send children to stay with Irish-speaking families and attend summer language courses over the border. Donegal has proven itself a constant, supportive companion to Irish speakers across the north.

The task of building and equipping a school – maintaining it, paying teachers' wages, drawing up a syllabus – is a daunting one, even with state recognition. The school finally received official maintained status in 1984, the year Bunscoil Cholmcille, or Steelestown primary school, was established in Derry. The Irish language was growing. When the first set of pupils graduated from the Bóthar Seoighe primary school they faced two options: move to the south for secondary schooling through Irish or join a local English-medium school. The Bóthar Seoighe community decided on a third option: setting up their own *meánscoil* (secondary school) on an entirely voluntary basis.

The school found teachers with Irish language skills working in nearby English language schools and asked for help. These teachers gave their time for free, organising a timetable for pupils, who were taught all their subjects in Irish. Where the language skills were shaky, help soon followed. The volunteer science teacher had poor Irish, so one of the parents drew up a glossary of terms and sat in on classes as an interpreter. This experiment in volunteer secondary education lasted two years, too demanding to be continued on an indefinite basis even for the men and women of Ulster. However, a point had been made – the demand for a secondary school was evident, along with the capacity to organise it. In 1991, Coláiste Feirste, the first Irish medium secondary school, opened its doors to just nine pupils. As the school opened for another academic year in September 2016, student numbers had risen to 650, a remarkable growth rate.

The task of reviewing the development of the Shaw's Road Gaeltacht and *bunscoil* is made easier by a field study undertaken by Gabrielle Maguire, who interviewed children and parents in the 1980s, producing *Our Own Language* (1991), covering the first two decades of the project. Maguire analysed the social background of the parents who sent their kids to the Shaw's Road school and compared them to their peers in an Irish-speaking primary school in south Dublin. The contrast was remarkable – in the Belfast school, 34 per cent of fathers were unemployed, 38 per cent unskilled or semi-skilled and 15 per cent professional/managerial category. In the *bunscoil* consulted for the survey in the Republic, 65 per cent of parents were professionals, leaving just 8 per cent unskilled or semi-skilled, and unemployment wasn't mentioned. Maguire discovered that the two biggest factors that persuaded parents to send their kids to the *bunscoil* in Belfast were 'Irish identity' and 'quality education', with only 9 per cent of parents citing Republicanism/Nationalism, even though 25 per cent of fathers had learned Irish in jail.

The armed conflict brought its own problems to Shaw's Road: a Loyalist attack on one occasion, periodic Republican riots and barricades and even a firefight between two units of the British Army, who mistakenly believed they had come under enemy fire. That skirmish left bullet holes in several homes. The houses all had a communal alarm system, a kind of panic button to be activated if one house came under attack.

Parents living outside Shaw's Road told Maguire that the opportunity to send their children to the *bunscoil* frequently proved the catalyst that started them speaking Irish to their kids, supporting their language development and growth. However, it remained a constant task, second-language learners attempting to keep Irish to the fore. Parents said that rituals like homework, story time, prayer time, meals, shopping and family walks were occasions for speaking Irish, whereas television and non-Irish-speaking guests broke the spell. The school bus driver described how kids coming to the school from non-Irish-speaking homes would get on the bus speaking English and then switch to Irish as they approached school. On the return journey home, English came to life as they drew near their homes in the afternoon. Maguire's research remains relevant today, and offers important clues as to how learners and parents might be supported. She discovered that parents who were shy of starting conversations in Irish with others would invariably have kids who showed the same reluctance. The same parents were consciously aware of using Irish, and each interaction had the air of a practice run rather than a natural flow. In addition, after a long day, by the time parents and kids were sitting down together, enjoying precious free time, they were often tired, and could do without the constant effort required to speak Irish.

These issues did not apply to the Gaeltacht homes in Bóthar Seoighe, where Irish was the first language. The rise of An

Chultúrlann, an Irish language hub along the Falls Road, the launch of a daily newspaper, *Lá*, alongside a credit union, small shop and clubs dedicated to cycling and swimming, all served to make the use of Irish more of an everyday, normal occurrence. Since the launch of the Bóthar Seoige *bunscoil*, Irish language learning has advanced in leaps and bounds in the north. The chief engine behind this development is the unstoppable growth of Irish-medium education.

In the early years, Bóthar Seoige was a small but determined team, alone on the pitch, sweating and struggling while thousands cheered them on, an expansive ripple of well-wishers, many of whom subsequently took up Irish themselves. 'These supporters', said Liam Ó Flannagáin, a language activist in Belfast at that time, 'are every bit as much part of the community of the Irish language even if they don't speak the language.' This support team raises funds and contributes energy to the language along with a *cúpla focal*, the greetings and farewells that keep the language visible and audible.

From a modest starting point there has been a 100 per cent increase in the number of children attending all-Irish schools in Northern Ireland in the past 10 years and, equally as important, 72 per cent of the Irish-medium schools are non-denominational, welcoming Catholic, Protestant and dissenter.

The mid-Ulster area is the single fastest growing region of all, with a 500 per cent increase in pupils opting for Irish-medium education between 2013 and 2016. There is no cut-off point in sight. Gaelscoil Eoghain in Cookstown, County Tyrone, had 13 pupils in 2013, a figure that rose to 67 in 2016. Gaelscoil Aodha Rua in Dungannon, with 12 pupils in 2011, enrolled 88 in 2016. International research commissioned by the Department of Education for Northern Ireland has shown that Irish-medium children were more open to cultural diversity, a perk as important as the Irish language that fostered it. Irish-medium education offers a system that improves children's skills in both English and Irish, while also providing the skills to learn further languages with greater ease. In the context of Northern Ireland's segregated school system, these outcomes are critical. Lest anyone feel smug from the comfort of the Republic of Ireland, the school system here is totalitarian rather than segregated: the icy grip of the Catholic Church still controls over 90 per cent of our schools.

The number of Irish-speaking homes along Shaw's Road has doubled in the past two decades, from 11 to 22, most of them located further up the road rather than side by side. Meanwhile the first children have grown up, and some of the older residents have died. Only one of the homes still houses parents who launched the project in 1969. 'It will be a challenge to maintain the linguistic integrity of the place,' admits Diarmuid Ó Bruadair, raised on Shaw's Road where he now lives with his Brazilian wife and three kids. This cluster of Irish-speaking homes now has Chilean, Welsh and Spanish parents living a trilingual existence. The north is wide awake, and if you include Oideas Gael across the border in Donegal, the province of Ulster emerges as the beating heart of the contemporary Irish language movement. Where one flower withers, another grows. While the better-known Gaeltachts are simply places where Irish is spoken, the growth of Gaelic in Belfast carries the mystique of a forbidden language spoken against the odds, and with a hint of subversive mischief. This blend of language and subversion found an early home in the Maze prison, or H-Blocks, witness to some of the key incidents from the province's recent past.

CHAPTER 12

From Jailtacht to Gaelictown

T he fastest-growing Irish language project in the world during the 1980s did not take place in the Gaeltachtaí of western Ireland or in Dublin's ambitious southside suburbs, but inside the cold, damp confines of the H-Blocks, home to over 2,000 Republican prisoners during the recent period of conflict. This community of captive learners and speakers was second in numbers only to those captives serving time inside the school system in the Republic. As language enthusiasts bemoaned the decline of the Gaeltacht, prisoners in Northern Ireland celebrated the birth of the *Jail*tacht. Irish had been taught and practised in other jails before, notably Frongoch and the Curragh during internment, but the H-Blocks brought together a critical mass of highly committed prisoners with considerable control over their surroundings and serving long sentences for serious crimes.

Toby MacMahon was one of the first Irish speakers to take the initiative in 1978, dismantling half the cubicles in Cage 11, one of the Nissen huts that housed Republican prisoners inside a former RAF base 10 miles from Belfast. The Jailtacht was an open-plan dormitory capable of sleeping 24 prisoners. Only Irish was spoken in this area, and a further big cell normally housing four prisoners served as a classroom as a roster of daily classes was established. At 8am each morning the Irish language came to life, as breakfast was accompanied by *Now You're Talking*, a series of Irish language TV programmes for beginners produced by BBC Northern Ireland, using the Ulster dialect. These were played until lunchtime, and were followed by more advanced language recordings of a morning chat show from Raidió Na Gaeltachta. Multiple copies were made, so that learners could walk around the yard with headphones on, practising their Irish. 'It was great, some people were fully fluent and they were taking others along who weren't fluent and slowly building up the language,' explained Anthony McIntyre, who moved into the Jailtacht. The use of Irish intensified during the blanket protests and hunger strikes (1976–81), a useful tool for secret communication. By then the old huts had long been knocked down and the H-Blocks built in their place, with two wings dedicated to the Irish language community. There were *ranganna comhrá*, conversation groups of up to a dozen people, alongside language classes for beginners. The prisoners also shouted up and down the wings *as Gaeilge* and played memory chess, shouting the moves from the door of each cell. McIntyre recalled one 36-hour chess marathon with Paddy Agnew, a future TD for County Louth.

The language was another weapon in the Republican arsenal, even if many of the Jailtacht members enjoyed it for its own sake. 'It was great to be able to shout over to the other blocks in Irish and talk to each other when the screws were about, passing messages in Gaelic during visits, dealing with IRA business.' McIntyre ended up in H4 of the blocks, with Gary Roberts, whose enthusiasm helped both of them improve their language skills. 'The interesting thing is that people who never learned anything were picking up Irish. They could understand it even if they never spoke it. If you shouted something or news came across in Irish they could work it out.' In a bilingual atmosphere Irish was passively understood even by those who didn't learn it.

I wondered was there an element of compulsion or duty about the use of Irish. 'No, there wasn't, it wouldn't have worked,' said McIntyre. 'It was all on a voluntary basis. At times they tried making certain classes compulsory but you could never sustain them.' McIntyre lived a bilingual life in the blocks, particularly in the early 1990s. There were 500 prisoners there at that time and McIntyre estimated that, while 60 per cent of prisoners picked up Irish during the blanket protest, 100 per cent were 'contaminated' or saturated in it because of its visibility and constant use. 'Some prisoners learned Irish out of interest, others out of boredom,' added McIntyre. 'You had to occupy yourself somehow.' The make-up of the Jailtacht was always shifting, as prisoners were released and others, suffering 'gate fever', lost interest in activities as their release date approached, and with it the long-awaited opening of the gates to freedom.

'The biggest impediment people had was that they were nervous, shy – you don't want to sound stupid. The whole thing was, you don't sound stupid on this wing, because we all sound stupid; we've all got daft, limited Irish,' recalled Féilim Ó hAdhmaill, a former prisoner and Jailtacht member. One of the policies adopted by the prisoners was to put everyone to work teaching Irish. 'Whenever someone was able to put a few words together, we said, Right, now you take a class. The notion was, you learn more from taking a class than from just attending a class. It's active learning then.' The advanced learners taught the improvers, and they in turn taught the *bunrang*, or beginner class, until the *bunrang*ers themselves taught people with no Irish at all. The classes, with 10 to a group, were complemented with one-on-one tutorials, to speed up fluency. 'It was a full-time job,' recalled Ó hAdhmaill.

On Friday nights the Jailtacht hosted a Gaelic cabaret, featuring table quizzes, music and games. One person would be given a sweeping brush, a sock and a pot, and would begin a story, before passing on other props to the next storyteller. There were heated political debates and a regular trad session with half a dozen musicians, who ultimately recorded an album, *Live from the Blocks*.

Féilim arrived late to the Jailtacht; the peace process was well underway, and he was amazed at what he saw: 'It wasn't like a jail at all,' he said. 'It looked like a kasbah, a kind of marketplace … with bags everywhere, clothes all over the place, mattresses turned into home-made sofas.' The prisoners were allowed out of their cells 24 hours a day, and had even fashioned a door out of spare wood to separate the Jailtacht from the rest of the prison. Before entering prison, Ó hAdhmaill had learned Irish at Cumann Chluain Ard in Belfast, attending classes twice a week, but also attended an intense course held in Bóthar Seoighe, five nights a week, for two weeks. 'It was brilliant – you were constantly speaking, you were going over phrases in your head, you kept a diary every day, and then every time I met certain people I was only speaking Irish to them.'

I spoke to Ó hAdhmaill in June 2016 at his office in University College Cork, where he currently works as a lecturer in social policy. A mild-mannered, soft-spoken individual, Ó hAdhmaill's life story seems scarcely credible when recounted within the relaxed, academic confines and leafy avenues surrounding UCC. 'From a very young age you realise there was something not right about the society in which you lived,' he said. 'The language is a way of expressing an identity that is being obliterated by the state and the institutions of the state.' Born in Belfast, Ó hAdhmaill moved to England in 1994, where he was caught in possession of explosives and sentenced to 25 years in jail. 'I thought that was it for the rest of my life,' he recalled. 'I'll be a pensioner when I get out.' By then he had a family, including two kids with whom he only communicated in Irish. His life in jail began in Belmarsh, but Ó hAdhmaill was frequently on the move, spending time in half a dozen different jails, each one with shifting rules on the use of Irish. In Belmarsh the Irish language was completely prohibited. 'I spent all my life speaking in Irish. I'm not going to change now,' he told the authorities. A standoff followed, and he was allowed letters, phone calls and personal visits, but those rights were soon withdrawn. On one occasion his wife came for a monthly visit, which was compressed into three visits inside 24 hours, a concession in recognition of the long journey from Ireland. When the visit began, Féilim and his wife sat opposite each other while six prison guards and a dog surrounded them, waiting to pounce should they speak Irish. There was a microphone hanging from the roof, a relic from an era in which visits in Irish were permitted but recorded. The couple held hands and gazed at each other for the two hours, without saying a word. The second visit followed the same pattern. At the end of the final visit they began speaking Irish to each other. 'The alarms all went off, they dragged me away, they dragged her away.' Ó hAdhmaill began to doubt the wisdom of his decision not to speak English. 'I was beginning to wonder, is this the sensible thing to do, because I'm in jail for 25 years, I'm making a stand saying I'm not going to speak English to my family, but they're not letting me speak to my family other than through English so, it was a bit complicated.'

Ó hAdhmaill's life had been centred upon Irish, the only language he spoke to his children. 'It was our psychological connection. I've never spoken English to my kids, and still haven't.' In the early days of his Republican activities, 'speaking Irish was about a blow against oppression and about saying I am Irish', but as time passed he feared he might never get a chance to speak to his family again. The peace process rescued Ó hAdhmaill, who was transferred to the H-Blocks and joined the Jailtacht before his release in 2000. Ó hAdhmaill initially suffered in the move from Belfast to Cork: 'When I came down here the big shock was the lack of interest in Irish. I couldn't believe it.' In the H-Blocks, he lived close to 100 per cent of his life through Irish, a situation that has declined dramatically in Cork. 'My life's virtually all in English. It's a bit depressing in that regard. There was a vibrant Irish-speaking community in Belfast, but you don't have that in Cork, no bars, a couple of *ciorcal comhrá*. But it all costs money; in Belfast everything is free.' At Cumann Chluain Aird, a bag was handed around and spare change put in, 'but no one expected it, it was just to pay for the tea ... It would be hard to learn Irish in Cork if you don't have money.'

Jail house school

Irish classes in the Jailtacht began with the 11 irregular verbs, and teachers used *an modh díreach*, a conversation-based learning style. There was no compulsion about it. 'People wanted to learn it, but they didn't want it preached to them,' recalled McIntyre. 'There's enough preachers in life without someone turning a language into a new religion.' There was a copy of the Dinneen dictionary and *Buntús Cainte*, a series of beginner lessons still available today, with CDs attached.

Micheál Mac Giolla Gunna, another former H-Block resident, recalled the nervousness of some of those who found themselves in the Jailtacht. 'There were some people who arrived into the wing and didn't leave their cells for a fortnight,' he recalled, because they couldn't speak any Irish. 'Little by little they got their confidence up, caught on to the conversations, and in two or three months they were speaking it. That's how immersion works.' There were 24 people on each of the two Irish-speaking wings, up to 48 people at a time becoming fluent, many of them with no Irish before they arrived. They would gradually leave and be replaced by others, continuing the process.

The Belfast peace accord should have put an end to that enthusiasm, as prisoners walked free and melted back into their English-speaking communities. In fact, the opposite has occurred. McIntyre, released in 1992, began to teach Irish to people in their homes. 'People would gather in a house, maybe five or six people at a time, and I'd take a class.' There was never any issue of charging money, another key aspect of the northern experience: the language is free, sociable and available. Only the occasional intense summer schools charge modest fees, while drop-in classes may leave a box for donations. McIntyre moved to Drogheda, where he lives with his wife Carrie and two children, Fírinne and Ronan. He still uses his Irish from time to time, and his children attend Irish-medium schools, surpassing him in fluency. When Ronan was six or seven he and his father would walk their dog, *as Gaeilge*, for an hour each day, a daily father-and-son ritual, a shared time for Irish. McIntyre now calls on Fírinne to pick out words or phrases he cannot understand in Irish language news items. When Anthony speaks Irish to Ronan, his son answers him in English, while Fírinne has started speaking Irish in conversation with him. 'But who talks to their daughter at 14?' he asks wrily. 'Teenagers are usually grunty – I don't want to be grunted at in Irish or English.'

Former Republican prisoners enjoyed occasional conversations in shops and pubs *as Gaeilge*, but beyond the Cultúrlann and the Shaw's Road, the city lacked a broader canvas for its language ambitions. Irish came to life through social occasions at the Cumann Chluain Ard, with its weekly céilís and language classes. Belfast was a city under siege in the 1970s and 1980s, with metal gates and bars pulled across the roads at night, locking residents into and out of certain flashpoint areas. 'It was dangerous to go beyond those metal doors,' recalled Liam Ó Flannagáin, raised in Belfast but now

part of the Carn Tóchair Irish-speaking community in rural
Derry. 'It was very much about creating your own world and
your own atmosphere with people who shared the same sense
of belonging as you did.'

All that has changed since the peace process.

Rather than simply disappear into the cracks and crevasses
of the big city, the former prisoners and language enthusiasts hit
upon another Big Idea. In a stroke of marketing genius, Belfast
created 'Gaelictown'. Ask anyone who has travelled to New York
for a holiday and they will describe the marvels of Chinatown,
a network of streets immersed in Chinese life, where the food,
smells, atmosphere and people allow a glimpse into another
world, a mysterious feeling that by simply crossing from one
pavement to another you are transported to a different country.
As soon as you step onto the Falls Road Gaelic is visible on
murals, posters and shopfronts, alongside images of the leaders
of the 1916 Rising and the more recent Republican battles, since
1969. Gaelictown is a distinct Gaelic-friendly area with schools
(800 pupils, 60 teachers), restaurants, shops, pubs, murals, cafés
and offices, and even an Irish language Indian head massage
clinic for when the language starts to wear off. And all within
walking distance of the city centre. In an area with a population
of 30,000, half that number apparently uses Irish on a daily
basis, from a *cúpla focal* to total *líofacht*. Irish is spoken IN A
VERY LOUD, CHEERY, ENERGETIC TONE. I defy anyone to
find a cranky Gaeilgeoir north of Dundalk. This palpable joy at
the mere act of speaking a *cúpla focal* demonstrates that the only
way to revive Irish is to have it banned. There was zero tolerance
for *an Ghaeilge* in the days of Protestant rule, and certainly no
grants or benefits to be had. This feat is all the more impressive
when you consider that when the first gaelscoil opened in the
1970s, it had exactly nine pupils. Micheál Mac Giolla Gunna
describes the Gaelic Quarter as a 'synergy', a critical mass of

Gaelic energy where schools, sports, business and social life intersect in a distinct and highly visible way. The strongest pillar is Coláiste Feirste, Northern Ireland's first Irish-medium secondary school. Mac Giolla Gunna, currently vice-principal, told me that the confirmed intake for the coming school year (2016–17) was 122 new pupils, marking a 20 per cent rise in admissions.

The local primary and secondary schools are the basis of a small but steadily growing army of Irish speakers, many of whom will live and work and study in the area, giving an energy and momentum to the language. Coláiste Feirste has a staff of 70, including 48 teachers, most of them under the age of 30. There is a canteen that belongs to the Department of Education and is staffed by English speakers. 'They do their best,' says Mac Giolla Gunna, who points out that at a salary of just £7 an hour the school is grateful for their good will and hard work in whatever language. There is no entrance exam, students with learning difficulties are offered extra help and anyone who wants an education in Irish is free to attend. Pupils must, however, first attend the *naoiscoil* (three years of age and upwards) and a *bunscoil*, for seven years. 'There'd be no sense in students coming here without Irish,' he explained. 'They wouldn't manage without the language of the classroom and of general communication.'

Mac Giolla Gunna studied Irish at Queen's University in the 1980s, becoming politicised as Thatcher, the hunger strikes, the Dunnes Stores picket, the Reagan visit to the Republic and student politics galvanised him into action. 'I left college a Gaelgeoir, a Republican and a socialist,' he told me, and they are the principles he brought with him to Coláiste Feirste. 'We are trying to change the world, and as a teacher this is [the] place where I can make a difference.' If, for example, a young pupil arrives at the school at the age of 11, from a poor economic background, 'this might be the first person from that family or neighbourhood who goes on to university – that is a life-changing event. That is revolutionary.'

Mac Giolla Gunna was arrested for minor language-related offences in his student days, but was convicted of possession of a weapon in 1990 and sentenced to 14 years in prison. He served seven years, enjoying early release thanks to the peace process. Inside prison he joined the Jailtacht and completed an Open University course in teaching Irish, while also editing the prison magazine, *An Guth Gafa*, the captive voice. My interview with the vice-principal ended at lunchtime and I strolled round the school, meeting pupils as they enjoyed their break. The atmosphere between teachers and pupils seemed relaxed, and Irish was spoken everywhere I went, but a brief visit is no basis on which to judge a school. The history classroom grabbed my attention, as Bernadette Devlin gazed out from one side of the blackboard while Che Guevara watched from the other side. I can already see the panic in the eyes of southside Dublin should they view this radical pair adorning any classroom wall, but being two of my greatest influences I can only cheer quietly and wish I was there.

West Belfast is an area with a huge number of learners and a relatively small number of speakers. 'We are awash with Irish up here,' Áine Nic Liam told me, shortly after I parked my car beside a mural along the Falls Road. I asked her a question in Irish but she apologised and told me she had only the *cúpla focal*. Áine studied Irish as a teenager but left it behind 50 years ago, coming back to it in the past five years. 'I heard the sounds again at a class and fell in love with it,' she told me. Now in her 70s, Áine attends several Irish classes each week, along with a Spanish conversation group given by an Argentinian woman. She enjoys learning languages but told me she had no major ambitions around speaking them.

The Falls Road has more signs of Irish language life than Dublin, Cork and Galway combined. The number of Irish speakers rises steadily, as Coláiste Feirste dispatches 100 more young adults into the area each year. Forbairt Feirste, a business development centre, is another all-Irish enterprise, while the Cultúrlann, sitting across the road, has a restaurant, book shop, childcare, info centre and classes.

The secondary school recently received the go-ahead to build a sports centre and a small housing project, stepping up to the implicit challenge on the sign as you come up the school driveway, 'An Ghaeltacht.'

There was only a *cúpla focal* to be heard along the Falls Road, but there was vast goodwill, the bedrock for future language growth. It is early days yet. Mac Giolla Gunna compared spoken Irish in west Belfast to the forgotten Gaelic civilisation described in Daniel Corkery's *The Hidden Ireland*, a landmark book that uncovered Ireland's buried Gaelic past, in decline but alive until the late 19th century. 'Irish is in hiding here,' he explained, 'you have to know where to look.'

As a teacher with a personal connection to hundreds of pupils, current and past, Mac Giolla Gunna frequently ends up speaking Irish in shops like T.K. Maxx and Topshop in the city centre, where several shop assistants are former pupils of the school. He also knows which of the parents are comfortable speaking Irish, 'but anyone else in the shops wouldn't know to speak Irish to them'. Anywhere he goes he finds current or past pupils, from shops to taxis and buses. Mac Giolla Gunna articulated something else that is immediately evident on the streets of west Belfast: 'Irish is important to the people. They are proud of it, even if they don't speak it. They will use a few words, a few phrases.' Irish has been made visible, normalised by its visual presence along the main road, the shop signs and street signs, murals and posters. 'We have created an environment in

which people are comfortable speaking Irish.' In comparison
to the Republic of Ireland, this counts as a major achievement.

CHAPTER 13

East Belfast Mission – the Final Frontier

The short walk from Belfast Central Station to the long and winding Newtownards Road takes you through Loyalist housing estates and workingmen's clubs where the Union Jack, lots of red, white and blue bunting, and an occasional Israeli flag define local political identity. Twenty years ago, maybe less, I would have taken a taxi. I'm sure nothing would have happened, but … you wouldn't take the chance. During the years of conflict, Belfast people, Loyalist and Republican alike, kept a close eye on strangers coming into their neighbourhoods. At some point in recent history it was a matter of life and death. 'What about ye?' wasn't just a friendly greeting, it was also a divining rod that helped anticipate motives and movements in areas permanently on edge, strained by the prospect of unexpected outbursts of violence. In the early 1990s I stayed with a family in St James's Park, just off the Falls Road, in a Republican stronghold. I woke one morning to find the house empty and that I was locked in. I opened up a sitting room window and climbed out. A young child, maybe six years of age, watched my movements. When I got to the gate, he spoke to me: 'You have to wait here,' he said, 'I have to get my daddy.' I understood what was happening. The boy's father appeared out of a house down the road, chatted briefly to me, figured out I was staying in the house and what had happened. We laughed it off. But the message was clear. This is a place where constant vigilance is the norm, even from an early age.

The same principle applied in Loyalist areas, where strangers were eyed with suspicion, their business to be determined as a matter of routine. Old habits die hard, and old resentments are nowhere near resolved in the north of Ireland, simmering quietly under the lid of the peace process but easily reignited. On this particular sunny late August afternoon, however, Templemore Avenue was relaxed, children were out playing on the street, and I felt entirely at ease. This is the heart of Loyalist Belfast, where road junctions and gable walls boast murals featuring balaclava-clad gunmen waving weapons, promising death before dishonour. There was no sign of glasnost here, just a tight-lipped resignation to the changing times. But you wouldn't push it. The city's mural committee, which discusses and negotiates images and text for new murals, or *mórphictiúirí*, across the city, was not asked for its opinion on some of the murals going up around here. The Newtownards Road hosts scruffy charity shops, Union Jack bric a brac and many shuttered premises, which lend an air of dereliction to the area. Whatever else might be said, it certainly didn't seem like the ideal place to launch an Irish language revival. The notion of pushing Irish on the locals seemed preposterous, possibly dangerous, and almost certainly doomed to failure. In these parts the Irish language conjures up images of Republican marching bands, a volley of shots on behalf of the 1916 martyrs and maybe a speech by Gerry Adams.

I reached the Skainos building, a drab, solid, grey-brick enclave set back from the road. There is a café tucked in on the right, a homeless shelter at the back and shrubbery sprouting beside a pathway, which leads to the reception area. The open square in front of the main door is a community space, where kids mess around on bicycles and teenage trysts are discreetly arranged. A busy vegetable allotment can be seen over a perimeter fence. There are benches and parasols, and on that warm afternoon it felt like a plaza in a European town. The restaurant and nearby chipper were attracting a crowd but the Skainos Centre, a one-stop community support network, felt like a small university campus. This is the home of the East Belfast Mission, which offers services to the homeless, youth and family support, community development, employment aid, age action, drama and writing groups, counselling and more.

On the second floor of the building is 'Turas', the headquarters of Belfast's fastest-growing Irish language movement. When I arrived into the office Linda Ervine gestured at me to sit down as she answered the phone, checked her diary and made notes on her computer. A slim, energetic woman in her late 50s, Ervine is a tireless and fearless advocate for the Irish language. Like a guerrilla commander surveying disputed territory, Ervine observes as new villages fall under the Gaelic spell. There are classes in Lisburn, Ballymena, Portadown, Antrim, Bangor and Monkstown (not the leafy Dublin suburb), with many more likely to submit to her charm in the coming months.

I asked Ervine to give me a snapshot of her working week – that one began with a visit from a Swiss delegation, followed by a talk with a women's group at a Methodist church in Lisburn, then came another with a group in Ballymore before a trip across the border to attend a civic dinner and an awards ceremony in Dublin, including the reading of a poem in Irish at the Abbey Theatre. Then she was back in Belfast for her own Irish diploma course lectures, not forgetting her weekly Irish conversation class at the Cultúrlann and the Irish language singing group that meets in this building each week. Ervine has an air of perpetual motion about her, and a single, deadly weapon in her armoury: 'the Miracle of Turas', a photo presentation and talk. I defy anyone to watch it and remain unmoved. It is a beautifully pitched tale of a personal journey (*turas*) from non-believer to converted, delivered by a quiet but confident Christian who firmly believes in redemption. The subject, however, is not God but the Irish language. '*Thit mé i ngrá leis an teanga*,' she told me, 'I fell in love with the language.'

Ervine delivers the Turas talk to audiences around the north, and by the end of the evening the public has invariably been won over and are demanding an Irish language class of their own. Where possible Ervine will provide a teacher, preferably someone local, or as near to local as is possible. Ervine and her team are achieving something that most people in the country would probably deem impossible – turning people from a Protestant and even Loyalist background on to Irish. 'I didn't even know there was an Irish language until I was in my 40s,' Ervine told me. In 2012 Ervine attended a cross-community Irish taster session, six classes in which she learned the basics of the language. 'I wanted to have this language,' she said. While Ervine immediately switched on to the language, it was only after discovering place names and surnames and reading up on the history of Protestants and the Irish language that she discovered her inner ambassador. 'I felt shocked and sad that I had been denied this because of politics,' she said. The links have been there forever, the language *fite fuaite* (interwoven) with the planter population. The emblematic Shankill Road, or *seanchill*, comes from the Gaelic Sean and Cill, or old church, while the name Glentoran, a traditionally Loyalist soccer club, comes from the Gaelic Gleann, or valley, of the river Roar. The Gaelic League had links to the Orange Order, and the language itself has close links to Scotland. 'This gave me an opportunity to take ownership of the language, that it didn't belong to one side or the other, and I wanted to share that information.'

The default Loyalist position, until recently, was to deny the existence of the language, claiming it was a kind of pidgin made up by Republicans. Gregory Campbell, MP for the dominant Democratic Unionist Party publicly ridiculed the language, only to be reminded by Ervine that his surname, Campbell, is Cam Béil in Irish, meaning crooked mouth. Prejudice is deeply embedded in the north, and when Ervine followed up her taster lessons with a *dianchúrsa* at An Droichead, a primary school and adult language centre based in north Belfast, she assumed it was a Catholic school. 'It was the names, Seán, Bernadette, Aoife,' she explained. Ervine then discovered it was an Irish-medium school, but was not affiliated to the Catholic Church.

Ervine gave her first talk to some hundred members of the Shankill Women's Association in 2012, quickly followed with an address to the annual conference of the Progressive Unionist Party. The invitations came thick and fast, and since then Ervine estimates she has spoken to 7,000 people across the six counties. Initially the classes were publicised by word of mouth, discreetly, as the owners of the building 'were a wee bit frightened,' recalled Ervine – but numbers kept rising, as one class became two classes and then three, with 50 people attending weekly language sessions. The classes were first held in the furniture restoration shop beside the current building, which was completed in 2012. Ervine, an English teacher in a nearby school, took up a post at Skainos as Irish Language Development Officer. She was joined by Matthew McCaughey, a fluent speaker, even though there were no funds to pay him. 'I'm not looking for any money, I'll come and help you,' he insisted. Soon after, another fluent speaker, from Fermanagh, asked if she could volunteer her time as a teacher, marking out east Belfast as identical to its Republican counterparts in viewing the language as a vocation, an activity that needs to happen regardless of money. All classes are free, with a donation box sitting on the table to cover tea and biscuits during class breaks. This attitude stands in stark contrast to the south, where funding and salaries and fees seem to be unavoidable prerequisites to any learning taking place. There is funding, of course, for the building, and for leaflets and research, but that type of structural aid is not conditioned by a demand for financial return. The return is in the community taking a huge step towards breaking down prejudice and discarding attitudes that separated them from the 'other' – their Catholic neighbours across the city. As the September 2016 season kicked in, there were 200 people registered for Irish language activities, which include a dozen classes each week, covering all levels, alongside tin whistle, singing and dancing. However, the organisation wants to inspire others who may not sign up for classes. In the coming months, they will host 'Snapchat Gaeilge', in which employees and visitors to Skainos can enjoy 10-minute Irish language warm-up sessions, letting them know what it's about. These will also occur around Christmas and holiday times, when classes are over but people want a blast of Irish.

It hasn't all been smiles and sweetness. Ervine recalled several angry phone calls from wealthy donors who advised her they would never again contribute a penny to the East Belfast Mission as long as Irish classes were being held there. 'We haven't got a magic wand,' said Ervine, 'we just opened the door for people who have never had the chance and said there you go, if you want to come in, the language is here.' A lot of people still say Hell no, while 'others hang around the door, intrigued, eventually finding their way in'. Still more come in, learn a little and give up. 'It's not easy learning the language, but at least they've come in and found something positive.'

The East Belfast Mission has proved an able publicist for the language, focusing on sharp, well-produced booklets and leaflets introducing people to the language. When I made a second visit to the Skainos Centre in August 2016 the local men's shed were in Ervine's office, listening to a talk about the language. These were older men from the locality, their lives marked by the Troubles. It was their first exposure to the Irish language. At the end of the session, a conversation began about the surnames in the room. Gordon McCoy, an Irish teacher and Protestant from Tyrone, handed out books about the origin of surnames, and soon the men were immersed in the task of finding out the Gaelic origins of their names. McCoy also handed out a new leaflet he has written, 'The Languages of Ulster', which includes Gaelic words in Ulster Scots and Ulster Scots words in Irish. By the end of it, the men have clearly been energised by the meeting, regardless of whether they follow up on the Irish.

Ervine's public talks end with an appeal to begin an Irish class immediately and people often sign up on the spot. It reminds me of Angela Davis, the prominent Black Panther activist, who advised her fellow activists, 'Don't let them out of the room without signing them up.' As I spoke to Ervine, she gathered up her things and prepared to drive to Millisle, a nearby holiday town, where she would address a group of primary school children and their parents at a youth club. It is very much Unionist territory. 'There will be some hostile questions,' she assures me, 'but I'll be ready.'

Oh, and she has written a play which is about to be staged, called *What the focal?*

The Skainos Centre seems like a particularly effective cross-community project, as Ervine's work challenges and changes one aspect of the deep-rooted fear that lies at the heart of sectarianism. Ervine might quietly have gone about learning Irish for herself, but instead she has chosen to reclaim it for Northern Ireland's Protestant community, as much a symbol of their identity as it is of the Nationalist community.

Ervine's work feels like the implementation of the peace accord, one new learner of Gaeilge at a time. The public talks, while effective, are just the first step; the real action happens during the Q and A sessions that follow. Someone will invariably denounce Ervine's work as a betrayal of Unionist values and a sell-out to Sinn Féin. Ervine knows precisely how to defuse and disarm her critics, however. 'It's 100 per cent positive after the Q and A,' comments Ervine, who has heard it all before, the insults, the fear and rejection from people who associate the Irish language with a Nationalist takeover bid. And yet the 1998 peace accord has largely taken the poison out of a language once viewed as another weapon in the arsenal of the IRA. When the Irish classes first began, the reactions ranged from encouraging to indifferent to hostile. One local woman tried to rally a protest on Facebook, using the following argument: 'It's an OUTRAGE, there are children starving in Africa and Irish classes are being organised on the Newtownards Road.' The comments beneath were largely supportive of Ervine, and the protest never materialised. Significantly, the classes received support from the Ulster Defence Association old boys' club, renamed Charter NI. A class was arranged inside their building and some of the learners even travelled to the Gaeltacht in Donegal, to pursue the language. Beyond the issue of Protestants stepping outside their comfort zone, Ervine has become sharply aware of class differences among those who attend the Irish classes. 'You have educated people here with PhDs alongside someone who doesn't have a qualification to their name,' said Ervine, 'but the language is a great equaliser, because they're all struggling with it, but I look around and wonder, where else would these people ever get together in the same room?'

One of the key elements of their success is that the classes are happening in the heart of a Unionist neighbourhood, allowing people to attend a class that is often no more than five minutes from their home. Unlike most political parties and social movements, Skainos operates on a principle of accessibility and availability.

The day after I met Ervine, I watched a television programme in which former Sinn Féin Mayor of Belfast Máirtín Ó Muilleoir squared off against Peter Weir, newly appointed Education Minister. Weir, a DUP member, played down the significance of the Irish language, but Ó Muilleoir made the startling statement that 'more people were signed up for Irish classes in east Belfast than in the Cultúrlann' (west Belfast).

Ervine took off for Millisle while I stayed behind with teacher Gordon McCoy. There were two classes planned, one of them held in the crèche area of the centre, a large, bright room with a kitchen attached. As I arrived in at 6pm, a group of parents and children sat around a table eating dinner. A volunteer chef from the hostel for the homeless attached to the centre prepared a tasty-smelling stew for the participants. A teacher presided over the dinner, introducing vocabulary, explaining syntax and drawing out the learners. The children were sitting comfortably on the floor, hunched over drawings. They have been given a task to do, labelling rooms and objects in the home, using Irish words supplied by their parents.

An Irish class at dinnertime in this traditional Loyalist heartland should be a complete failure, but the provision of a casual conversation class with a free hot dinner attached is a masterstroke. 'We see Irish as part of a social environment, not something separate,' says Ervine. As soon as the drop-in dinner class is finished, I retraced my steps upstairs to the Skainos office, which also serves as a classroom. A group of 15 learners, ranging in age from mid-twenties to mid-seventies, were crowded around the long table for their weekly two-hour class. While most of these people were local, one had come from Portstewart, even though Lurgan was far closer. The geography of conflict continues to affect the movement of people. Lurgan remains a flashpoint, a deeply divided town where only the public library is regarded as a comfortable, safe space for all, and is therefore hugely oversubscribed by groups desperate to find a suitable place for community events.

The Skainos classes are all free of charge, and there is a quick break for tea and biscuits during the evening class. The Nordies have, without a doubt, mastered the art of social Irish. In Monkstown, County Dublin, inside the elegant headquarters of Comhaltas Ceoltóirí Eireann, I attended an Irish conversation class facilitated by Máire Ní Bheaglaoich, a member of the Gaelic nobility of west Kerry. The class took place in the kitchen, and a kettle lay within arm's reach, but David, a friend who invited me along, warned me to forget all hopes of a *cupán tae*: 'There will be no tea whatsoever.'

Love/Hate

On the morning after the class in Skainos I returned to Linda Ervine's office to meet Robin Stewart, whose offer to make coffee was foiled; we couldn't use the kettle, as it was on loan to an Irish class taking place in the room next door. Stewart ranks as the least likely Irish language learner I have ever encountered, a self-described 'former tattooed, skinhead, Loyalist thug'. A former British soldier and member of the Loyalist Red Hand Commando paramilitary group, Stewart is a man with a lot on his conscience. He seems keen to take responsibility for past mistakes, while outlining the remarkable distance he has travelled since he first began rioting in Belfast in 1969.

Stewart, who has the appearance of an ageing member of the Millwall FC hooligan fraternity, doesn't seem like the ideal person to win fresh recruits to the Irish language revival. His bald head and muscled body promise aggression rather than a *cúpla focal*. *Ach is ait an mac an saol*, it's a strange life and it's about to get a whole lot stranger. 'When I used to think about the Irish language,' Stewart told me, 'I used to see a balaclava and an AK47.' Sinn Féin's occasional sound bites didn't help either, as when one prominent member told followers, by way of encouragement, 'every phrase you learn is a bullet in the freedom struggle'.

Stewart is a charmer who would be equally at ease having tea with Sharon Stone or Michael Stone, or even Bobby Sands for that matter. He greeted me with a firm handshake, and once the hunt for a cup of coffee was over he settled down to a thorough conversation.

Born locally to a working-class family in 1957, Stewart shared a two-room home with his four siblings and parents, relying on an outside toilet. He came of age with the Troubles, engaging in years of rioting against the British Army, which ended when he joined their ranks. Many of his friends joined Loyalist paramilitary groups, but his rioting was no more than a distraction from the tedium of life in east Belfast. Once in the army he spent 12 years fine-tuning his skills in explosives, weaponry and war. By then, many of his old friends were deeply involved in the escalating violence. 'You didn't see anything wrong in what they were doing', recalled Stewart, 'they were all around you in the community, you played football with them.' As the conflict intensified in the 1970s, Stewart developed a gut-level hatred of Catholics, nourished by the inflammatory speeches of Ian Paisley and others. 'I would be calling for the deaths of Catholics, using colourful language, get the Fenian bastards.'

However, nothing in Northern Ireland is quite as it seems. Stewart joined the Royal Irish Regiment, a British Army unit that embraced its Irishness, celebrating St Patrick's Day and warriors like Brian Boru. The regiment used the Irish wolfhound as a mascot, and its motto, written in Irish, is *Fág an bealach*, or clear the way. It's another topsy-turvy reminder that Ulster is a proud old province where Irish was once spoken by all. This was Stewart's first contact with the language. Each time he returned home his old friends would seek his advice and expertise, and they weren't looking for cookery tips. 'The endgame was to stop the war,' he said, pausing, choosing his words carefully. 'If that meant that we sickened people then that's what had to be done.' Stewart left the army and returned home, formally joining the Red Hand Commando.

Stewart advocated bombing the Republic of Ireland. 'Thankfully no one listened to me,' he says, partly ashamed but still prepared to defend his philosophy. 'I wanted to end the war quickly, and that would certainly have brought things to a head.' It could be argued that the IRA bombing of London's financial district served the same purpose, high-profile acts of terror that focused minds in the corridors of power. Stewart told me he went out on active service armed with weapons and explosives. 'I was involved in all things expected of an organisation in a time of war,' he said. 'I sound like Gerry Adams,' he added. Was he involved in the targeting of individuals? 'I would have no problem with that.' I find myself mentally matching Loyalist massacres to Stewart's years of active service, but the effort seems pointless, the years gone by. There was a long silence. 'I didn't want my kids to grow up the same way I did.'

Stewart now works with Reach, a community development organisation made up of former prisoners, representing another stage in moving away from conflict and grappling with hopes for the future. Stewart's ambition around learning the Irish language was modest: 'I always thought it would be nice to order a drink in Irish,' he said. A chance meeting with Linda Ervine in the steam room of a local gym kickstarted the process when she invited him to join a beginner language class.

The proximity of the class, just five minutes from his home, was a key motivator in getting him in the door. 'I was curious about it. I was always fascinated by Irishness. This was the opportunity and there were no excuses,' he said. Some of his friends criticised his decision to sign up for Gaelic classes, but he stood firm. 'I told them youse are afraid to learn your history because you won't like the British as much as you think you do.' Stewart also asked them about their identity. 'A Welshman is Welsh, also British, a Scotsman is Scottish, also British, what are you? British? Irish is a dirty word. All they have is what has been taught to them by others, the negative feedback: If Sinn Féin like it then it must be bad. One side says it's good, the other says it's bad.'

After a year of classes he was ready for a cross-border Gaelic incursion, heading to Sligo for the weekend. He entered a local pub and asked for his drink in Irish. 'Nobody spoke it the whole time I was there,' he said, sounding disappointed. As we finish up the conversation I spot 'Love' and 'Hate' tattooed across the knuckles of his hands. 'The right hand is "hate",' he explains. 'It's the gun hand, the trigger finger, the hard-hitting hand.' The ink is fading on hate but Love is still visible. 'It must be a prophecy,' he concluded.

Stewart was by no means the first Loyalist paramilitary to tackle the Irish language. As with the Jailtacht tradition, Loyalist prisoners also learned Irish inside jail, at least for a time. William 'Plum' Smith spent five years in Long Kesh prison camp, convicted in 1972 of shooting a Catholic man eighteen times. Remarkably, the victim survived. In prison, Smith learned about Irish history and began learning Irish. The IRA prisoners offered him safe passage into the Republican 'cage' for classes but the authorities refused. Undeterred, Smith sat by the fence and learned his Irish from an IRA member instructing him from the other side. He was a key figure in facilitating the Combined Loyalist Military Command ceasefire in 1994, chairing the press conference when the move was announced.

The past is a recent place, of course, and painful memories are close at hand. During a break in the conversation I overheard Ervine recall the days when fear of the stranger kept everyone firmly on their own turf, and one local thug was recalled as 'the Prod who killed that guy with cheesewire'. I asked Stewart if attitudes towards Ervine and the Skainos centre had improved in recent times. 'Yes, there's been progress,' he said. 'People aren't putting the windows in or throwing rocks or golf balls at us anymore.'

The work of Ervine's language team dismantles sectarian prejudice, *focal* by *focal*, but the outreach work is just as important. The Skainos institute brings learners to west Belfast to meet other learners, and they in turn come to visit the Newtownards Road. 'At first there would have been a reluctance to go, but you hardly hear anyone mention that anymore,' said Ervine. There are also Irish classes in Protestant schools, raising awareness of place names and surnames as part of a citizenship module. Two schools located in Loyalist areas have Gaelic names hiding behind anglicised versions, the Sullivan Upper School (*Cnoc na gCoiníní*) and Lisnasharragh, Cregagh, or *Lios na Searrach,* the ford of the foals. The school badges gave the game away, as Sullivan used rabbits on their school jumpers, while Lisnasharragh had four horses as its school emblem.

Ervine phoned the Sullivan school and spoke to the school secretary, who told her she was aware of the Irish name. 'Do you tell the children?' she asked. 'Certainly not,' was the response. The school principal, with a holiday home in Donegal and an interest in the Irish language, agreed to allow Ervine to visit the school and explore its Gaelic heritage. A bus tour has been developed, highlighting the links.

Another aspect of the changing attitudes towards the language is the greater ease with which learners of a Protestant background express their politics. 'I've noticed people wearing poppies when they come to class, being quite open about their Unionism,' said Gordon McCoy. 'Before they would have under-communicated that.' Learners with a Unionist background face an uphill struggle to find people they can practise with outside class. In summer 2016, however, McCoy noticed that many of his students were attending the McCracken Summer School, elsewhere in the city. 'I didn't even bother holding a class that week,' recalled McCoy. 'Most of them had gone to the *dianchúrsa.*'

The East Belfast Mission now sponsors a weekly drop-in coffee morning and a *dianchúrsa* of their own, in the autumn, so that learners can practise outside class. The big difference in recent years is the ease of movement around the city as people are far happier to travel into areas once regarded as suspect if not off limits altogether. McCoy himself is constantly seeking ways to improve his language skills, even after completing a degree in Irish and making regular visits to the Donegal Gaeltacht. 'You are always a learner,' he said. 'That's why you say "*Tá Gaelic agam*", I have some Irish, but not "*Tá an Ghaelic agam*" – you never have the whole of the language.' McCoy signed up to Gaelchultúr's translation course in Dublin, attended an intense summer translation course in Donegal and constantly records programmes from RnaG, listening to them on headphones when he goes out for walks.

In its language planning document, published in 2012, the ULTACH Trust (since disbanded) recommended the approval of policies that might 'reduce negative preconceptions about the language and its speakers, with a particular although not exclusive focus on the Protestant and Unionist community in Northern Ireland'. It seemed an obvious starting point for a language often construed as an extension of the Republican struggle rather than the shared heritage of two communities living on a small strip of land. The document, written by Aodán Mac Póilin, also called for 'the nurturing and development of Irish-speaking networks and communities', as the centre of the language planning process, and that all other language planning activities be built around that core priority.

The future of the Irish language in the north of Ireland looks healthy and budget cutbacks rather than sectarian prejudice mark the limits of progress. It seems unlikely that Ervine and her team will draw down the blinds and relax. While the 'G word' (gaelscoil) has yet to be mentioned, there is talk of an integrated school with an emphasis on Gaelic, at an interface point between neighbouring Catholic and Protestant communities. Ervine's ultimate goal, however, is to cease being newsworthy. For now, Skainos is a symbol of hope in the heart of Loyalist Belfast, an exception in a region coming to terms with centuries of distrust and violence. 'What we do and where we do it gives permission for others to do it elsewhere,' says Ervine, 'but the real mark of our success is when people are no longer interested in us because other groups elsewhere overshadow us, doing their own fantastic things.'

CHAPTER 14

The Secret of Carn Tóchair

Ulster is a province where language ambition knows no bounds: from Bóthar Seoighe to the Jailtacht and Gaelictown to the Newtownards Road, no scheme is too far-fetched and no delirium too fantastic to be undertaken. Meetings are held, plans are drawn up, funds are raised and the work begins. It's a curious alchemy, one which seems to include, among the necessary ingredients, the total indifference of the state. In the early 1990s a group of people in Carn Togher, a loose gathering of homes west of Maghera in south Derry, drew up plans to reinstate the Irish language in their community within two generations, a span of about 50 years. Nowhere in rural Ireland has Irish reasserted itself as the primary language of communication inside a community that has become only English-speaking. The challenge would appear doomed to failure until you meet the people involved, the children, teenagers and middle-aged enthusiasts, and by the time you leave you wonder why you didn't think of the idea yourself in the first place.

The end of Irish in this area adjoining the Sperrin Mountains lies just beyond living memory, tantalisingly close to the parents and grandparents of those living here, yet also firmly out of reach. Liam Ó Flannagáin, a Belfast native, moved to Carn Togher in 1992, where he came across a local woman, Annie

Lagan, born in 1900. She lived on the side of a nearby mountain and recalled Irish being spoken when she was growing up. 'We knew the old people spoke it,' she told Liam. 'We would be put to bed in the loft at night-time and you could hear the old ones downstairs speaking a language we didn't understand.' As a small child Annie was convinced she would end up speaking this language when she got older, a physiological development acquired after a certain age, like arthritis. At the turn of the 20th century the Irish language had the status of a secret, private language, spoken after hours and outside of public view.

Carn Togher is a traditional farming area named for the mountain that shelters the community. It is an area of stunning natural beauty, and the Glenshane Pass, which I ascended as I travelled from Belfast, offers the visitor a breathtaking vista. The word *tóchar* means a path, or raised causeway. Carn Tóchair is a rural scattering of homes stretched between two parishes, its inhabitants largely invisible in the surrounding countryside. I drove past the area twice before figuring out that the small car park with a few buildings attached constituted the centre of the community. If you keep your eyes peeled as you travel along the Tirkane Road that runs along Carn Tóchair, you will spot a school, a sports field, a few barns and clusters of trees.

Irish remained strong in the Sperrin Mountains until the beginning of the 19th century, but the census from that time reveals a sharp contrast – in 50 per cent of rural townlands, almost everyone over the age of 30 spoke both Irish and English, but those under 30 spoke nothing but English. The language faded, but there were still speakers scattered throughout the area. Ó Flannagáin told me he can vividly imagine the transition in the 19th century, as English replaced Irish, when parents 'used a broken language they had barely learned to start trying to raise up the next generation at the end of the 1800s'.

When Niall Ó Catháin was a child in the 1970s, many of the old men living near his home would speak to him about his grandfather, a fluent Irish speaker who gave classes locally on behalf of the Gaelic League. Roger Casement visited the area in the early 1900s and rewarded the local branch with a coveted copper shield in recognition of their progress in restoring the language. The seeds planted during that era are finally bearing fruit. Niall studied no Irish at primary school but took classes in secondary school and pursued the subject as part of his university studies. He was one of a half dozen locals who decided 'to bring the language back', holding meetings to determine how best to achieve this goal. After a visit to Shaw's Road in Belfast they decided that educating children in Irish was the most effective route to reclaiming the language. The Carn Tóchair community group set up a *naíscoil*, or pre-school playgroup, in 1992, on a small patch of land donated by the GAA for the purpose.

There were seven children signed up for the pre-school, and a year later the community established a primary school, Bunscoil Luraigh, an independent gaelscoil in nearby Maghera. When it came to establishing the new *bunscoil* the community once more applied the lessons from Shaw's Road – don't wait for permission, just do it. Niall was working as a surveyor in the construction industry and found mobile classrooms at a former hospital in Derry, while nearer to home 'a fella had a site', which was levelled by a bulldozer; foundations were made, an advertisement placed for a teacher and doors opened in September. 'We were very lucky with the people we had,' explained Niall, as one parent was a senior teacher (since appointed principal) of a nearby English-medium school. She became the chairperson, overseeing educational standards. The autonomous school ran for eight years, the annual £30,000 running costs supplied by the community through fundraising efforts. 'It was the worst seven years of my life,' explained Ó Catháin, who uttered an audible sigh every time he recalled that tough, initial period. The school grew rapidly, student numbers multiplied and two new teachers were hired.

By the year 2000 running costs associated with the maintenance and administration of the school had escalated to the point where the volunteer effort was no longer sufficient to sustain the costs. The community was forced to take a strategic decision that went against the grain of their philosophy. As of 2001 the *bunscoil* would become an *Aonad*, or unit inside the local English-medium school, an Irish language stream in an English-speaking environment. The understanding, according to Carn Tóchair parents, was that once the school had a steady supply of pupils of all ages, it would be granted facilities to set up a separate school.

More than a decade later that hasn't happened. At the beginning of the school year in September 2016, the school welcomed 27 new pupils, bringing the Irish language section to a total of 125 pupils, easily outnumbering the English-speaking section, which has a total of 80 children. Niall Ó Catháin jokingly referred to himself as a 'Jehovah's Witness' when it comes to enrolling newborn infants in the school, visiting friends and neighbours with small children and inviting them to information sessions about the benefits of bilingual education. Carn Tóchair and Maghera now have two *naíscoileanna*, catering for about 35 children per annum, along with the Irish-medium *bunscoil* unit. Irish classes for adults begin before the school term, giving parents a chance to learn the *cúpla focal* as their children start school. The community bookshop sells *Gaschaint*, a guide to everyday Irish around the house, available with a CD and choice of three dialects. You can brush your teeth in Connemara, have breakfast in Corca Dhuibhne and enjoy bathtime in Donegal.

The decision to fold the primary school into the local English-medium school had one major advantage: it freed up community organisers to focus their efforts on expanding other areas of work. Rather than impose an Irish language rule, the community has avoided the term Gaeltacht in its planning, considering community development association a broader label in an area that requires a bilingual, inclusive approach. 'It's going to take generations to restore Irish as the daily language here,' observed Ó Catháin. When the Carn Tóchair project began there were half a dozen people who spoke Irish, or 'maybe less', a figure that has grown to about 180, a combination of kids immersed in school, adults who have achieved fluency and a sprinkling of native speakers who moved here upon discovering the language rebirth. The Carn business centre has a craft shop, bookshop, library and computer training lab. The Irish language classes run twice weekly for 60 people, while an immersion course is held each summer during the annual Carn Tóchair Festival. Evidence of the progress made can be heard each year at the Feis Charn Tóchair, an annual showcase of talent where 200 children aged four to 12 years recite poetry and song. There are several classrooms in the business park offering classes from sewing and art courses to computer animation workshops. 'Most of the stuff for adults is in English, to welcome people through the door.' The community has also built a centre for the Arts with a venue and bar attached, selling out all 220 seats at the monthly concerts. Recent guests included Sharon Shannon and John Spillane. There is also a cross-community project with a group on the other side of Maghera that is very similar in profile but 'Protestant/Unionist', while Carn is broadly Catholic and Nationalist. Together the groups organised a heritage trail featuring a guided tour with an app and map.

When you visit nearby Maghera you notice a total absence of Irish signs in shops. The high visibility of Belfast's Gaelictown, its shopfronts and posters, led me to believe that Carn Tóchair's Irish-speaking community would also maintain a public display of Gaelic pride. On arrival into the small town I dropped into a shop situated directly opposite Maghera Orange Hall. I asked after the Irish language district. 'I've no idea,' said the woman behind the counter, before pointing towards the opposite end of town. 'I'd say it would be out there along the road.' I asked Liam Ó Flannagáin why there were no signs of Gaelic life. 'This is part of the northern context,' he explained. 'Once you move outside the big Nationalist bloc areas of the cities you are into areas with mixed Unionist and Nationalist people, and there's a real fear, reticence and concern that if you fly the flag, if I put up my sign in Irish, I might be boycotted by some people, I might attract a stone through my window.' The atmosphere of distrust surrounding the language reflected something 'deeply ingrained over centuries', a narrative of suspicion that lingers despite the peace process. Ó Flannagáin believes that the job of showing that the spread of Irish is a positive and peaceful activity comes down to the Nationalist community: 'We have to keep working on it until people realise that this [Gaelic] doesn't threaten my identity in any way, that it's part of the scenery, it's not about politics.'

Like other places where Irish is present yet invisible, Ó Flannagáin has a network of his own thanks to the close-knit nature of this rural community. 'You recognise someone who was at the *bunscoil* working in a shop in Maghera and you do your business in Irish. That has become much more common ... That way people get the message, that Irish is a real and living language, in everyday use and normal.' He was keen to reassure anyone who confused the speaking of Irish with a separatist agenda: 'We're not talking about throwing away the English language,' he said. 'It's one of the most important languages in the world and we already have it, it's in our hip pocket. Everything you have through your own language is on top of that. I defy anyone to come up with a downside of it.'

Ó Flannagáin was living in Belfast when Aoife, his first child, was born. The infant was signed up and ready to go to the Shaw's Road *bunscoil* when an opportunity arose to buy land and settle in Carn Tóchair. 'It was the biggest loss and the hardest decision to make, the loss of that connection,' he said. Liam and his wife Áine were abandoning Belfast for an area without Irish, or so they thought. Áine, who didn't speak Irish, was local to Carn Tóchair. 'It was a gradual thing with Áine. She mixed with my friends, she went to classes, and it became a natural thing over time.' Like so many other parents of mixed-ability Irish, the arrival of a child sparked the language flip, 'because that's exactly how we lost the language,' he says, recalling the parents who stopped speaking Irish to their children several generations before. Liam has always spoken Irish to the kids, while Áine speaks English, and they move effortlessly between the languages. Liam was lucky in that he arrived in Carn Tóchair in 1992, just as the local Irish language project took off, and with it a school for Aoife.

I wondered was there a teenage kickback against the parents' deeply held beliefs. 'That's the importance of the Irish-medium education,' explained Liam. 'They can drift away, that's natural, but you have to provide a caring atmosphere in which they have a bedrock of the Irish language to be with on a regular basis.' Once the teenagers move out into the world, 'they start to think a little more about values and what's important in the world', and invariably come back to the language, particularly if they start their own families. That evening Liam received a Skype call from Aoife, now a woman in her 20s and living in Australia, where, according to Liam, she enthusiastically seeks out Irish speakers to maintain her connection to that native root.

The Carn Tóchair organisers have handed on responsibility for youth planning to the first generation of new local Irish speakers, and one of them, Joe O'Doherty, showed me round the business park, which has accommodation attached. The youth group is a key element in developing a social life in Irish, away from parents, as kids move into adulthood. 'The people of my age group need to be kept in the background,' said Liam. A group of Carn Tóchair youths travel to the Cabaret Creacáilte, organised by Rónán Mac Aodha Bhuí in Gaoth Dobhair, an edgy Irish night of music, with different groups playing each month. Belfast is also within reach, while their own venue attracts visitors from elsewhere.

Niall Ó Catháin met his partner Siuán through the medium of English, but made a conscious decision to switch to Irish when their children came along. The language flip worked fine during the day, but like a former smoker eyeing up friends having a fag outside the pub door, temptation crept in at night. When the children went to bed English became the late-night language of comfort, a brief return to a familiar port of call. One morning, however, his daughter, aged three, announced that she had heard them speaking English as she sat on the top of the stairs, eavesdropping, as children do. The incident reminded me of Annie Lagan, listening in on the adults speaking Irish late at night. This was Niall's final pain barrier, the opportunity to dive into the deep end for good. 'They [the kids] laugh at me now if they hear me speaking English,' he says. I spent the night at the home of Niall and Siuán and their four children, who converse with an ease that is way beyond me, the easy banter and half snatches of conversation that come with a mother tongue. The television went on later that night, BBC Northern Ireland, and I half expected parents and kids to suddenly switch to English now that Big Brother had arrived into the room. It didn't happen. When I asked Niall whether the TV and visits from outside affected the language, he seemed surprised by the question. 'No,' he said, 'they wouldn't even think of it.' This is the ultimate goal of the Carn Tóchair language shift, to restore Irish as a natural, daily, community language within a broader bilingual context.

Since the year 2000, when Niall began speaking Irish all the time, conditions have changed, as a critical mass of speakers now share a social life beyond the home. 'It is easy to bring your family up in Irish,' says Niall, 'because there is a core group who speak Irish as a first language and children who speak Irish all the time.' The opening of the Gaelcholáiste, a secondary school in nearby Dungiven, is a major boost to the language, as children can now complete their entire education cycle through Irish.

Niall's immediate neighbours speak Irish, and the ripples have spread to embrace cousins, aunts and uncles. I asked him if they had ever experienced the rebellious phase so common among Gaeltacht kids elsewhere. 'As soon as they could talk we explained to them the context, the reason why we speak Irish. It makes a huge difference.' Niall told his kids how their great-grandfather would have spoken more Irish than English, and that further back, only Irish was spoken. The landscape around them, the surnames and family nicknames, all owe their origins to Irish. When the language repossession was under discussion, the locals came across various theories that sought to explain such a shift, from the cultural dimension (enriching the soul), to the reconciliation discourse (promoting tolerance and diversity) and finally the philosophy they ultimately settled on – the post-colonial option: 'that's the one that puts a fire in people's bellies'.

That theory maintains that the language and culture were there in previous generations, but that hostile language planning eroded and destroyed it. 'It was taken from us, and

if we want it back we have to speak it.' The area has a strong
Nationalist base, with the GAA at the heart of the community,
along with traditional music and an old custom of *meitheal*, or
cooperation. 'It's alive in the farming communities at the wakes,
a tradition of community and collective effort.'

The Carn community group also has a nature reserve,
with loughs and ancient remnant woodland next to bogland,
while allotments have been created around a farmhouse and
buildings. The community advertised for an Irish-speaking
farm manager but found Glen and Kelly and their two young
children instead. The family was living in Devon at the time but
had the skills for the job. They didn't have Irish but Kelly's family
had roots in the area and Glen, an environmental scientist, had
woodland and farming skills to offer, and is a skilled forager
and qualified personal trainer. They sent their kids, aged three
and five, to the local Irish-medium school and attend their own
Irish classes. On the night I met him, Glen was organising a
couch-to-5km run for locals. I thought back to Diarmuid
Johnson, his insistence that learning to speak Irish was akin to
running a marathon. The people of Carn Tóchair have taken
the language, shaken it down and dusted off the cobwebs, from
the couch to the community, from the *cúpla focal* to the slowly
growing *líofacht*.

The View from Cúil Aodha

'What is your book about?' asked Peadar Ó Riada, as I took off my coat and switched on the tape recorder. I stumbled over a brief, dissatisfying outline. 'Answer me this question,' he continued, '*Cad é an difríocht idir bundúchasach Gaeltachta agus duine Gaeltachta?*' Hang on, I thought to myself, I'm asking the questions here – ideally in English. My mind went to work. I'm pretty sure he's asking me the difference between an indigenous Gaeltacht person and a person raised in the Gaeltacht, something like an Irish-speaking blow-in.

The question felt more like a password request than a conversation opener. Interviews are tricky beasts, and a skilled operator keeps the thorny issues until the end so that even if you get thrown out you still have the guts of a job done. There was a further difficulty: my Irish is fine for casual conversation but lacks the breadth of expression required for philosophical discourse. I had been advised that Peadar was, variously, 'deadly serious', 'scary', 'up in the clouds' and 'away with the fairies', that he tolerated no small talk and cared little for the opinions of others. Normally an opening question like this is simply a prelude to a speech. Sit tight and all will be revealed. A minute later, an eternity, and Peadar is still looking at me. Another half minute passes.

'I think you are a *duine Gaeltachta*,' I said, 'but Liam O'Flaherty was probably a *bundúchasach Gaeltachta.*' More silence, more intense stare.

'Y–e–ss,' he said, slowly.

Jesus, I think, relieved, let the show begin. At this point I let Peadar know the interview needed to be done in English, as the book is going to be in English and there's no sense in my translating his words into a language we both speak. No problem there. He elaborated on his opening question, a magisterial account of the difference between a native indigenous Gaeltacht person and a person who is raised or living in the Gaeltacht. He does this with such insight and eloquence that I quietly congratulate myself for resolving an issue that has been circling around previous interviews but has never been pinned down to my satisfaction.

That was when I noticed the tape recorder was still on pause.

I said nothing, but as we moved on to other matters I was distracted by the knowledge that at some point before leaving Peadar's house I would have to ask him to repeat what he said at the beginning. The last time I forgot to press play during an interview was in 1989, when the Berlin Wall was still standing. I was doing a course in journalism in Dublin and contacted the head of RTÉ, who agreed to talk to me about Section 31, the legislation that authorised censorship of Sinn Féin and IRA spokespeople on Irish radio and television. My interviewee was gruff and curt, checking his watch several times during a conversation that lasted less than seven minutes. Right at the end I noticed the timer on my recorder remained at 00.00. I thanked him and left.

Peadar Ó Riada landed in Cúil Aodha in 1961, uprooted from suburban Dublin to this remote village. 'My father came in to school to collect me and take me home because like that [clicks his fingers] he was leaving everything, fucking off to the

Gaeltacht.' Peadar attended the local school, where his teacher, Pádraig an tSionnaigh was a poet who applied his craft when instructing his charges. The school days had a distinct rhythm. At 10.30am someone in the class was dispatched to the Oifig an Phoist to get the day's newspaper, along with 10 Gold Flake and a packet of Goldgrain chocolate biscuits for his daughter, who taught another group of children. 'He would read the paper, everything, even the death notices, and from that we'd learn all our commerce and history.'

Peadar's father, Seán Ó Riada, was a household name in Ireland, composing 'Mise Éire' (1959), the soundtrack to the memory and mythology of the Irish freedom struggle then still fresh in people's minds. The epic score somehow reflected the hopes of a new society. Ó Riada also created Ceoltóirí Chualann, a traditional ensemble in which he played harpsichord and bodhrán; forerunner to the Chieftains, they put traditional music on the world map. At home in West Cork he composed music and verse for the Irish mass sung by Cór Chúil Aodha, the choir he established. Ó Riada's ensemble played their final performance in 1969, released as a live album, *Ó Riada Sa Gaiety*, a treasure of Irish music that influenced a generation.

Ó Riada died at the age of 40 in 1971, passing the torch on to Peadar, still a teenager, months away from sitting his Leaving Cert exams. 'I had to sit into the thing and do it. I didn't think it was tough at the time, I just had to squeeze my arse tight shut and get on with it.' Peadar studied music at college and was offered a scholarship to travel to Amsterdam. His lecturer called out to his home to persuade him to take up the offer. 'It was a fine, sunny day, and just outside the window my mother was lying out in the sun.' Ruth, his mother, had been diagnosed with cancer. Peadar chose to stay, sensing that whatever he decided would determine the course of his life. He had dreamed of travelling to the Americas and following the path of Carlos

Castaneda, a spiritual writer who delved into hallucinogenic drugs and shamanic awareness. The alternative was to stay in the mountains and rivers of West Cork, carrying the legacy entrusted him by his father on his deathbed. 'I'll stay in the mountains,' he decided. 'That was the most important decision I ever made in my life, because I met all those things, they came here.' What might have happened if he had taken off at that moment? 'I'd probably be gone to America and become some kind of a hippy with trad connections, and make pots of money or attempt to make it, and kill myself in the meantime with whatever excess.'

Seán Ó Riada left big shoes to fill, but Peadar now wears his own, carving out a prominent role across a range of interests. He has a weekly radio programme on RnaG, plays solo and with Triúr, alongside Martin Hayes and Caoimhín Ó Raghallaigh, members of The Gloaming. He leads the Cór Chúil Aodha, which plays in churches around the country, and is chief guardian and guarantor of his father's legacy. His most recent release, *Peadar on Piano* (2016), is a double album of music on a piano he purchased through the Crowdfundit website. 'I have been chasing windmills all my life,' he says on his website. 'Some of the projects were more successful than others.' One of those projects, the Acadamh Fódhla, a 'Hedge School University', combines schools of History, Energy, Land Knowledge and Sean-Nós.

Féile na Laoch, August 2011

Five years before my interview with Peadar, in August 2011, my brother and I travelled to Cúil Aodha to attend Féile na Laoch, the Festival of Heroes, an event organised by Ó Riada and the local community. As we left the nearby town of Baile Bhuirne we crossed a small bridge over the river Súlan, and felt we had entered into another world. The busy Cork–Kerry road gave way to the low hum of murmuring water and a mild breeze caressing the green hills beyond. A powder-blue sky lit up the distant trees, sending shafts of pale colour onto the surrounding fields. Sean Ó Céilleachair, poet, gave voice to this river and its seasons: '*An samhradh sámh taitníonn go mór liom / Is deas é an gáire is an comhluadar*' (The peaceful summer greatly pleaseth me / The laughter and the company). The rivers of Ireland are almost all feminine nouns, but the Súlan river, its source in Cúil Aodha, is an exception, a man-river. Legend has it that the Súlan demands a human sacrifice every seven years, and Ó Céilleachair's poem ends on a grim note as harsh winter arrives, and with it the time of the sacrifice. The river, '*fuar, fada fireanna*' (cold, long and manly), takes its share; *Tháinig an t-am is sciobas an duine* – 'The time came and I swept him away'.

When I went looked back over my diaries from recent years I noticed that singer Damien Dempsey had rescued two people from the Slaney River in 2014, halfway through the seven-year period. I wondered if the deaths averted in another river might count at the time of the next reckoning. Féile na Laoch seemed like an act of appeasement or defiance to the wildness around us. The festival was timed to commemorate the 80 years since Seán Ó Riada's birth, and the 40 years since his death. It will be held every seven years. There was a film festival and exhibition in the village hall, and music in the local church. The male choir brings together a group of men in their 50s and 60s, along with their children and grand-children, an anchor or rope binding Peadar and the community to this place, these mountains and the Irish language. The choir has been together for over 40 years and each member knows the other inside out, guiding new arrivals along their way.

As the choir set up in the church one of the men arrived with an infant in his arms. 'A father brings his son with him on his shoulders,' explained Peadar, 'and when they are big enough they sit in the first pew, then, depending on how shy they are, they come over the pew to the piano to where I am with the boys.' The kids gathered round Peadar's piano with little solemnity in sight as they coughed and whispered and nudged each other in relaxed fashion. Ó Riada has a natural gift for putting children at ease, and they can be heard on his recordings. The theme to his weekly radio show, *Cuireadh Chun Ceoil*, features the shrieking kids in top form. No one is left behind, regardless of changed circumstances, and at a performance during Galway's 2016 Arts Festival Peadar explained that an older member of the choir, suffering Alzheimer's, still accompanies the choir on stage, with one concession – his microphone is switched off.

The rough and rugged voices fill the church, the sound resonating across the grassy slope outside. The village has no tourists, no shops and no holiday homes. Many local children speak Irish first at home and then learn English at school. The village and wider area came to global attention in the 1980s when a science documentary named it one of the seven safest places in the world in the event of a nuclear strike. This announcement was enough to send convoys of hippies into the area, but the horizontal rain and high winds soon became a greater deterrent than imminent nuclear meltdown. As evening fell that Friday, a veil of mist clung to the mountains, drawing a discreet curtain over the landscape.

The centrepiece of the weekend was the concert in a nearby field, an all-night event, a temporary Bardic school celebrating the seven Muses: Storytelling, Sport, Singing, Poetry, Music, Dancing and Acting. The artists performed on a purpose-built stage, which rotated throughout the night before greeting the rising sun at dawn. The event was a Who's Who of the arts community of Ireland, featuring Martin Hayes, Glen Hansard, Christy Moore, Phil Coulter, Barry McGovern, Paul Muldoon, Michael D. Higgins and many more, as sean-nós dancers and harpists took a turn, along with a spectacular aerial display in which Tash Bourke wrapped herself in silks and danced in the air, her umbilical silk cord attached to a crane parked below.

There was food available in a tent, an all-night beef stew washed down with buckets of tea. The event was free of charge and most of the people in attendance seemed local. Christy Moore drove by in a large four-wheel drive and almost ran me over. We were a long way from Lisdoonvarna. There was no security presence and no sign of alcohol, the latter explaining the former. The event generated little publicity considering the range of talent on show, and the crowd didn't exceed 400 people. Not a hipster in sight. It had the atmosphere of a village fete, friendly and intimate, even private. As the sun rose the next morning, Micheál Ó Muircheartaigh took the microphone as whoops came from the nearby hills. At some unseen signal a group of hurlers and Gaelic football players came running down from different hills and gave a display of ball skills on the field to the accompaniment of Ó Muircheartaigh's breathless commentary.

The entire event took place through Irish, the language of daily life here. It was the first time I'd been in an Irish-speaking district since I had attended the summer school in nearby Baile Bhuirne nearly 40 years previous. *Chuaigh sé go mór i bhfeidhm orm* – It had a powerful effect on me. Someone told me there were 2,000 poets buried in the local graveyard, and that a major battle had been fought in the area, one of the bloodiest in Europe. The nobles among the dead were sent home embalmed in barrels of brandy while the lowly fighters were buried nearby. After that weekend nothing would surprise me about the place, and if Cúchulainn himself had appeared, jogging down the road with a *camán* and *sliotar*, it would have seemed entirely in keeping with the mood. On Sunday Ronnie McShane, gifted bones player with the Chieftains, gave a virtuoso display of his

craft and recounted his time in the company of Seán Ó Riada.
He described how Ó Riada would hide in the bathroom of his
home, to compose in peace, his kids running wild elsewhere. It
was a memorable image, Ó Riada composing the soundtrack of
the Irish freedom struggle, 'Mise Éire', all the while locked inside
his bathroom. The Festival of Heroes held a closing ceremony a
month later, which I didn't attend, in which the community put
away the flags and pictures taken out during the Féile weekend.
If you view it online you can hear the nails banging shut the
Cófra Mór for another seven years, alongside the quenching of
the festival torch and a parting song.

On the way home from that first visit to Cúil Aodha the
language was on my mind, the seed firmly planted. I imagined
returning to interview Peadar *as Gaeilge* and maybe investigate
that private world of Cúil Aodha. I have come across him a few
times since then, with one memorable event in Tulla, County
Clare, the handover of a former convent to the local community.
Peadar was invited to speak at the event. A large crowd gathered,
the plain people of east Clare. Ó Riada launched into a speech
with two main themes: the pointlessness of watching television
and the need for revolutionary change in Ireland. Too much
television, said Ó Riada, makes you stupid. He spoke to the
crowd as if he was chatting at a local cattle mart, but he built
in pitch, a leader rallying his troops towards the barricades. Yet
Peadar belongs to no political party or movement, ploughing
his own furrow among his own people. A passionate beekeeper
and nature lover, Ó Riada incorporates everyday sounds into
his music, from the birdsong of An Draighean, his rambling
country home surrounded by hedges and water, to the coughs
of the parishioners during choir performances.

In November 2015 Peadar was invited to UCD to give the
Léacht Uí Chadhain, an annual talk in honour of Máirtín
Ó Cadhain, broadcast live on RnaG. At that point my

comprehension skills had improved, and I was reading fitfully in Irish, picking up books but rarely finishing them. Several months later, and once more back in Latin America, I listened to the UCD lecture in which Peadar outlined his vision of Irish society. I decided to transcribe the whole thing, a forensic linguistic DIY project, studying noun, adjective and intonation. Hunter S. Thompson copied F. Scott Fitzgerald's *The Great Gatsby* word for word to marvel at the sentences, the beauty and simplicity of the prose. This process is all the more beguiling when done in another language.

The lecture was titled 'Fuaimeint Gaeil', and I looked up old Dinneen to find out what *fuaimeint* meant – vigour, force or foundation. I listened carefully, picking out the gist of the talk, but couldn't catch the detail. The first words he spoke set the tone: 'There is something fundamental that is wrong in our lives.' Peadar spoke of how the land where we live has shaped us and our ancestors over years and decades and lifetimes; this process fashions a 'coat' we wear, its material and folds moulded and shaped to suit our needs through the ages. The coat we currently wear, says Peadar, is unsuited to our body. I listened back to the talk a few times, grasping a little more each time. The different coats represent the encounter between ancient Ireland, with its language, ways and customs, and contemporary, anglicised Ireland. What has been lost? The task of writing out the lecture, word for word, brought me to another pain barrier, and after 1,000 words, barely 10 minutes of the talk, I was exhausted. It took me six months to finish the transcription, but the writing itself took only two days – one in January and another in June.

The lecture raised as many questions as it answered. Ó Riada told his audience that the English and Irish languages were utterly incompatible – that English sounds came from the roof of the mouth, suggesting control and authority. 'This is why it is easy to lie in English,' he said. Irish, however, came from deeper down, like the sounds made by a Tibetan monk, ummmming from the chest. 'It is easier to pray in Irish,' he told an audience at another public event in Galway. An audible murmur passed through the audience, but no one took him up on this remarkable claim. It sounded like the type of notion that sees Italian as a romantic language and German associated with order and control. There is something in it. But all sounds come from the mouth, with Irish and Arabic stretching to the pharyngeal cavity, but no language goes lower, where you find yourself in the lungs. There is something behind cultural stereotypes, whether it is the Latin lover or the well-organised German, but lying is hardly a linguistic talent, more like an acting skill.

Back in Peadar's house, the tape recorder now rolling, he teased out ideas of land, identity and belonging. When Peadar speaks of the land and its significance I hear echoes of the indigenous people of Latin America, who contrast the addiction to ownership of everything (land, songs, resources) with their own perceived role as caretakers of the natural world. 'We don't own the land, the land owns us,' says Peadar. 'It's a much more potent energy, it survives through generations'. The indigenous culture is transmitted from generation to generation, 'through blood,' says Peadar. 'By blood I mean genetics, so whether you are an earthworm or a guinea pig or a human a lot of your information is inherited from those that went before you.' In that sense language is one of the final vestiges or cloaks, a reflection of what is going on in the inner side of a being. Peadar enjoys immense respect among and beyond the Irish language fraternity, but I often heard caution expressed around his vision, that it might be too closely connected to the Catholic Church. Cór Chúil Aodha, a mass choir, always seen and heard in churches, probably feeds this notion. I told Peadar that since my teenage years as a punk in Dublin, the Catholic Church has always represented a repressive burden, an enemy of sorts. He perked up immediately. 'Sid Vicious's godmother is a Cúil Aodha woman,' he says.

Really? Ó Riada informs me that Lizzie O'Brien, a local woman, was godmother to Sid Vicious. He then described himself as a Christian, drawing a sharp distinction between 'the centralised, rule-bound, controlling church' in Rome and the legacy of Colmcille and St Gobnait, older monastic influences representing a decentralised church. 'In our own laws a woman could divorce a man if he wasn't satisfying her in bed,' explained Peadar, 'but in everything the bigger priority was not to hurt people. Our language reflects it and our music reflects it, love was a big element in life and there's a respect for that concept.' St Gobnait, a medieval female saint from the 6th century, was a local beekeeper and healer, her shrine and holy well now a popular place of pilgrimage.

As the interview drew to a close I swallowed my pride and asked Peadar if he would repeat what I had missed at the beginning, about the fault lines between native speakers born with the language and those who, like himself, merely grew up with the language. 'The native speaker lives unconsciously,' said Peadar, 'their knowledge and information, their heritage and culture come from their blood, inherited in their genes, whereas the Gaeltacht person, and I count myself there, is aware of the difference between Gaeltacht and Galltacht, and therefore the intellectual process has come into play and controls the whole thing.' This intellectual attachment to the language results in a diligent approach to speaking Irish and a different set of worries from the indigenous person. 'They [non-indigenous] are worried in case the language dies, in case it won't thrive, they feel a duty to push people to speak it, they worry about all that stuff.' The committed speakers still think along the same lines as the Western culture they seek to leave behind, something he sees reflected in the increasing tendency to impose English syntax on Irish speech. 'The extra verb tenses in Irish are not being used because the concepts behind them, the urge to use them, is not felt in the same way.'

In contrast the indigenous Gaeltacht person doesn't worry about the language, 'because to them the language is something that just happens. They don't think about it, they dream and live through the language unconsciously.' By contrast the intellectual Irish speaker 'becomes strident with it, or they can become subservient with it and post-colonial'.

Ó Riada laughed as he recalled an incident that highlights what he has said. As a child in Cúil Aodha he attached himself to the neighbouring Ó Cíobháin family, helping them on their farm. 'I remember being down the field one day and looking up to see my father coming down,' he said. The Ó Cíobháins had given them the local hostel to live in during winter but come spring they were moving in to another home. Seán Ó Riada had borrowed the donkey and cart from the Ó Cíobháins and piled all the mattresses and accoutrements on top before sitting on the pyre with a book in his hand. 'I'm sure he didn't pile them up,' said Peadar, 'I'm sure my mother and various other women did that work.' Seán held the reins and ignored the donkey while he read his book. 'I remember being embarrassed and saying, Goddammit couldn't he even at least drive the bloody donkey properly.' On reflection, Peadar realised that the donkey and Seán were doing just fine as they were. 'I was intellectualising, saying it's not the right thing to do, but an indigenous person wouldn't think like that at all, because nature does its thing anyway.'

Ó Riada had an idea for the 1916/2016 celebrations involving Cailís na Trócaire, a 'chalice of forgiveness' made in the shape of the Ardagh Chalice. The chalice would have been

the centrepiece of a street pageant and a global call to gather
in expressions of forgiveness. Anyone could send a card to the
GPO forgiving someone some slight or injury, old or new. The
chalice of forgiveness would be paraded down O'Connell Street
with President Michael D. Higgins adding the final note before
it was sealed. The messages of forgiveness would be lowered
into a boat in the Liffey and burned at sea. 'It would be a fresh
start, a catharsis.' The state would also open up all the places
of power to the general public for a week and turn them into
places of creativity, from Dáil Eireann to banks, churches and
galleries. The trains and buses should be free, giving ordinary
people access regardless of income. It would have been a
memorable week.

Peadar closed the interview by speaking of the importance
of maintaining songs and stories exactly as they are, without
changing a word or line. When culture and tradition are
passed on orally, the accuracy of the original is critical. If that
system is disrupted the knowledge is lost forever. 'You may not
change the word of a song because if you do you change the
knowledge and the history that is transmitted in the song,' he
explains. I was wondering what purpose was served by such
a strict accounting of law and song and story when I came
across research conducted into folk tales in Australia. Marine
geographer Patrick Nunn and linguist Nicholas Reid found 21
indigenous stories, handed down word for word through 300
generations, that record dramatic rises in sea levels dating back
somewhere between 7,000 and 18,000 years ago, a period in
which the sea rose by 120 metres. The stories survived thanks
to a key feature of indigenous storytelling, a 'cross-generational
cross-checking' system. In the research paper, 'Aboriginal
memories of inundation of the Australian coast dating from
more than 7,000 years ago' (*Australian Geographer*), Nunn and
Reid argued that the stories provide empirical corroboration

of a postglacial rise in sea levels as documented by marine geographers.

The manner in which the stories were passed on through generations reflects Peadar's idea of the importance of songs and stories unchanged over time. 'The idea that 300 generations could faithfully tell a story that didn't degenerate ... that was passing on factual information that we know happened from independent chronology ... we don't find this (consistency) anywhere else in the world,' said Reid, based at the University of New England. 'At any given point in time my father is telling the stories to me and his grandkids are checking,' added Reid. 'Three generations are hearing the story at once ... that's a kind of scaffolding that can keep stories true.'

In Peadar's mind, if the roots remain attached to an idea, tune, poem or song, they will remain intact over generations: 'That idea and concept is foreign to Western culture, because in that system the idea is that you *own* everything, you own the piece of land, you own the house, you own the tune. If you don't you take it and then let someone try and take it off you again.'

I left Peadar's home and drove back over the Súlan river, the bridge taking me back to a more familiar existence. Peadar sounds like a prophet in the wilderness, one of a growing number of voices demanding a halt to runaway consumerism and growing global indifference to the pain of others. His vision is at once simple, almost childish, yet bold and challenging, inspired by his father's call to be *uasal* or noble, decent and respectful in all things. Peadar's appeal to an older Gaelic civilisation is a response to the crisis of our times, a notion of collective, shared bonds which might alleviate the alienation, loneliness and depression so common among people today. 'People need to be equipped to adapt to an ever-changing world, particularly nowadays, when there is no such thing as a pensionable life-long job, and they can only do that by being sure of who they are and what's behind them, so they can go forward.' The culture of Gaelic Ireland, forged over more than a thousand years, offers this anchor or rope, firmly secured in the past, with a hook in the future. 'The English language is important because it's the language of commerce and communication worldwide,' concluded Ó Riada, 'more important still is our own language, because that is our very being trying to communicate with the world around us, whether it is in our mind internally, with our family, with our otherworldly beings, God of some form – our atheistic God if you like.'

CHAPTER 16

Let's Get Serious

had worked out the first steps and danced my way to something approaching conversational Irish.

I had the tips and the daily practice, the social scene and the old books, Dinneen's daily Tweets and RnaG's daily gems. I was on the road to speaking Irish but still had more of the road in front of me than behind. The problem with this journey is that the more you know the more you realise how much you don't know. I enjoyed the native speakers on RnaG but sensed their Irish belonged to a place of childhood, to infants learning their first words and naming the world around them. That time can never be recaptured by an adult learner, even if they are lucky enough to witness it through the birth of a child. People mentioned friends of friends, a range of people who learned the language from scratch to a really advanced stage, native speakers in all but name.

Was there anything different or unique about them? I thought their stories might serve as templates for others, a pathway dotted with signposts and stepping stones. Most importantly, I was curious about the spark that kindled the interest in Irish. Regardless of how sympathetic one is to the language, Irish is not necessary to communicate with others in this country. There are many people for whom Irish is a more comfortable language than English, but there are few, if any, who cannot understand English. There has to be some driving force that motivates the learner and pushes them through the pain barriers, a force required to learn anything, but one which seems extra demanding when it comes to Irish.

Sorcha

I visited Sorcha de Brún, a woman in her 40s, living between Dublin and Belfast. A friend of mine told me she was passionate about Irish and had a story to tell about learning it. She had just completed a doctorate on Irish language literature. It was the night before New Year's Eve, the rain lashed down on the grey city and I could barely see the road before me. I got out of the car outside a shop and raced inside to get further directions, soaked in an instant, somewhere between Terenure and Tallaght. Sorcha and I eventually sat down with Christmas cake and tea and got to work. She recalled how she first became interested in Irish as a young child, when she looked at a map of the world and noticed the many languages spoken by different peoples. 'It didn't make sense to me that we didn't speak Irish,' she said. Her aunt, Teresa Conden, worked at the Royal Irish Academy, delving into manuscripts. She visited the house and spoke Irish to Sorcha, who didn't understand a word, nor did her parents. The attitude at home, however, was always positive. At nine years of age Sorcha began to record programmes in Irish on the radio. 'Then I would go up to my room – this was my hobby – I would sit down and write out the whole thing from beginning to end and often I wouldn't understand a word.' Her parents were unaware of her pastime: 'If my parents had said to me, You should be talking Irish, we want to send you to a gaelscoil, I wouldn't be talking Irish today. That's the honest-to-God truth.'

When Sorcha came across words she didn't understand, she would write down the sounds and store them in her head. At that time she was attending the Royal Irish Academy of Music, where she was obliged to write down pieces of music, note for note, a discipline she holds responsible for her efforts at transcribing Irish language programmes. On summer holidays Sorcha's parents would take her to remote villages where she saw buildings abandoned during the Famine. One year, when Sorcha was 10 or 11 years of age, they travelled to Dún Chaoin, and she and her parents spent time in the houses of local fishermen. 'My father said to me, and I never forgot it, you should listen to these guys speaking Irish.'

Some combination of the above kick-started a lifelong fascination for Irish. At the same age as she began transcribing radio programmes she also wrote letters to virtual strangers in French and German. 'I was really into writing letters as a kid,' she explained. 'Any time I met people I'd get their address and persecute them with letters.' Sorcha didn't know any French but that didn't deter her, as she borrowed her brother's schoolbooks, teaching herself the language. She had an uneasy relationship with her school and was not permitted to do honours Irish or French, in what she says was an act of punishment. 'School didn't work for me. I stopped going in sixth year.' In a very Irish fashion, her parents chose to ignore the defiance taking place under their noses. Each morning Sorcha would put on her school uniform and come down to breakfast, acting out the normal school routine. Once her parents, both working, had left the house, Sorcha sat down and began her own routine, listening to Irish and writing up to 40 pages a day in her diary.

Tadhg

Tadhg Mac Dhonnagáin grew up in rural Mayo, where he didn't have any Irish but he did have the next best thing, 'rural English', a language built around the rhythm and structures and syntax of the Irish language. He heard a neighbour talking about a man who 'came home from England and a big car at him' – a word-for-word translation of '*tháinig sé abhaile ó Shasana agus carr mór aige*'.

Young Tadhg was unlucky in that his school, St Louis, Kiltimagh, a former boarding school for girls, was just phasing out all-Irish education when he arrived. A few boarders remained, speaking Irish to each other. 'It seemed such a cool thing to be able to do.' But it was the music of Clannad that opened the door to a teenage passion for singing: 'They sounded so modern and so old and so exotic', their dialect incomprehensible but attractive. Mac Dhonnagáin discovered Slógadh, an Irish language festival featuring rock music, drama, storytelling, choirs, visual arts and contemporary dance, created by Gael Linn and open to anyone under the age of 25. This was where Hothouse Flowers, Clannad, Iarla Ó Lionáird and Dolores O'Riordan enjoyed their first audiences. Slógadh was a competition with local, county, provincial and national rounds, and Tadhg's school would put on a show, lasting 90 minutes, showcasing the talent that found its way to the national festival. Thousands of teenagers attended Slógadh each year, and the staff were only a few years older than them, native speakers from around the country. 'They spoke Irish at rapid speed, and it sounded like a real language'. Mac Dhonnagáin became 'obsessed' with becoming fluent and being able to fully participate in this cultural world.

Róisín

The more I thought about the Sorchas and Tadhgs and others that I met, the more they appeared like exceptional figures, with individual narratives of passion and persistence. This type of personal journey made the task of learning Irish look more difficult, if that was possible. At some point I started asking everyone I met about their experience of learning Irish, hoping to stumble on a different pattern. The morning after making this foolhardy decision I walked into the Jervis Street Shopping Centre in Dublin to get a key cut. Upstairs on the second floor there was a small handwritten note on the key cutter's stall: 'Back in two minutes.' Several minutes passed. There were two women behind me, each one staring over the other's shoulder, in that uncertain way when we are unexpectedly thrown together with a common purpose, however trivial. '*An bhfuil aon Ghaeilge agat?*' I've said it before I can change my mind about saying it. The older of the two women, in her late 60s, explains that she used to speak Irish, that she studied secondary school through Irish, that she loved it but had long since forgotten it. 'I have no one to practise with' she said, sounding sad. The woman beside her told me she had almost no Irish but that I should meet her daughter, who had taken it up at secondary school and loved it. A month later Róisín Grady is sitting opposite me, home for a brief holiday from London, alongside her partner Lauren, having agreed to discuss her attachment to Irish.

Róisín attended an English language school in Lucan, where she learned songs and stories in Irish and, significantly, received encouragement at home. It was in secondary school, however, when teacher Sean O'Casey, an inspiration, took the language to an entirely different level. 'He had this amazing passion for the language,' recalled Róisín, arranging a school concert for the annual Seachtain na Gaeilge. 'He brought in a magazine and we would read about Britney Spears and the like. It was far more interesting than Tír na nÓg or Cúchulainn.' O'Casey had a 'barter' system, swapping a song or a story at the start of the class for some grammar before the end. By fifth year Róisín had helped form an Irish language debating team, which won the All-Ireland championship. They practised at lunchtime and after school, and their passage through local and county heats was announced through the school loudspeaker system, giving everyone involved a sense of achievement. Most significantly, they had support at home, even though neither parent spoke Irish. 'They had a few little sayings, *codladh sámh* in the evenings, *an-mhaith*, stuff like that,' said Róisín, 'and they would listen to me practise for the debates even though they didn't understand them.' Her enthusiasm was not shared by most of her classmates, who still hated Irish, despite the enthusiasm of Mr O'Casey. The story of the inspiring teacher came up repeatedly, from every corner of the country, names easily recalled even decades later, and in some cases contact maintained. In my own case, Bernie Cosgrove, my first Spanish teacher, has remained a friend all my life. The teaching of language to school kids is the Holy Grail, the way and the light. Get it right, and kids are hooked; if it goes wrong, kids are lost, unless they find their own way back in later life. However, teachers appear not only in the classroom but outside as well, in the form of relatives, siblings and neighbours.

Adrian

I hadn't met anyone, apart from my brother, who had tackled the language with a system like my own until I came across Adrian Mallon in Belfast. I was walking past An Chultúrlann one morning when I spotted a group of people drinking tea inside. It was break time for one of the language classes. It turned out to be an *ardrang* arranged for Liú Lúnasa, a new festival organised by Misneach (Courage), the activist group working on Irish language issues. The group's slogan is simple – *saol trí Ghaeilge atá uainn* – we demand the right to live our lives through Irish. The four-day festival, held in August, had an impressive array of activities, from music workshops to mental well-being sessions, soccer, comedy, meditation and face painting, political discussions, late-night gigs and, perhaps the most intriguing of all, Tomaí Ó Conghaile hosting a debate entitled '*An bhfuil gluaiseacht na Gaeilge ró-mhacho?*' (Is the

Irish language movement too macho?). The title itself, because of Irish grammar rules, sees 'macho' become 'wacho', which in Buenos Aires Spanish is Guacho, often used as an insult, meaning a lowlife. The joy of language.

As I poured myself a cup of tea and explained my mission, a woman pointed at a man sitting nearby and urged me to go chat to him. Adrian Mallon introduced himself and began telling me about his return to the language. I quickly sensed I had discovered my lost second brother, some Nordie doppelganger left for dead in Cullybackey in the 1950s. Mallon was working on precisely the same task as the McCaughan brothers. Born in north Belfast he studied Irish, 45 years previous, liked it, went to the Gaeltacht, but abandoned *an Ghaeilge* after school. A nagging curiosity remained. Two years ago he took a year off work to see just how far he could take the language. Mallon used schoolbooks from the 1920s and 1930s which belonged to his grandfather and great uncles, and part of his motivation in learning the language was to bring those voices back to life. 'I also want to see, as an adult learner in my 60s, is it possible to really pick up the language and speak it?'

If our brief conversation is anything to go by, Mallon has succeeded. 'Every week I get better,' he told me. 'It's a simple equation: the more time you put into it, the more progress you make.' One class per week was not enough for Mallon, who studied the shifting timetables and geography of the Belfast language scene. Each Monday now begins with an early-evening singing class in Irish at the Skainos Centre in east Belfast. When that ends he heads to the Áras Mhic Reachtáin, the McCracken Centre in north Belfast, for a conversation class at 8pm. On Tuesday he begins the day where he left off, attending a basic learner class in the morning. 'I don't care about the level, I'm happy to struggle with whatever is going.' That afternoon he goes up the Cliftonville Road to an advanced class with Brendan

Ligott, 'who gives a lovely class'. On Tuesday evenings he returns to the Skainos Centre for Gordon McCoy's conversation class. Wednesday begins with a Gaelic League class on the Antrim Road, a coffee morning with a dozen people, while later that evening the same organisation holds a class with Sean McCorry from the training college at the University of Ulster. On Thursday Mallon finds himself attending a 'wonderful class' led by Stiofán Ó Díreáin, formerly of Queen's University, at the Linenhall Library, an *ardrang* conversation class.

That evening is the turn of the Cumann Chluain Ard, Belfast's premier language centre, temporarily absent from its usual home in west Belfast, operating at the time from the McCracken Centre. It will move back into its own redesigned premises (with bar attached) before the end of 2016. The Cumann has a fearsome reputation, according to Mallon. 'People used to be put off by the fundamentalist attitudes people had towards the language,' he said. 'They were very intolerant.' That mood has changed entirely, says Mallon, and 'now it's a very different atmosphere, much broader, more inclusive, more encouraging to a wide range of people'. The weekend is embraced by a three-hour session on Friday nights in Casement Park with the legendary Albert Fry, a social gathering with seasoned veterans. 'I'll be listening more than anything,' says Mallon. 'The level is beyond me.' On Saturdays Mallon takes a day off classes, opting instead for private study and conversation at home, where his wife Bride, from Galway, has become a talented sparring partner. 'She went through the school system and hated it,' says Mallon, 'yet oddly here in Belfast she is embracing and rediscovering it.'

God might rest on the Sabbath, but the hard-working Gael must go on. Mallon attends the weekly Irish language mass at 11.30am in the centre of town. 'I'm not a believer,' he says, referring to religion rather than Gaelic. The weekly mass is followed by a gathering in the nearby Havana Café, 'a really good social meet-up, wonderful Irish'. Mallon's weekly immersion has no parallel anywhere in the country, and is carried out virtually free of charge. A growing library of Irish books is Mallon's most expensive vice. 'It's about leading by example, committed teachers, people who clearly believe in what they are doing.' In addition, it is a cross-community activity in a place that has created few opportunities for such meaningful encounters. In summertime the classes take a rest, but the *dianchúrsaí* take over, week-long intense courses covering a range of abilities. Mallon spent a week in Rosgill, County Donegal, at a free course sponsored by the GAA, but the highlight of the summer is undoubtedly the Áras Mhic Reachtain summer school, attended by 250 people in Belfast. If you cannot get to the Gaeltacht, the Gaeltacht comes to you.

Mallon deserves fluency and a medal for his diligence. His learning experience also shows that the school experience, with its meagre results, need not be the end of the Irish story. Motivation is clearly a key starting point. If you were ordered to learn Japanese for no particular reason it would probably prove immensely difficult. Why bother? Now imagine you have just received a letter confirming that dream job you applied for in Japan. The posting involves checking out hotels, restaurants, clubs, cafés and places of scenic beauty for a travel company. The job is well paid but there is one condition – you must speak Japanese. Suddenly the prospect of turning Japanese takes on an entirely different hue. But before the victory lap, check out the language. Japanese has three separate parts: the first is a pictograph system, or kanji, which consists of 7,000 characters; the second and third parts are separate syllabic alphabets, each with 48 letters.

Nuala Ní Dhomhnaill was born in Lancashire to Irish-speaking parents, who sent her at the age of five to her grandparents in the west Kerry Gaeltacht, 'ashamed that their daughter mightn't learn Irish'. For six weeks she refused to speak any Irish, convinced her sudden exile from her parents was a form of cruel punishment. Her father visited after a month but she spoke only English to him. 'I went on strike. I'd be damned if I spoke Irish,' she recalled, 'but I could understand them perfectly well.' One morning at breakfast she demanded 'milk' but nothing happened. 'I said "*bainne*" and suddenly milk appeared in front of me. I said to myself, Aha, this thing works.' When her father visited again, a month later, he addressed her in English. 'I said to him, What are you speaking English to me for? This is Ireland.'

I decided to look further afield, to other learners in different circumstances. Laurie Lee, a poet and novelist, set out walking from his home in England to Spain in 1934. He travelled there, he explained, because 'somewhere or other' he had picked up the phrase in Spanish for 'Will you please give me a glass of water?' – a sufficient start for a new life overseas. With his violin wrapped in a blanket, Lee walked the back roads of Spain, every new village and town a challenge to his survival skills. He stayed with locals, and he described how on one occasion, drowsy with wine, he began fitting sentences together in his mind, 'like a string of ill-knotted flags'. This mirrors my own experience, the slow construction of language, word by word, like building blocks or a jigsaw puzzle, its pieces scattered on the floor, a corner here, an image there, until finally they dance their way out of your head and into the world, improbable sounds that never cease to amaze me.

Irish writer Liam O'Flaherty landed in Rio de Janeiro in 1918 after working his passage on a steamboat. He met an Irishman working at a language school who offered him a job. O'Flaherty had no Portuguese, so the school director seconded a servant to shadow him all day and teach him. 'In about a week I could converse with him,' recalled O'Flaherty. After two weeks he spoke the language 'quite well'. He soon tired of life in Brazil and left the country. After a further two weeks O'Flaherty became aware he had forgotten all his Portuguese, a reminder that language must be used or it is lost. Ixim, a young Mexican boy, came to stay with me in the Burren along with his Irish father, an old friend, in 2013. We all spoke Spanish and Ixim had very little English when he began school that year. Each afternoon the school bus deposited him back among the Burren rocks along with his frustration at being unable to engage with his schoolmates. After about three months, a local girl, Saoirse, jumped off the school bus and came skipping up to me, a broad grin on her face: 'He can talk!' she exclaimed. 'He can talk!' The barriers had suddenly lifted, and Ixim was now fully able to communicate in English.

Slahi

Mohamedou Ould Slahi, born in Mauritania in 1970, found himself learning English to save his life. Slahi was imprisoned in Guantanamo Bay in 2002, accused by the US authorities of involvement in terrorist activities but never charged with any crime. 'When I first met Americans I hated their language, because of the pain they made me suffer without a single reason. I didn't want to learn it.' Over time Slahi changed his mind, and learned English from his guards and interrogators despite a ban on books teaching the language. Why the ban on English learning, he asked his kidnappers. 'Because detainees pick up the language quickly and understand the guards,' came the reply. Slahi didn't need to be told twice. He already spoke Arabic, French and German, but had only a handful of English verbs. After a short time, he said he could 'speak like common folk.' Slahi was less than impressed with the poor grammar and crude language of his captors, with its emphasis on 'F this and F that', but before long he was writing down new words learned from the more eloquent among the guards. Books appeared over time, including *Catcher in the Rye*, and by 2005 Slahi had handwritten his memoir, *Guantanamo Diary*, in English, some 466 pages, or 122,000 words. Slahi endured the most complete nightmare of our age: detention without trial, torture without time limits and endless imprisonment. He was finally released on 17 October 2016. In his introduction to Slahi's book, Larry Siems, writer and activist, put the prisoner's achievement into context. Apart from his lifelong fascination with words, Slahi's feat stemmed from a desire to engage with and understand his captors, allowing him to remove the translator/interpreter from the interrogation sessions, 'opening the possibility that every contact with every one of his captors could be a personal exchange'.

CHAPTER 17

Fairytale of Ayapaneco

T he UNESCO World Atlas of the World's Languages in Danger charts the decline of 3,000 languages expected to disappear completely by the end of this century. Needless to say, Irish is not among them. By comparison with some of its cousins in the US, Latin America and Africa, Irish is in rude health. Lovers of *an Ghaeilge* may lament the steady expansion of English in Gaeltacht areas and the dwindling *saibhreas*, or wealth of expression, among new speakers, but the situation is far from critical.

Consider the plight of the Quileute people, living in Washington State, along the shores of the Pacific Ocean. The Quileutes once hunted and fished along hundreds of miles of coastline stretching from the glaciers of Mount Olympus to the distant rain forests. The tribe 'negotiated' (a euphemism for total surrender) the Treaty of Olympia with the US government, using a lingua franca, 'Chinook Jargon', which had only 500 words, many of them open to multiple meanings and convenient ambiguities. The Quileutes are now confined to a single village, La Push, covering little more than a single square mile. The population has been reduced to 2,000, but only a fraction still live within reservation boundaries. On the day when Kevin James, a composer, visited La Push, the best speaker of the language had just been airlifted away due to illness. 'And the population of native speakers went from four to three,' he observed. The next best speaker suffers dementia, and the remaining two were 'old women who had grown up at a time when they were punished for speaking the language'.

The Turkish whistling language is another case in point, a language that evolved in isolation, amid deep ravines and hilltop settlements, where whistled sounds carry for several kilometres. There are at least 10,000 speaker-whistlers in north-east Turkey. In Kuskoy, a village whose name means 'Bird Village', each Turkish syllable is adapted into piercing whistles, which can be understood four miles away. The language does not lend itself to secret longings, but it really has to be *seen* to be believed, and can be, thanks to the Internet. In one gripping snippet, the question 'Do you have fresh bread', or '*Taze ekmek var mı?*' in Turkish, is rendered into six separate whistles made with tongue, teeth and fingers. The target of this message is standing on a rooftop a long distance away. They are soon deep in conversation. The number of fluent whistlers has dropped dramatically in recent decades, while mobile phones, offering soundless privacy and instant communication, threaten its future. The whistled language has a unique scientific interest in that, unlike all other spoken languages, the whistled form of Turkish engages speakers equally on the right side of their brains as on the left side. Whistlers speak Turkish when they are together, and switch to whistling when they need to send a message over longer distances.

The Canary Islands also have a whistled language, Silbo. You can observe a classroom of young children in La Gomera, one of the Canary Islands, conversing in whistles under the watchful gaze of their whistle teacher. As a fluent Spanish speaker, the structure sounded familiar, and when one child whistled '*Bueno, bueno, ya voy,*' I could easily make out the structure of Spanish in the whistled utterance. This may be my next language challenge. It comes as no surprise to learn that it was declared by UNESCO a Masterpiece of the Oral and Intangible Heritage of Humanity in 2009. In 2003 the Convention for the Safeguarding of the Intangible Cultural Heritage was signed, taking effect in 2008. The Silbo speakers come in two categories: those born before 1950 and those who have attended school since 1999. In between those years, the language was looked down upon as a backward, rustic relic, unfit for use in the contemporary world. The fightback began in the 1990s, when expert speaker-whistlers began teaching the language on a free and voluntary basis at a centre set aside for the purpose. This grassroots movement prospered and spread the language to schools, prompting the government to adopt and promote its own revitalisation programme. In 1997 the subject was added to the school curriculum, and two years later it became compulsory for all schoolchildren. A project began to digitalise all recorded audio material on the language, while a teacher-training college consolidated the comeback.

It is hardly surprising that endangered languages have attracted the attention of composers, who set them to music. An Australian opera includes fragments of Turkish whistling, while 'Counting in Quileute' was performed live in Brooklyn, New York, an immersive experience in which a set of audio speakers were placed around the audience, producing an immersive chanting of Quileute words accompanied by the music of an instrumental ensemble.

The Ayapaneco language, spoken for centuries in Tabasco State, in southern Mexico, survived the Spanish conquest but is now on its death bed, with only two speakers left alive. The situation is more critical than even that bare statistic suggests, as the two remaining speakers, who live 500 metres apart, refuse to talk to each other. One would expect a long-running feud or a land dispute, but the context for the lack of communication may be more mundane. 'They don't have a lot in common,' explained Daniel Suslak, a linguistic anthropologist from Indiana University. One is 'a little prickly', while the other rarely leaves his home.

'When I was a boy everybody spoke it,' Manuel Segovia, aged 75, told *The Guardian* in 2011. Segovia still speaks the language with his wife and son, but while they have a passive understanding of it, they speak no more than a *cúpla focal*. The virtual disappearance of the language in less than a lifetime is a sobering reminder that languages are practised or lost.

Isidro Velazquez, aged 69, shared the Ayapaneco language with his brother until his death a decade previous. The swift end to the language occurred largely due to a prohibition at school, in favour of compulsory Spanish and widespread migration from this impoverished region.

Suslak is involved in an Ayapaneco dictionary project, which, when it appears, will accommodate two different versions of the language as disagreed upon by Velazquez and Segovia. Mexico's Instituto Nacional de Indígenas was planning one final attempt to get classes going while the speakers were still alive. Segovia had attempted to intiate classes in the past but was unable to raise either funds or enthusiasm: 'The classes would start off full and then the pupils would stop coming.'

The story might well have ended there.

I checked to see if there were any developments since 2011, fearing that one or other of the elderly speakers might have died. A surprise awaited me. A campaign to bring the two speakers together in 2014 had been successful. More than that, the first school of Ayapaneco had been built, and a crowded class of young children took instruction from Manuel and Isidro, now 80 and 74, respectively. Popular pressure from the community made it happen. And to complete the fairytale, the two agreed to help write a single dictionary of Ayanapeco.

CHAPTER **18**

Ceol and Soul

The soul of the language speaks through story, song and dance, through place names and poetry, the word singing the world into existence – but it can't always be heard. As Marcus Ó hIarnáin said, 'We know nothing about the music we play, but it's there, it's coming out through us.'

When I was growing up I associated traditional Irish music and the Irish language with Republican orthodoxy and conservative Catholicism, some hybrid of Diddle-Aye, 'The Men behind the Wire' and céilís at the crossroads under the supervision of a parish priest. It was the last place I wanted to be. The shifting sands of adolescent identity called for a radical break with tradition, as rock and punk music became the vehicles for questioning and challenging everything around me. Back then I was asking different questions, yet some of the singers I listened to were skating on the surface of the Irish tradition, particularly Kevin Rowland and Shane MacGowan, The Pogues delving further all the time, bringing me closer to the roots. The Pogues began life as Pogue Mahone, a phonetic reading of *Póg mo thóin* ('kiss my arse'); it was too much for the BBC, who refused them airplay until they amended the name.

The Irish tradition seeped through in the unlikeliest places. At the age of 12, when I bought a copy of Thin Lizzy's album *Johnny the Fox* (1976), its artwork stopped me in my tracks. The cover featured a glossy collage of Celtic symbols and spirals created by artist Jim Fitzpatrick. In interviews at that time Lynott spoke of his desire 'to strengthen Lizzy's Celtic identity' but lamented the absence of a direct connection to the tradition: 'I don't play a f … in bodhrán, I love the Chieftains but their music is handed down father to son.'

Three years later Thin Lizzy released *Black Rose* (1979), featuring another Fitzpatrick cover and a title track reimagining 'Róisín Dubh', a 17th-century poem. 'Tell me the legends of long ago,' sang Lynott, 'Play me the melodies I want to know / So I can teach my children *óg*.' Lynott name-checked Cúchulainn, Queen Maeve, Joyce, Yeats, Behan, O'Casey, Shaw and Wilde. The album cover referenced the myths and legends of old Ireland, and in the years that followed Dexys Midnight Runners and The Pogues offered further glimpses of fiddle and accordion and jigs and reels. It would take a couple of decades in Latin America and a move from Dublin to County Clare to connect with notions of land and music and belonging. My immersion in the local music scene and return to *an Ghaeilge* prompted a new set of questions, more in keeping with middle age than with teenage years. The questions then fell away as something altogether different began to emerge, a kind of soul-searching in which my growing connection to language and lore wrapped itself in music and writing, old and new.

Recently, on following the thread of Thin Lizzy's evolution, I discovered that the *Black Rose* LP might have been released under its Irish title 'Róisín Dubh' if Lynott's label hadn't previously prevailed upon him to omit lyrics in the Irish language. Lynott was steeped in Irish folklore and language, and searched for a means to express it through rock music. 'Subconsciously I know it's very dominant but consciously I don't try to do it at all,' he told one journalist. Jim Fitzpatrick recalled how Lynott asked that the *Black Rose* cover reflect the singer's love of the poem 'Dark Rosaleen', by 17th-century poet James Clarence Mangan, a poem about the yearning for freedom from English rule that Lynott knew by heart. An epic seven-minute saga, the title track referenced a number of old Irish tunes, among them 'Will You Go Lassie Go' and 'The Mason's Apron'. Lynott, a fan of Seán Ó Riada, had a GCE in Irish, and enjoyed writing in the language, but was frustrated by record company management. 'I'd also written "Éire" for the first album completely in Irish, and they wouldn't let me put that down because they said the kids wouldn't understand it,' he said. He did sprinkle a word or two of Irish in his songs, and frequently sang about his cultural roots:

> Gather all the men folk
> Speaking the Celtic tongue
> The land is Éire
> The land is young.

(Thin Lizzy, 'Éire', 1971)

Even as a kid I wondered why only the menfolk were summoned to the language – what about my sisters and mother and grandmother? The point, however, was clear: the interconnectedness of land, language and lyric.

Irish sean-nós singing, those soulful unaccompanied voices, cut through the centuries, and take us directly to some place of ancestry. You know it when you hear it, something otherworldly, beyond language itself. 'People who sing sean-nós are doing it because it has an intense relationship with the people that went before them,' said Tadhg Mac Dhonnagáin, 'they will sing a song because their grandfather sang it, because their uncle, who is now dead, sang it. That song for them has huge echoes, personal echoes but also echoes that are weaved into a tapestry of community and memory that is profound.'

I had difficulties connecting with sean-nós; it seemed spare, austere, almost barren. There was, however, one song I came back to again and again, a track from *The Otherworld*, a collection of songs and stories in CD and book form published in 2012. There was something about the singer, the pace and rhythm he imposed on the song, allowing him to take effortless ownership. Just behind the voice I sensed an overwhelming mood of sadness, of unfulfilled ambition or dashed hopes. I listened to the song frequently, but it was only while writing these lines that I bothered to look up details of singer and song: Ciarán Ó Con Cheanainn, singing 'An Aill Eidhneach'. If anyone had asked me what Ó Con Cheanainn might look like, I would have assumed a middle-aged man with the best part of his life behind him. Ó Con Cheanainn was in fact the youngest-ever winner of the Corn Uí Riada, the sean-nós singing competition at Oireachtas na Gaeilge, the annual celebration of Irish language and culture. A sparse biographical note announced his death in 2009, at the age of 27.

In 2012 I attended a gig by fiddle payer Martin Hayes in Crusheen Church, County Clare, at which he invited local musicians to join him on stage throughout the evening. The music came alive; it spoke to something inside me. This growing sense of a connection finally clicked into place when I came across the music of Lorcán Mac Mathúna, a towering figure, yet virtually unknown. When Pearl Jam singer Eddie Vedder met Pakistan Qawwali singer Nusrat Fateh Ali Khan, to record a track for the *Dead Man Walking* soundtrack, Vedder described the experience of watching Ali Khan warm up his vocal chords. The hum and vibration, hinting at everything Ali Khan learned from his parents and grandparents before him, left Vedder in tears. Mac Mathúna has a similar effect on these ears. On his album *The Arrows that Murder Sleep*, track six, 'Battle Lines', Mac Mathúna hits that spot, and the soul of the language seems to leap out of the stereo. Mac Mathúna's Irish is impenetrable but that doesn't matter, as the energy is transmitted through the sounds, and the lyrics are written inside the CD booklet.

The events described took place over a thousand years ago, at the time of the Cogadh Gael re Gallaibh on Good Friday, 23 April 1014. This was the time of war between the Gael and the Foreigners, while another track, 'Ordeal by Cohabitation', references the 9th-century story of Liadán and Cuirithir, two poets sworn to marry each other. But Liadán entered a monastery and Curithir followed suit. In a test of their religious vows they share a cell for the night, watched over by acolytes. The lovers, wrote Mac Mathúna, 'contemplate spending eternity in each other's company in this cell'.

What is it about sex and the Gael? And yet there was hanky panky afoot if the first comprehensive English–Irish dictionary, produced in Paris in 1732, is to be trusted. Conchubhar Ó Beaglaoich's work included an entry for the dildo, described as 'Óirnís ar chuma slaite fir noch do bhíos ag mnáibh drúiseamhla chum caitheamh aimsire', which translates as 'Gadget in form of a man's stick/rod that lusty women do have for passing the time.'

And you thought the *bata scóir* was the only tallystick in Gaelictown.

Ancient Gaelic Ireland was fond of absurd proofs of chastity and daring bloody deeds on the battlefield, of Cúchulainn and his 'war face' and killing spasm, of song and poetry and bravery of fathers orchestrating the death of their own children, of epic grief and the feral howl, the dark omens of imminent death, of animals and humans in conversation, land and people intertwined. And all this happened, or some version of this happened, on the ground upon which we walk. Myth and reality, spinning around inside our psyches. I still don't know if that means anything at all today but it has a grip on my imagination, and with it a growing curiosity for the language that created those tales. And I found myself asking a bizarre question: 'Where has this language been hiding all my life?'

Marcus Ó hIarnáin's *Coigil an Tine* was my favourite album of 2016, his self-styled 'pure ancestral Connemara dance music', a wild, bare-knuckle ride that feels like the tradition's response to contemporary techno music. It reminds me of the punk music that still owns most of the available time on my record player, music unhinged and free. I haven't the patience for set dancing, but Marcus's music belongs in the mosh pit. In his sleeve notes to an earlier Ó hIarnáin album, *An Chearc Fhraoigh* (1989), Seosamh Ó Cuaig cited old Dinneen: '*is treise dúchas ná oiliúint*', instinct is stronger than education, explaining how Ó hIarnáin enjoyed the rare gift of instinct and education, his musical family 'beacons of hope in a world of chancers and exhibitionists'.

There are many others, so many others. As soon as the words '*an bhfuil sibh réidh?*' are spoken on their *Scaoil Amach An Pocaide* album (the only words spoken on the album), recorded live in 2005, button accordion player Tony Mac Mahon and guitarist Steve Cooney lift the roof off another ceiling. Then came *Caithréim* (2016), Síle Denvir's interpretation of Pearse's writings, followed by Slow Moving Clouds, *OS* (2015), an Irish–Nordic collaboration which provided the soundtrack to Swan Lake/Loch na hEala, an extraordinary dance theatre production performed in Dublin in October 2016. In the early prose sagas of Ireland, transmitted orally through the ages, the mythological cycles drew on the otherworldly powers of music, from the *geantraí* (music of happiness) to the *goltraí* (music of sadness) and the *suantraí* (music of sleep and meditation). These changing moods live on inside a rooted yet restless tradition, anchored in the past but always looking forwards and outwards.

John Spillane is a singer-songwriter who has delved into the same well for inspiration, moving easily between English and Irish, his songs naming the fields of his childhood, each one associated with a personal memory or a local story. When you see the eight members of Kila spread across a stage, each one playing two or three instruments (no, not at the same time), the many influences present, from jazz and funk to trad and classical, offer a bridge across a global culture, before returning back to the source. Liam Ó Maonlaí's latest band Ré is another inspiration. The term 'working within a tradition' applies to poets too, as Ailbhe Ní Ghearbhuigh observed: 'I can use a word or a phrase and it's ringing a bell of a song that was sung for centuries or harking back to an ancient poem – that's very powerful.'

Readers will probably anticipate what's coming – could it be that Irish music is having a moment, like the language, or is it all in my head? Colm Mac Con Iomaire, former fiddle player with The Frames, has released two solo albums, which take the tradition and push it outwards, towards classical music and moody Western soundtrack. On stage Mac Con Iomaire switches between Irish and English, and on one occasion he described the Irish language as 'a kind of first aid kit for the Irish people … our emotional makeup'. His music feels like a balm to the wounded soul. The poets are always close at hand and *rapfhile* Séamus Barra Ó Súilleabháin, the latest on the block, channels the dispossessed, the confused and the lost in a contemporary idiom, a satisfying combination of John Cooper Clarke and Eoghan Rua Ó Súilleabháin.

Music seems a far easier doorway to open into the language than any other medium. Clannad and Enya, hailing from Gaoth Dobhair, put their native music scene on the global map in the 1970s and 1980s, inspiring local teenagers, who saw their language on Top of the Pops, validated by a broader audience. 'Clannad radically changed a lot of people's perceptions of the language,' Éamonn Ó Dónaill told me. 'They were singing local songs which we didn't really value that much previously, and suddenly they were on the international stage and it made me rethink my relationship with the language ... Without thinking it through too much I decided to devote my life to trying to promote the language.'

There was however one musical risk attached to turning on RnaG each day, and that was the likelihood of hearing John Beag Ó Flatharta, the Garth Brooks of Connemara, a revered figure in the Connemara Gaeltacht. I can't believe how often he's played on my radio station. As soon as I hear his voice I lose the will to live. Outside of sport on the radio it is the only moment when my hand instinctively reaches out to switch off. John Beag sounded like that person who climbs on stage after the band has finished and the lights are on and simply won't leave until dragged into a waiting car boot. This opinion finds no echo anywhere despite my best efforts. Rónán Mac Aodha Bhuí, a keen follower of music new, weird and wonderful, tells me I've got John Beag all wrong. 'He is Johnny Cash na nGael', an ordinary man singing about the lives of his people – their pain, their hangovers and their hardships, the fishing and digging at home, exile and emigration abroad. Mac Aodha Bhuí, no fan of Irish country music, makes an exception for John Beag.

I did recall one evening in An Cheathrú Rua when I was staying at Mairéad and Pádraig's home while studying at the nearby Acadamh. They dressed up to go out one night, their faces a picture of joy, visibly excited at the evening ahead. They were going out to see John Beag at his weekly local gig. He speaks to their lives. It's a reminder that there's no good or bad music, just different tastes, like the *blas* that distinguishes one Irish speaker from another. And you don't have to cite manuscript to touch the soul. You don't even have to sing in Irish.

The death of the Gaeltacht has been widely predicted, but when you witness social occasions, the mix of *ceol* and Irish, it's hard to see it. 'Every time people tell me it's going to die, I think of social occasions in Connemara,' said Toner Quinn. 'I love the sessions, the music and language mix. At a recent gig in Inverin, Irish was on fire … everything was through Irish, all the conversations … If someone walked in and said, You know this will be dead in 10 years, it would have been hilarious.' Quinn and others, notably Donncha Ó hÉallaithe, a lifelong activist, have established Ceoltóirí Cois Fharraige, organising weekly music sessions in Irish for children and teenagers, a natural way to ease both age groups into leisurely, social Irish, the baton handed on to another Irish-speaking generation.

CHAPTER 19

Cúpla Focal – Cold Comfort or Cool Brand?

T he idea of the *cúpla focal*, a few words of Irish, has been a symbolic acknowledgement of the national language by people unable to speak it – a greeting, a thank you, a hello before switching to English. The same impulse drives visiting tourists in Spain to ask for a *cerveza* or a *habitación*, not much, but still a show of respect for the local people. In Ireland the *cúpla focal* enjoys ambivalent status. On the one hand it has become a formal gesture hauled out on occasion by officials who show no further interest in the language, and on the other, the few words serve as a sign of life. In my local supermarket in Gort, County Galway, I hear Bridget as I approach the checkout, using the *cúpla focal* to almost every customer during an eight-hour shift in which she brings the language to life in a small, uncomplicated but noticeable way.

The 1916 proclamation, with its three words of Irish at the top, could easily be seen as another example of the *cúpla focal*. The gap between desire and ability, aspiration and application, remains enormous. The Irish language is largely invisible despite its official status, as we glance at bilingual road signs but see only the English names, while most people change the channel when the odd news bulletin is broadcast in Irish and regard the subtitles on TG4 as a lifeline rather than a source of irritation.

The callout for a *cúpla focal* has been adopted by Irish language lobbyists as an encouragement for people to use whatever Irish they have. The merest hint of Irish spoken by anyone resembling a celebrity is treated as a hopeful portent. In a major coup for Conradh na Gaeilge, global superstar Ed Sheeran recorded one of his best-known songs, 'Thinking Out Loud', in Irish, 'Ag Smaoineamh Os Ard', on a CD released to mark the annual Seachtain na Gaeilge, distributed free to school children.

The CEOL 2016 initiative was sponsored by Conradh na Gaeilge, its online radio station Raidió Rí Rá and RTÉ's 2FM. At the time of writing (August 2016), the English language original had 1,226,723,812 views. I had to check this figure several times: it appears to be, Jesus it is, one billion, a couple of hundred million and spare change. When John Lennon boasted that The Beatles were bigger than Jesus, he clearly hadn't anticipated Sheeran, who is bigger than Jesus *and* The Beatles combined. Sheeran has strong Irish connections, his grandparents coming from Gorey, County Wexford, and he busked as a teenager on the streets of Galway. When he launched a film of his 2015 tour he was asked to send a message to his Irish fans. I wondered might there be a *dia duit* or a *conas atá sibh* or even, let's face it, hope dies last, a shouty *CAD É MAR TÁ TÚ* for the northern compañeros, but no, all we got was a bog standard 'Whatsup?' 2FM's Eoghan McDermott said that getting Sheeran and others to record in Irish 'shows that the use of the Irish language is being revolutionised at the moment ... This album shows that anyone can speak *as Gaeilge* and that we should all give it a go.'

The reality is that Sheeran merely sang a set of phonetic lyrics on a once-off basis. A more honest assessment might have been that anyone can learn a brief set of lyrics for a pop song in any language. The low visibility of Irish in the social life of teenagers becomes dense fog when it comes to social media, so the Sheeran coup was a major boost in territory normally bossed by English. Then I checked the number of views for Sheeran's Irish language effort – 18,224. It was tiny, less than tiny, infinitesimal, barely in existence. This seemed odd. Surely a few hundred million of Sheeran's devoted fans would be curious enough to click on this. If Pearl Jam or Kila recorded a version of 'Mary Had a Little Lamb' in Swahili I'd probably watch it more than 18,000 times myself alone. However, even my cold and calculating heart was moved when I found a version of Sheeran's song recorded by primary school kids at Scoil Bheanna Bhoirce, which had a mere 385 views. Are numbers everything?

The unquestioned champions of the *cúpla focal* on social media are Coláiste Lurgan, the Irish college in Connemara, which runs summer courses for teenagers and has become a legend for its innovative musical arrangements of pop hits. The Coláiste translates and records hugely popular pop songs using quality production values and professional video recordings. The outcome is a polished, crisp version of songs like 'Wake Me Up' by Avicii vs Lurgan, uploaded to YouTube and viewed over 5 million times, with 5,612 comments posted. Douglas Hyde would be dancing in his grave with joy. It's the musical equivalent of the *cúpla focal*, a snazzy pop marketing sound bite. I tried out another song, 'Pompeii' by Bastille (TG Lurgan), and found the Irish version sounded every bit as awful as the original. I am probably not the best person to pass judgement. The Coláiste Lurgan vibe feels like an attempt to make Irish popular and hip by grafting English pop songs onto videos of young, beautiful people having a good time together *as Gaeilge*. In a separate video about the successful videos and the school, a teacher was filmed as the pupils gathered for the end-of-course performance. He demanded the attention of all present, reminding them they had better speak Irish throughout the event. At the end of each video I expected to see a logo for a mobile phone company or a beer manufacturer, language as brand. That said, this musical *cúpla focal*, with its millions of clicks, clearly serves its intended purpose.

There is a brief online snatch of Conor McGregor responding in Irish to a question from a TG4 reporter at a press conference in Dublin ahead of a fight with Brazil's José Aldo in Las Vegas. '*Tá mé go hiontach*,' says McGregor, when asked how he feels. Was he looking forward to the upcoming fight? '*Tá mé ag súil lenar troid*.' He then slipped into English, but the reporter persisted. What would he say to his opponent, *as Gaeilge más féidir*? He smiled and took a deep breath. 'I'm a bit rusty,' he admitted, saying he could understand what she was saying. '*Tá mé chun buail é san cheann … le mo chos, istigh ceathar mináid … round uimhir a haon*' (I'm going to hit him in the head … with my foot, inside four minutes … round one).

It was a magisterial performance by the standards of Irish speakers, probably lifting him into the top 20 per cent of those who claim some knowledge of the language. Apart from one detail – on the brief bio handed out to journalists covering the press conference, McGregor listed English and Irish as his spoken languages. The Irish was *ceart go leor*, reasonable enough, but no more than that. It seemed a telling detail that at the end of these few words he added, for no apparent reason, laughing as he spoke, '*an bhfuil cead agam dul go dtí an leithreas?*' before lamenting a lost era – 'I was fluent'. McGregor attended Coláiste de hÍde in Tallaght, then Coláiste Cois Life in Lucan. 'I was in Irish school me whole life and now … I have it there, I just need to brush up on it.'

The significance of the segment can be seen in the number of views: 292,201, of which 690 paused to comment. Many of those who tuned in had never before heard Irish spoken, and others were unaware of its existence. The comments ranged from the impolite to the unprintable, while many confessed to total confusion. 'What does it mean the sentence about going to the toilet and why is it a part of Irish humour? Is this famous phrase or something?' asked Stanislaw Rewiski. Many people commented on McGregor's poor Irish, but one person defended the fighter's Gaelic thus: 'Hes being getting punched in the head for the last 9 years since he had to speak Irish I would say he done pretty well'.

But the king of the *cúpla focal*, by an Ulster mile, is George Chittick, Grand Master of the Belfast Orange Order. In February 2014 Chittick warned Protestants to stay away from Gaelic because it was a Republican tool, part of an ominous agenda on a par with Hitler's expansionism in 1930s Europe. If the language continued to grow, said Chittick, 'eventually they'll try and make it the same status as English and you'll not be able to get a job unless you speak the two languages'. At that point, he insisted, the situation would be just like the Sudetenland in the 1930s: 'They were German-speaking so Hitler went in … that could happen here.' Chittick suddenly changed tack. 'I can use the Irish language as well,' he said, saying '*Faugh a Ballagh*' (clear the way) and '*Lámh Dhearg Uladh*' (Red Hand of Ulster), before informing the reporter that his 'predecessor', Dr Rutledge Kane, had been an 'ardent' speaker of the language and signed the minutes of the Orange Lodge in Gaelic. That, he said, was before the language had turned 'political'. I was amazed at this piece of information, that an Orange Grand Master spoke Irish in recent times. When I went looking for Dr Kane, I discovered that he had been in the job some time ago, as he had died in 1898. Chittick's closing *cúpla focal* were also a surprise – '*tiocfaidh ár lá*,' he said, our day will come, a slogan frequently invoked by IRA supporters.

I watched this brief vox pop via YouTube, waiting for a knowing nod or wink – surely he can't really believe what he just said? There was no nod or wink, however, and it seemed clear that Chittick, representing a swathe of Loyalist opinion, was speaking to an issue that exercised his support base. The brief outburst was actually a masterclass in political grandstanding. The Irish language took hold in east Belfast in 2012 just as the Union Jack was removed from Belfast City Hall, sparking violent street demonstrations. Soon after, it was announced that Belfast now had a Catholic majority, while youth unemployment in working-class Loyalist areas stood at 25 per cent. Chittick's wild leap of logic stoked the oldest fears of a settler population. When the Unionist majority ruled the roost over a century ago, the language was a harmless badge of regional identity, but once the political arrangements had shifted, the Irish language, like the tricolour, acquired the status of an imminent threat.

The Chittick video attracted 83,018 views and 1,101 comments, drawing vitriolic responses but little in the way of informed debate. We enjoy a laugh at the expense of the funny Orangemen, but should probably keep an eye on events in our own backyard. Chittick would be heartened to hear that in Cork City waiter Cormac Ó Bruic gave up his job in the Flying Enterprise bar after the owner, Finbarr O'Shea, insisted he stop speaking Irish. 'I'm running a business,' said O'Shea. 'We have a dress code and a language code. All staff need to speak English.' Ó Bruic, a native speaker from the nearby Gaeltacht, spoke Irish on occasion to an Irish-speaking colleague and a few customers who expressed an interest in the language. 'People often told me how lovely it was to hear Irish being spoken,' said Ó Bruic, while two or three staff members at the bar were also keen to try out their *cúpla focal* with him. However, the manager claimed he had received complaints 'from a number of people who felt uncomfortable' with Irish being spoken around them. Ó Bruic, who had been working for eight months in the bar, felt he had no option but to leave the job, as a matter of principle. 'I love the language,' he said. Thankfully, he was immediately offered a job in Dingle, where his Irish was welcomed. A couple of months later, I was chatting to a friend about the Ó Bruic incident. He was astounded when I explained the full story. 'I thought he (Ó Bruic) had refused to speak English to customers in the bar,' he said. The full story played out on RnaG, out of earshot and understanding of the monoglot majority. Whatever way the news and views had floated through the English language airwaves, it had left my friend convinced that another Gaelnazi had received his comeuppance. For reasons of habit or carelessness, the old stereotypes hold firm.

From Learning to Yearning, the Never-ending Scéal

When I started out on the *bóthar ar ais go dtí an Ghaeilge* my goals were modest – to outdo my older brother. It was a pattern that had repeated itself since childhood: one or the other of us would discover some new enthusiasm, in music or books, and both of us would tune in to the same thing within a short period of time. Gerry is now reading epic tales and sagas from old Irish manuscripts, in old Irish script. At some point, you have to recognise when you're beaten.

I enjoy the written word but I am impatient to speak more Irish. For many people the motive for learning a language is pleasure, curiosity or travel, prompting a relaxed approach. I wanted more. As a journalist who reports from Latin America, I set myself the task of achieving a level of competence that would allow me discuss Latin American affairs in Irish.

That day seemed a long way off.

I was often asked about my progress but had little to say except 'It's coming along.' I was reluctant to commit to any particular level of proficiency, yet curious to discover where I stood. How far had I come and where was I going? Initially, I gauged my progress during brief chats with friends, aware of the point where I needed to turn to English to sustain a conversation. A dictionary was required to follow the most basic article or book, and while my understanding of RnaG improved, I spent a lot of time guessing and filling in gaps. My written Irish was incredibly slow and laboured. It took me half an hour to write a short email, and when I approached my interviewees for this book in Irish, through email, it took longer still. When I read back over the words on the page, the language appeared dry and tasteless.

On my last day of classes in Baile an Fheirtéaraigh, County Kerry, in July 2015, we were asked to contribute to a vox pop for RnaG's *An Saol Ó Dheas*, about learning Irish. It was brief – '*is breá liom an teanga*', I love the language, and a few other platitudes. I liked the course, improved my Irish and hoped to learn more. It was all over in less than two minutes.

Raidió Na Gaeltachta relies on a relatively small pool of possible interviewees, and the station's presenters are always on the lookout for new voices. The invitation arrived well before I had expected it – *tar isteach* and talk to Rónán Mac Aodha Bhuí. He's a Cork man who was raised in Gaoth Dobhair and now speaks the local dialect with the speed of a bullet train. I couldn't think of any reason to decline the offer. It would be the first time I spoke on radio without the safety net of a pre-record.

Rónán has a special interest in revolutionary matters, and often signs off his programme with signature Gaelic rebel yell, '*DORN SAN AER DO NA GAEIL!*' – A FIST IN THE AIR FOR THE GAELS! I was terrified. By way of compromise Rónán agreed to stick to three topics over a 15-minute slot during his hour-long show. It looked simple. Just learn enough vocabulary to hold my own in discussing my time in Mexico, Colombia and the Gaeltacht. I spent some time with Úna, my friend and language coach, and counted the days. I listened to his show, tuning in to the dialect, and noticed how he kept calling his guests 'a hash key'. I wondered if this was dialect or something to do with the reggae music he plays on the show.

When the time came to check in to the studio at Casla, Connemara, I felt like I was back at school sitting the oral Irish exam. Back then, however, the audience consisted of the examiner and me. Now, on RnaG, it would be at least twice that number. Rónán phoned me from the studio in Gaoth Dobhair, exactly one minute before the show was due to begin. He was clearly *ar bís*, '*HAIGH A HASH KEY GUJAYMARATÁTÚ?*' The plan had changed. He wanted to talk about Venezuela, oh, and Cuba, and maybe Argentina. 'Oh, *agus rud eile*,' said Ronan, his irresistible signature tune starting in the background, 'can you stick around for the whole show?' I stared at my script, carefully calibrated to last the 15 minutes. I prepared for one exam but they switched papers at the last minute. '*Cinnte*,' I hear myself say, 'sure thing.'

I had promised myself two things – no Béarla and no awkward silences. By the end of the show I was sweating profusely, heart beating dangerously fast, but it was done. I can't bear to listen back to it, but a milestone had been passed. The next day I found myself keener than ever, dictionary in hand, RnaG on the go, continuing this mysterious journey to some unknown destination.

The How of Irish is still unfinished business, a matter of time, patience and perseverance. The Why, a deeper issue, has become clear along the way; the impulse that sees me reach for the radio each morning, gets me out of bed and in to the *ciorcal comhrá* in Ennis on Saturday, the same feeling that gets me on the road to the annual Oireachtas na Samhna, when I could just sit back and *Say Yes to the Dress*.

The system, the How of it all, falls into place by itself. There are as many ways to learn a language as there are learners, and the system ideally should be uncovered rather than selected from a shelf of previously worn systems. This book describes the system that has suited me, the one that fell into my lap. It had already begun before I even realised it was a system.

La muda

The Spanish word *muda* means a change of clothes, while *la mudanza* refers to moving home. Learning Irish feels like a kind of *muda*, or moving out, swapping one set of clothes for another. As competence in Irish grows I find myself speaking it with old friends who have only ever spoken English to me before. The language shift happens progressively, a few words here, a phone call there. One of the most difficult switches happens with old friends during deeper and more complex conversations, exceeding my capacity *as Gaeilge*. It happened with Úna, an old friend who has helped me constantly with my Irish. I first met her more than 30 years ago and over the years we have developed a close friendship, but exclusively in English. In recent times, as I grew more interested in Irish, we would try chatting for a few minutes *as Gaeilge* before moving back to English when the topic and depth demanded it. The Irish bits expanded, and at some point in 2016 we went cold turkey. The process demands great patience from Úna, who has to carry the greater share of the conversation and she is also charged with rooting out all my grammar mistakes. Everyone needs at least one grammar fascist in their life. She seems to relish the job. I appreciate it – well, most of the time.

Over the past year *la muda* is on the march. In a small act of historic repair, I began speaking Irish with old friends Éamonn and Deirdre, the same couple who raised their children through Irish and tolerated my annual incursions into their home while visiting from Latin America. At first it felt like an exercise, a little stiff, but over time Irish becomes more natural and *la muda* is now taking root.

Closer to home, my brother and I enjoy part of our conversations in Irish and my sister Mary has joined the club, also using Irish at her workplace on occasion. We enjoy regular phone chats *as Gaeilge*, switching to the language of the oppressor only when necessary. Older sister Catherine is fluent already, having studied Irish many years ago. That makes 66 per cent of the family speaking Irish some of the time, and if you factor in niece Caroline, a fluent speaker who attended Gaelscoil de hÍde, we are approaching critical mass, a mini-Gaeltacht perhaps.

In December 2015 I returned to Wynberg Park, the leafy suburban road in Blackrock where I was raised. Once a year I drop in on my former next-door neighbour Mrs Regan (she's always been Mrs Regan, I can't change that now), mother of my old friend David. Mrs Regan always sounded posh to my ears, and I associated her, unfairly, with all things English. By now, however, not even Mrs Regan was going to escape my obsessive inquiry into the Irish language, and before a *cupán tae* had been served I had it out in the open. Mrs Regan answered my inquiry *as Gaeilge* and explained that she, David and one of her grandsons were attending weekly conversation classes at the Comhaltas Ceoltóirí Éireann centre in Monkstown. This news only increased my feeling that Irish was happening all around me, rising up, returning and flourishing. Beyond the siblings and the old neighbours my constant brushes with strangers bent on learning or liking the language added to the growing sense of a renaissance.

When I began the language 'flip' with some old friends and stuck to it, they seemed surprised. 'Are you doing a Daniel Day-Lewis on the Irish?' asked one friend, referring to the actor's immersion techniques. When Day-Lewis was due to play a boxer in Jim Sheridan's eponymous film he took up boxing and achieved a top-20 ranking in his weight. If Day-Lewis was playing the role of a Gaeltacht figure he would probably be a native speaker within three months. The rewards and motivation for his system, the target he might set, would be entirely appropriate to the job at hand – it's too late to begin the Irish classes when the camera is rolling. I have opted for a slow accumulation of language rather than a sprint to the finishing line.The process of learning Irish reminds me of making a jigsaw puzzle but with one key difference – you never get to see the final image and you only get to hold one piece at a time. When one piece is done, the next becomes available. It is, in some strange way, just like DIY.

If there is one thing the Irish language is lacking it is brass nerve, at least in the Republic of Ireland. The north of Ireland has a can-do philosophy. At a time when bilingual signage was illegal, a group of Irish speakers in Belfast's Twinbrook Estate came together in the 1980s and went door-to-door, asking for a pound per family towards the cost of rebel signage. The amount collected fell short of the anticipated cost but was sufficient to begin the process. The signs went up and the local authorities, facing far more immediate challenges, let them stand.

The Gaeldar (Gaeilge and Radar)is an essential piece of kit, named after the Gaydar (a combination of 'gay' and 'radar'), meaning an intuitive ability to guess the sexual orientation of others through visual cues, body language and tone of voice. The Gaeldar is the ability to recognise or connect with fellow learners and speakers. The first language you speak to someone tends to be the language that sticks. This was the reason behind the *fáinne* badge, historically worn by Irish speakers as a way of meeting others. It's time for an App based on the Tinder model, making it easy to meet fellow speakers. After Tinder, *Gliondar* perhaps, (meaning gladness or joy), a software application for mobile phones that might help fellow speakers find each other in public places.

There are even jobs available with the Irish language, whether it's translating official EU documents in Brussels or Church of Scientology documents from the comfort of your own home. No kidding, Old Brother Hubbard wants to spread his good news *as Gaeilge*. And as my mother used to say, when life falls apart, 'there's always teaching'.

I was struck by the consistency with which contemporary Irish emigrants expressed a longing for Irish culture. Johanna O'Connor lived in Sharjah, part of the United Arab Emirates for 10 years, but decided to return home when her son was born. This event was a turning point, causing 'a cosmic shift in our mindset'. Sharjah had everything she needed, sunshine, jobs and quality healthcare, but once their son was born, the decision was soon made: 'I want him to enjoy cups of tea at the kitchen table with his granny and grandad … appreciate Irish music and art … I want him to go hurling with his friends and learn Irish at school.' Johanna wanted her infant child 'to grow up with all of the things we took for granted but never will again'.

When Catherine Connolly was elected mayor of Galway in 2004 the event crystallised her ideas around the language. 'I have a voice now,' she said to herself, 'and that voice should be in English and Irish.' Like all learners, she had her own personal tale of difficulty: 'I didn't have the fluency and I don't like making mistakes.' But what was particularly striking, in a major city on the doorstep of the Gaeltacht, was that nobody expected any Irish from her. 'That speaks volumes in itself,' she said. Connolly can't stand the *cúpla focal* approach to the language, but respects anyone who gives it a go. When she returned to the language she began taking classes, travelling to Muintearas, a supportive educational organisation, to learn from Máire Feirtéar and other teachers. 'As soon as I crossed the first bridge to Ceantar na nOileán I felt I was going home,' she said of her weekly trip to the class.

In her successful campaign for Dáil Éireann in 2016, Connolly cycled around Inis Mór, canvassing locals in Irish. 'It was the highlight of the campaign,' she recalled. 'That's where I began to feel this Irish is ok, I'm beginning to grasp it.' She has been named chair of a new Joint Oireachtas Committee on the Irish language, an opportunity, she says, to listen to the organisations who are in tune with the language. 'We need to know where we are and where we want to go,' she said. Connolly's other great hope in the years to come is to kick-start a return to the Irish language in the Claddagh, once a fishing village, now a sizeable neighbourhood near the centre of Galway City. Connolly lives in a terraced home here, tucked into a quiet street near the playing fields, and she points out several homes around her where Irish is still spoken.

The one really surprising discovery as I researched and wrote this book was the following – if you speak Irish in Ireland, you will be treated as a second-class citizen. Despite the good will evident in the census figures, the legal status afforded the language, the translation of official documents, the ceremonial pride and, of course, compulsory Irish at school, this is no country for Irish speakers. There is some psychological block at the heart of this contradiction, so rarely discussed or even noticed by the monolingual majority. We are a colonised people, a condition that outlasted the declaration of the Free State in December 1921. We have two governments on this island, a direct consequence of occupation and plantation. One can agree or disagree with the existing arrangements but one cannot deny the reality of a divided country which carries with it the imprint of a brutal past and the legacy of a post-colonial mindset. This condition is buried deep within and emerges in strange ways.

A friend, working in a bar in Ennis, County Clare, often speaks Irish to customers and colleagues. The owner is happy to hear Irish spoken but my pal recalled the occasional grumble from customers; 'Don't you think it's rude to speak that language?' On another occasion, a customer, half joking, wholly in earnest, grumbled when two members of staff spoke Irish together, inquiring as to whether they were 'messing around with Al Qaeda and making bombs', that subconscious association linking anyone speaking Irish to random terror. Where do these bizarre attitudes come from? How might they be challenged?

The refusal to facilitate Irish speakers as they go about their daily business, even in the Gaeltacht, makes a joke of endless government statements about the importance of the language. Ask most Irish people whether the Irish language is treated fairly and you may well be greeted with a litany of complaints invoking the 'mind-boggling' amount of money wasted on the twitching corpse. Hang out with an Irish speaker for a while and you will encounter a very different reality. One hundred years after the Rising and the War of Independence, the Irish language is barely tolerated and speakers still struggle to assert even the most basic rights.

In September 2016, GAA club Na Piarsaigh, based in Rosmuc, Co. Galway, played Bóthar na Trá, a team based in Galway City. According to witnesses at the game, the referee was unhappy that players were speaking Irish on the pitch. 'Stop speaking that language', he ordered, before taunting the Irish speakers by sarcastically adding the phrase 'a mhac' (sonny boy) to his decisions on the pitch. Initially I assumed the story was a hoax. Surely this couldn't happen in 2016, in Connemara of all places? But it was true. The next shock – the players, remarkably, complied with the language ban, along with club officials on the sidelines.

They stopped speaking Irish at the whim of a referee.

The club lodged a written complaint with the county board. A written complaint? Is that it? Why didn't they continue to speak Irish and defy the referee? Why didn't they walk off the pitch? Why didn't their opponents do the same, in a gesture of solidarity? The referee's attitude was unacceptable but the players' meek response was baffling. Get up, Stand up, *basta ya* agus *déan clampar* or go back to sleep. The subsequent commentary on RnaG and other radio stations, never even contemplated the possibility of an indignant, active response.

Elsewhere, Paul Williams, broadcasting on Newstalk FM, expressed surprise and indignation that anyone might criticise the referee for banning Irish on the pitch. *Go bhfóire Dia orainn*! Williams then struck up a jaunty Gestapo-style tone, falling back on the oldest cliché in the book – the Irish speaker as language Nazi. The leap of 'logic' was remarkable; a referee bans the native language in the Gaeltacht, a complaint is made, so, like, they must be, like, Nazis, you know, like Germany in 1939, rounding up Jewish people, I mean, it's almost identical, isn't it? Cad-*ever* as the gaelscoileanna kids say, in their daily re-creation of the language.

Williams, prevailed upon I suspect, invited Julian de Spáinn, general secretary of Conradh na Gaeilge, onto his show the following day, a right of reply of sorts. Williams, sounding impatient, advised him he had all of four minutes to deal with *an Ghaeilge*. I timed one of the commercial breaks during his show – four minutes and thirty seven seconds. The right of reply, if it could be called that, fell to George Hook, fellow Newstalk presenter, who rubbished Williams' outburst later that morning. If you add the Cormac Ó Bruic tale to the mix, the guy who left his job in a bar in Cork after being warned not to speak 'that language', it becomes clear that the Irish language needs an army of psychologists as much as a flying squad of willing teachers.

An Irish studies module in primary schools would be a start, explaining the history of the language, the events that led to its decline and its relevance to the Irish nation. The Irish language also needs a generation of instigators, people with energy, ideas and courage to inspire others. The gaelscoileanna movement is blossoming around the country, the artistic scene is vibrant, the North is enjoying a language boom and everywhere I travelled I met the same positive response to the idea of the language, if not its daily practise.

That is a strong enough basis on which to proceed. There may be no reversing the language shift but there is a growing confidence shift which is critical to the language renaissance. The Celtic Tiger era, for all its wealth and sham, brought a new conviction to the Irish people with regard to their country and its language. The blighted language of hunger and poverty became, in the minds of many people, the language of plenty, sparking renewed interest. The peace agreement in the North removed a key argument against the language, undermining the notion of it as an exclusively Nationalist badge of identity.

The growing strength of the Irish language, at home and abroad, is a small but significant contribution to the global struggle to preserve diversity in the face of our expanding McUniverse or what linguist James McCloskey describes as 'the dreary homogeneity of 21st century global capitalism'. In his memorable meditation on the fate of the Irish language, *Voices Silenced* (2001), McCloskey describes the losses that accompany the death of a language: 'an encyclopedia of histories, mythologies, jokes, songs, philosophies, riddles, superstitions, games, sciences, hagiographies – the whole cumulative effort of a people over centuries to understand the circumstances of its own existence.'

The future is unwritten and begins again, here and now, in every fresh instant, the language coming alive, one *focal* at a time.

Bainigí sult as!

Sources

While personal interviews played a key role in this book, there were many written sources that proved invaluable to the narrative, along with radio archives, mainly RnaG. In some cases, personal interviews were complemented by other sources as with Nuala Ní Dhomhnaill's *Selected Essays* (New Island, 2005).

Jhumpa Lahiri's initial take on learning Italian, 'Teach Yourself Italian', (*New Yorker*, 7/12/15) was boosted by her book-length meditation, *In Other Words* (Bloomsbury, 2016) while Liam O'Flaherty's gripping account of his wanderings after the First World War, *Two Years* (Jonathan Cape, 1933), provided the information about his attempt to learn Portuguese.

In Chapter 2, 'Buried Alive', the writings of Douglas Hyde were helpful, notably *Language, Lore and Lyrics* (Irish Academic Press, 1986) while Aidan Doyle's *A History of the Irish Language* (Oxford, 2015) traced the language shift through the centuries. J.J. Lee's *Ireland 1912–1985; Politics and Society* (Cambridge, 1989) includes a brief but eye-opening analysis of Irish language issues since independence. Seán de Freine's *The Great Silence* (Mercier Press, 1965) is a moving account of the language shift, while *The Handbook of the Irish Revival*, edited by Declan Kiberd and P.J. Mathews (Abbey Theatre Press, 2015) offers a sweeping review of the revival era. Recent biographies of the sixteen men executed after the 1916 Rising helped clarify information on their attitudes towards the Irish language, particularly Conor Kostick's *16 Lives: Michael O'Hanrahan* (O'Brien Press, 2015).

In Chapter 5, 'Fever', Pat Walsh's *A Rebel Act* (Mercier, 2012) outlines Michael Hartnett's farewell to English and the response of other poets to that gesture. Nicaraguan poet Ernesto Cardenal's *La revolución perdida* (Fondo de Cultura Económica, 2005) is an exploration of the legacy of the Sandinista revolution, including its literacy project.

In Chapter 6, 'Why we didn't learn Irish at school', Ruth Dudley Edward's *Patrick Pearse: The Triumph of Failure* (Poolbeg Press, 1990) remains definitive while Elaine Sisson's *Pearse's Patriots* (Cork University Press, 2004) skilfully examines the story of St Enda's school and the Cult of Boyhood.

In Chapter 11, 'A Fitzcarraldo in West Belfast', Gabrielle Maguire's *Our Own Language: An Irish Initiative* (Multilingual Matters, 1991) is key to understanding the success of the Bóthar Seoighe *bunscoil* and Gaeltacht, while *Northern Ireland: The Orange State* by Michael Farrell (Pluto, 1976) lays bare the reality of life in post-partition Northern Ireland.

Chapter 15, 'The View from Cúil Aodha', references research into aboriginal storytelling which first appeared in the *Australian Geographer* ('Revealed: how Indigenous Australian storytelling accurately records sea level rises 7,000 years ago', *The Guardian*, 17/9/15).

In Chapter 16, 'Let's Get Serious', information on the difficulties of learning the Japanese language came from Bill Bryson, *The Mother Tongue* (Perennial, 1990). The story of Mohamedou Ould Slahi is taken from his memoir, *Guantánamo Diary* (Canongate, 2015).

In Chapter 17, 'Fairytale of Ayapaneco', *The New York Times* reported on the fate of a number of endangered languages, ('Vanishing languages reincarnated as music', *The New York Times*, 3/4/16) while *The Guardian* covered the crisis in Ayapaneco: 'Only two speakers of Ayapaneco remain alive...' (*The Guardian*, 14/4/11) and 'Language at risk of dying out – the last two speakers aren't talking', (*The Guardian*, 14/4/11). The Silbo whistlers of La Gomera can be seen on You Tube.

In Chapter 19, McGregor, Chittick et al. can be seen online, just search for them by name and add 'Gaeilge'. The Ó Bruic story was widely covered in the media, from *An Saol Ó Dheas* (RnaG) to *Liveline* on RTE1 and the daily papers.

In the Afterword, the idea of '*la muda*' arose in a conversation with Eamonn Ó Dónaill while Johanna O'Connor wrote about Irish in the Generation Emigration section of *The Irish Times* (13/8/16).

James McCloskey's *Voices Silenced/Guthanna in Éag* (Cois Life, 2001) is a bilingual meditation on the Irish language and a useful starting place for anyone interested in the topic.

A range of daily newspapers and online sources kept me up to date on breaking stories, notably *The Irish Times* and the *Irish Examiner*, while the *Tyrone Times* supplied the statistics on growing numbers in Irish-medium schools in the north of Ireland.

There were other books which served as background reading but are not directly quoted in these pages, among them, *A New View of the Irish Language* (Cois Life, 2008), *Scéal Scéil: Rúndiamhra Na Meán* (Cois Life, 2014), Iarfhlaith Watson, *Broadcasting in Irish* (Four Courts Press, 2003), Gordon McCoy and Maolcholaim Scott, *Aithne na nGael* (Institute of Irish Studies/Queen's University Belfast, 2000).

A Brief Glossary

Amach anseo: In the future.

An teanga náisiúnta: The national language.

Ardrang: Advanced level. Irish courses often range from *glantosnaitheoir* (absolute beginner) to *bunrang* (basic), *meánrang* (improver) and *ardrang.*

Arís: Again.

Bean an tí: Woman of the house. Frequently refers to women in the Gaeltacht who offer lodgings, food and a helping hand to students coming to learn Irish.

Botúin: Mistakes.

Cailín: Girl. Interestingly, *cailín* is a masculine noun.

Ciorcal comhrá: Conversation circle.

Cois tine: By the fireside.

Comhghairdeachas leat: Congratulations.

Cúpla focal: A few words of Irish thrown in here and there.

Doras: Door.

Draíocht: Magic.

Fear an tí: Man of the house. Also used for MC (Master of Ceremonies).

Freagair an cheist: Answer the question. Feminine nouns take a 'h' with the definite article, i.e. an cHeist, but as with everything in life, terms and conditions apply. *An teanga* (language) is feminine, but doesn't take a 'h' with the definite article because of the 't' that comes after the 'n' of '*an*'. Other examples are *an tine, an trá* and *an teilifís.*

An fhuinneog: The window.

Gach lá: Every day.

Ginideach: The genitive case.

I dtús báire: Initially.

Is mór an trua é: It's a great pity.

An madra: Dog. As this is masculine, it requires no 'h' after the definite article.

Meánleibhéal: Intermediate level.

Múinteoir: Teacher.

Muna miste leat: If you don't mind.

Na mná: The women. The singular of woman is *an bhean.*

Oíche mhaith agus codladh sámh: Good night and sleep tight.

Ómós agus aitheantas: Honour and recognition.

Sagart na bhfocal: Word priest. The famous *tuiseal ginideach* in all its glory, the priest of the words.

Scéalta: Stories.

Scrúdú cainte: Oral exam.

Seafóid: Nonsense.

Seanfhocal: A proverb. When two words come together to make one, like *sean* and *focal*, a *séimhiú* or 'h' is added to the second word.

Stad anois é! Stop now!

Suigh síos: Sit down.

Táim just ag foghlaim: I'm just learning.